HOLLYWOOD
Special Effects

with Adobe®
Premiere® Elements 3

Peachpit
Press

Hollywood Special Effects with Adobe® Premiere® Elements 3
Carl Plumer

Peachpit Press
1249 Eighth Street
Berkeley, CA 94710
510/524-2178
800/283-9444
510/524-2221 (fax)
Find us on the World Wide Web at: www.peachpit.com
To report errors, please send a note to errata@peachpit.com

Peachpit Press is a division of Pearson Education
Copyright © 2007 by Pearson Education

Editor: Laura Norman
Production Editor: Matt Purcell
Tech Editors: Devon Westerholm and Davis Plumer
Compositor: Carl Plumer
Indexer: Rebecca Plunkett
Interior Design: Anne Jones
Cover Design: Anne Jones and Mimi Heft

ISBN 0-7897-3612-8

9 8 7 6 5 4 3 2 1

Printed and bound in the United States of America

About the Author

Carl Plumer has worked professionally as a writer, Web developer, multimedia designer, Help systems developer, and documentation manager for high tech companies including Oracle®, Computer Associates™, and Avid® Technology. At Avid, the company that makes the editing system on which virtually all Hollywood films and many television shows are edited, he helped design one of the very first home video editing applications, Avid Cinema™. Carl is the also the author of Que's Easy Adobe® Premiere® Elements 2 and writes regularly about Premiere Elements on his website, www.LearnPremiereElements.com.

Dedication

I have many people to thank for helping me on my way through this life, but there is one who has made all the difference: Kristen. This journey is perfect because I share it with you. Also, I can't imagine my life without my four loves by my side: Hannah, Kira, Joseph, and Davis. This book would have been impossible without your support, your willingness to help, and your positive energy. Come to think of it, my whole life would be impossible without you!

Acknowledgments

I want to thank Laura Norman for once again guiding me through this amazing process and for truly taking this book from concept to reality. Thanks, too, to Anne Jones, Matt Purcell, and all the great people at Peachpit Press and Que who helped put this book together. Thanks to the companies and individuals who enthusiastically contributed sample clips for this book: your contributions were essential to the success of these projects. And to the people at Adobe, thank you for putting Premiere Elements out here for all of us to use in the first place. Last but not least, thanks to Davis Plumer, whose long hours, hard work, and attention to detail in testing each and every one of the projects in this book contributed immeasurably to their quality.

Contents

Introduction

These days, you can find video just about anywhere. You'll find it on the hard drive of your computer, on the hard drive of your TiVo® box. You'll find it on your iPod® and on your cellphone. You can upload it for all the world to see on dozens of video sharing and video blogging sites. You can even view home-made video shorts on cable channels such as Current® TV and sometimes on CNN®.

The Sundance® Film Festival, the Slamdance® Film Festival, and Hollywood itself—once the exclusive domain of film—have now found themselves becoming more and more a part of the digital world. And digital video, with the advent of 24p and HDV recording and editing equipment, is increasingly closing the gap between it and film.

So here you sit with your camcorder and your computer, eager to join this exciting world, but finding, despite all this change and energy, the whole digital video experience for you personally is lacking something; missing that one key ingredient necessary to keep you involved and to keep you interested: fun.

The fact is, editing video is hard work. Getting the right shots in the first place is no easy feat. Then capturing your footage onto your computer, gathering all your music, creating titles, and duct-taping the whole thing together can take you hour after painstaking hour, even day after humbling day. Only in the end, to have a video production that still has you wishing you could have done it better, could have created something a little more special.

The Wonder of Special Effects (SFX)

Well, move over *Lord of the Rings*. Look out, *Star Wars*. Step aside, *King Kong*. This book will show you how to create your own Hollywood special effects that are fun to do, and which are sometimes down right funny to watch. They don't require much if anything in the way of special equipment and they don't require a whole lot of investment in time, either. But the small movies you create will impress your family and friends (and yourself) and will probably cause some new creative thinking of your own. (If you come up with some great suggestions, let me know. They just may end up in the next edition of this book!).

Along the way, you'll learn more about Premiere Elements than you ever thought possible. In fact, by learning how to execute these special effects, you'll learn skills that will translate well into your other editing projects that have no apparent special effects purpose to them. This is because while these effects projects take advantage of color and sound techniques for "slight of hand" magic, they utilize the same techniques that you would use to correct the colors in an oversaturated video clip, for example, or to get the colors to match in two clips that were shot under different lighting conditions. By following the instructions in this book, you'll learn to think about timing, splitting clips, matching audio to video, syncing clips, and other concepts that until now you might not have given much though to. These projects will teach you about Premiere Elements in a way that no other book can.

Where the Fun Is

But most of all, let's face it: special effects are where the fun is. It's where the "wow" factor is. Although these effects projects are organized to build one upon the next, you don't need to follow them sequentially. Just pick one that looks interesting to you and have at it. Relax and give yourself time to work through the steps and study the illustrations. If you skip a step or miss a setting for an effect, the thing might fall apart on you; but so what? Back up a step or two, and start again. It's worth it when you're all done, sitting in your living room with your family or showing your video on a portable device to some friends. They'll be wondering how you did it and marvelling at your skills. In fact, after reading this book you may have video skills that, to paraphrase Napoleon Dynamite, "are probably the best you've ever seen."

While it's important to follow the steps exactly, it's equally important, once you get comfortable with your new skills, to experiment. I've recommended certain settings throughout to achieve an effect that I think is appropriate or cool. Feel free to mess around with any or all of the controls and settings as you go—even throwing a few other effects into the mix. You may discover something that I'm not even aware of and create an awesome effect all your own! Don't forget to save it as your own preset using the My Presets function and you'll have it ready to go the next time you want to apply it.

In this book I've tried to gather together a number of the most-asked for effects out there (such as the COPS® Hidden Identity Effect), as well as some of the most well-known (the Star Wars® Opening Sequence Effect and the Star Trek®-style "Beam Me Up" Effect). I've also thrown in a few of my own making, to show you the power of Premiere Elements (such as the Enchanted Elf Effect, the Pencil Sketch Effect, and the Retro Title Effect).

There are 20 effects in all, but these are only a mere sampling of what Premiere Elements is capable of. Browse through the Effects and Transitions palette and apply them to clips on the Timeline and see what you come up with. Combine effects and play with the controls in the Properties panel. You'll be surprised what can be accomplished with a little creativity and a video editing package as powerful as Premiere Elements.

The Minimal System for Creating SFX

One final thing about special effects: they require a lot of horsepower. If you are already editing your videos, you are probably aware that video editing is a high-end task for your computer. Adobe recommends the following configuration for Premiere Elements, but keep in mind that this represents their "entry level" setup:

◆ Intel® Pentium® 4 or AMD® Opteron® or Athlon® 64 (SSE2 support required)

◆ Microsoft® Windows® XP Professional, Home Edition, or Media Center Edition with Service Pack 2

◆ 256 MB of RAM

◆ 4 GB of available hard-disk space (This is for installation of the program only)

◆ Sound card

◆ DVD-ROM drive (compatible DVD burner required to burn DVDs)

◆ 15" monitor running at 1,024x768 16-bit XGA display

◆ Microsoft DirectX 9 compatible sound and display drivers

◆ DV/i.LINK/FireWire/IEEE 1394 or a USB2 interface

Special effects, where changes are applied to each frame in a clip, and to many clips in a video track, and to many tracks in a project, and to both video and audio tracks at the same time, obviously requires a little more than the minimum.

The Optimal System for Creating SFX

If you want to really get down to work and enjoy the experience, consider upgrading to a system like this (in parenthesis I've also added what I would consider "dream" system components: not required, but the way to go if you wanted to go all out):

◆ AMD 64 3.0 Mhz or Intel P4 3.0 or better (dual processors)

◆ 1 Gigabyte of RAM (2 Gigabytes)

◆ 160 Gigabyte hard drive (2 drives, each 250 Gigabytes)

◆ 19 inch digital (DVI) monitor running at 1,280 x 1,024 32-bit (two 19 inch DVI monitors)

◆ 64 Mb NVIDIA® GeoForce® or ATI® Radeon® graphics card (256 Mb with support for two DVI or VGA monitors)

◆ DVD Burner (double-sided, dual-density)

The Secret of Working with Special FX

There's also a secret to creating your special effects clips. You need to think about creating your movie as the process of assembling a number of smaller clips into a final, finished video movie. Work on your special effects clips as separate projects—the smaller the better. If you have a scene where the special effects are only used for a minute or two, cut that section out of the longer clip and start a new project for that section.

In your special effects clip "project," add your effects, render, test, adjust, and render again; and then save. Bring your special effects clip into your original project and overlay it in the same part of the clip where you took it from originally. It will now behave just the same as any other clip, requiring no special rendering or processing, and therefore no extra overhead from your computer. Continue in this way, with all of the clips for your project, assembling them into the "master" project file only after they are completely done. You will find it much easier to work this way. You can even go back and make changes to these clips and re-import them as needed.

That's it! Have fun, be creative, think outside the box (there's a lot of great effects you can do with just your camera and no software at all), and think small and quick. And if you get a chance, write to me at Carl.Plumer@LearnPremiereElements.com with your experiences, comments, and new ideas.

The See-Through Title Effect

MEDIA:

autumn_leaves.avi
clouds.avi
jazz-theme.wav

1

COMPLEXITY:	Simple	Moderate	Complex
SKILL LEVEL:	Novice	Intermediate	Advanced
MATERIALS:	None	Some Props	Greenscreen

Introduction

In the same way that adding music to your productions immediately—almost magically—gives them depth and power, adding titles can also provide an instant professional touch. Fact is, many home movies suffer from lackluster titles or no titles at all. Taking titles to another level, this chapter will show you how to fill a title with a video clip. Doing so has a dramatic "wow" effect that your audience will appreciate. It also gives your production the feel of a broadcast television show.

Having this technique under your belt may inspire you to plan, maybe even storyboard, a real "show." The subject of the show could be something along the lines of a "welcome to my life" video that takes the viewer around your house and your town. Maybe you can be the "host" and your daughter the cinematographer. This could be an interesting video to post on the Web for folks to view, or to send in the mail on a DVD disc to your friends and family.

When creating family videos, think creatively. This doesn't mean you have to stage everything (in case you're worried about things feeling forced). Just get everyone involved in the project. Even a movie about cleaning out the garage could be a great family video if done right.

If you get a nice opening title going, you can reuse it and perhaps create a weekly five- or ten-minute "broadcast" of your own. A number of Web sites exist that are fairly inexpensive that make it easy to upload videos and video blogs, or "vlogs." Your friends and family might even get used to "tuning in" to your weekly online show!

What You'll Do

Create the Project and Set up the Tracks

Add the Background Clip to the Timeline

Create the Title Text

Add the "Fill" Clip to the Timeline

Fill the Title with the Clouds Clip

Create a Drop Shadow for the Title

Add Some Theme Music

Add a "Fade Out" to All Video and Title Clips

Make Adjustments, Render, and Export

Creating the Project and Setting Up the Tracks

As with all of the projects in this book, we'll start by creating a new project. For this project, we'll have an initial step of creating the four video tracks that we'll need for this project. In Premiere Elements, the default number of tracks for new projects is three, so we'll be adding a single video track. If you have changed this default to a number greater than three, you can skip this task. If your default number of tracks is less than three, add as many tracks as needed so that you have four video tracks to work with.

Name the Project and Add a Track

1 Start Premiere Elements and create a new project called **seethrutitle.**

2 If the **My Project** panel is in **Sceneline** view, click the **Timeline** button to switch to **Timeline** view.

3 **Right-click** in the track header area and from the contextual menu select **Add Tracks**.

4 The default on the **Add Tracks** dialog box is to add one track. Use the **Add Tracks** dialog box as follows:

◆ If this brings the total number of video tracks to four, leave this setting and click **OK**.

◆ If not, change this number as needed so that you will have at least four video tracks available for this project.

IMPORTANT *You should now have a minimum of four video tracks on the Timeline on the My Project panel.*

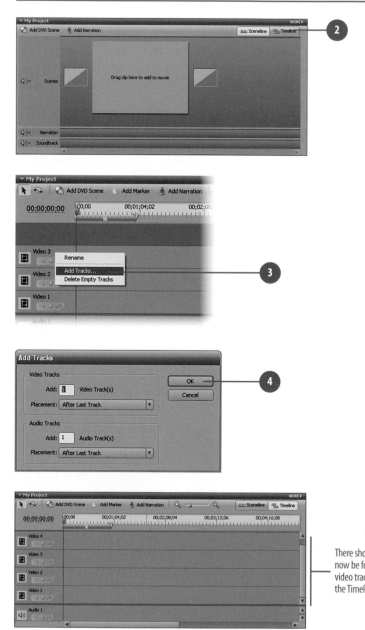

There should now be four video tracks on the Timeline.

Adding the Background Clip to the Timeline

In this task, we'll get the "background" clip and drop it on the Timeline. The background clip will supply the action over which your title will be superimposed. This can be any clip at all, but the more movement and action the better. If you are skilled at motion effects, the scenes can gently move across the screen or gradually get larger during the clip. Use your imagination and experiment: you may come up with an impressive opening sequence for your project this way. The background clip can also be a photograph or set of photographs. For this project, we have supplied you with a background video clip, **autumn_leaves.avi**.

Add Your Main "Background" Clip to the Timeline

1 Click the **Get Media from** button on the **Media** panel to access the **Get Media from** view, if it's not already active.

2 Select **DVD, Digital Camera, Mobile Phone, Hard Drive Camcorder, Card Reader**.

3 When the **Media Downloader** displays, click the **Advanced Dialog** button to switch to Advanced mode.

4 Select the **autumn_leaves.avi** clip for this project.

5 Click the **Get Media** button. Premiere Elements copies the **autumn_leaves.avi** clip from the DVD onto your hard drive and adds it to the Available Media list for this project.

6 From the **Media** panel, drag the **autumn_leaves.avi** clip to the **Video 1** track on the **Timeline**.

IMPORTANT *Be sure to drag the* **autumn_leaves.avi** *clip so that the front of the clip lines up with the very front of the* **Video 1** *track.*

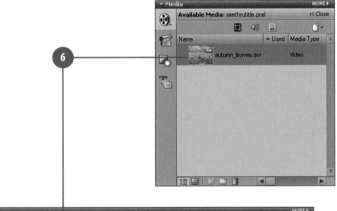

Creating the Main Title Text

For our title, we'll be using sturdy, block-style lettering (Arial Black) which will enable the viewer to better to see the video clip inside the title. We'll be making the title as large as we can while leaving plenty of the background clip showing. We also don't want to go outside the safe text boundary. For the purposes of our See-Through Title Effect, we are keeping it short and sweet with "AUTUMN DAYS."

Type, Color, and Position Your Title

1 Click the **Add Text** button on the **Monitor** panel.

2 In the text box on the **Monitor** panel that currently reads, **Add Text**, type "**AUTUMNDAYS**" in all capital letters.

3 Using the **arrow keys** on your keyboard, move the cursor so that it's between **AUTUMN** and **DAYS** and press the **ENTER** key on your keyboard. This places the two words on separate lines, like this:

> **AUTUMN**
> **DAYS**

IMPORTANT *If you click on or off the* ***Add Text*** *text box,* ***Add Text*** *will no longer be highlighted. Be sure to highlight all of the* ***Add Text*** *text again before you start typing the new text.*

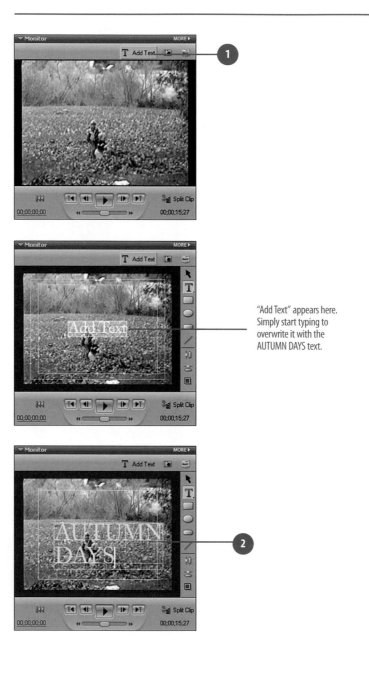

"Add Text" appears here. Simply start typing to overwrite it with the AUTUMN DAYS text.

Did You Know?

The See-Through Title Effect works best with short titles. Long words, and titles containing too many words, don't work as well as short ones. You want to be pithy, concise; brevity's the thing. Titles like "The Klondike Family's Incredible Summer Adventure" must be jettisoned in favor of "THE KLONDIKES!" or "SUMMER '07!" Think of your basic blockbuster title. You don't often see full, literary-style titles in blockbusters. You see, instead, titles like "The Ring," "Scream," "Titanic." *The Adventures of Huckelberry Finn* would today simply be, "FINN!" *All Quiet on the Western Front*, simply, "QUIET!"

Make Adjustments to the Text

 Click the **Center Text** button on the **Properties** panel to center the text.

2 **Right-click** the AUTUMN DAYS text and select **Font**.

3 From the list of fonts, choose **Arial Black**.

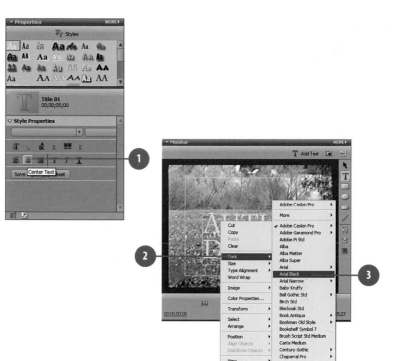

Did You Know?

You can customize titles with your favorite fonts. Any font that you install in Windows XP will also show up in Premiere Elements. If you install a new font while Premiere Elements is running, you may need to restart it before the font you installed shows up in the font list. This feature enables you to use any font you want, including free fonts, in your video productions. The right font can set the tone of movie and can make for a truly personal statement that identifies your films as *yours*.

Set the Font Color

 Click the **Color Properties** button

2 In the **Color Properties** window, color the text pure white by entering the following settings:

- ◆ **R: 255**
- ◆ **G: 255**
- ◆ **B: 255**

3 Click **OK**.

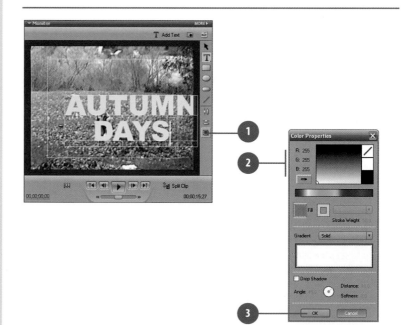

Reposition the Title Text

 Center the title vertically by clicking the **Vertical Center** button.

 Center the title horizontally by clicking the **Horizontal Center** button.

 Click the **Selection Tool**.

 Drag the title up so that it aligns with the top of the Safe Title Margin.

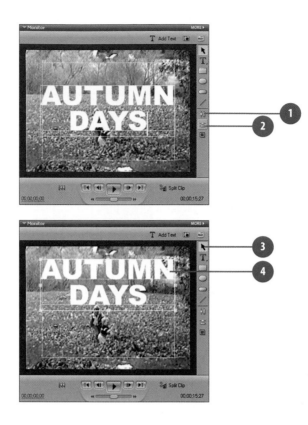

Move and Resize the Title Clip

 Click on the **Timeline** to exit the Titler.

 Drag the **Title 01** clip you just created from the **Video 2** track to the **Video 4** track.

> **IMPORTANT** *Be sure to line up the head of the* **Title 01** *clip with the beginning of the* **Video 4** *track.*

 Grab the tail (end) of the **Title 01** clip and stretch it across the **Video 4** track until it is the same length as the **autumn_leaves.avi** clip in the **Video 1** track.

Adding the "Fill" Clip to the Timeline

Now that we have created our title, we need something to fill it with—either a video clip or a still image. The brighter the fill clip, the better. Good examples of fill clips are pictures or videos of a bright summer sky, the ocean, fall leaves, the golden reflection of the sun on a lake. What you want is anything that will really stand out from the background. The title itself won't be very big so when you fill it with a clip, you want "the best and the brightest" you can find to put in it. For this project, we've provided a clip that we've created using royalty-free video courtesy of Artbeats (**www.artbeats.com**), which we're calling **clouds.avi**.

Add the Clip You Want to Fill the Title with to the Timeline

1 Again, click the **Get Media from** button on the **Media** panel to access the **Get Media from** view, if it's not already active.

2 Select **DVD, Digital Camera, Mobile Phone, Hard Drive Camcorder, Card Reader**.

3 When the **Media Downloader** displays, click the **Advanced Dialog** button to switch to Advanced mode.

4 Select the **clouds.avi** clip for this project.

5 Click the **Get Media** button. Premiere Elements copies the **clouds.avi** clip from the DVD onto your hard drive and adds it to the Available Media list for this project.

6 From the **Media** panel, drag the **clouds.avi** clip to the **Video 3** track on the **Timeline**.

7 Grab the tail end of the **clouds.avi** clip and resize it so that it matches the length of the **autumn_leaves** clip in the Video 1 track.

Filling the Title with the Clouds Clip

Now that you have your two media clips (the background **autumn_leaves.avi** clip and the title "fill" clip, **clouds.avi**) and your title on the Timeline, here's where the real fun begins. We'll be applying a basic Premiere Elements video effect, the **Track Matte** effect, to the "fill" clip on the Timeline. We'll then point it at the **Title 01** clip and the title text will display within it the **clouds.avi** video, clipped to play only within the bounds of the title itself. You'll like it and your audience will be awestruck.

Use the Track Matte Key to Fill the Title

1 Click the **Effects and Transitions** button on the **Media** panel to change to the **Effects and Transitions** view.

2 In the text box on the **Effects and Transitions** view, type **track**. The **Track Matte** effect appears in the **Keying** folder in the **Video Effects** section of the **Effects and Transitions** panel.

3 Drag and drop the **Track Matte Key** effect onto the **clouds.avi** clip on the **Video 3** track on the **Timeline**.

4 With the **clouds.avi** clip selected, access the **Properties** panel and click the triangle next to the **Track Matte Key** effect to reveal the effect's controls.

5 From the **Matte** drop down, select **Video 4**. Leave the other **Track Matte Key** options (**Composite Using** and **Reverse**) as they are.

TIP *Note that in the Monitor panel, the effect is instant. The clouds now show through the title text. You may have to move your CTI along the Timeline to see the effect if it happens to be placed off of the clips on the video tracks.*

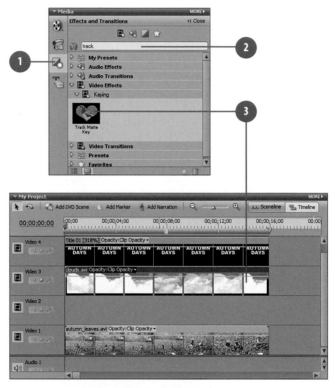

Creating a Drop Shadow for the Title

Now that the title has the clip in place, you might notice that while the effect looks good, it has no "dimensionality" to it; that is, it looks a little flat. There isn't much differentiation between the background and the title. In fact, if you were to use, for example, a clip of the ocean inside your title and your title overlaid a scene of the beach, it could be difficult to tell what's title and what's background. This can be fixed easily using the ever popular "drop shadow." To apply a drop shadow we first create a copy of our **Title 01** clip. Then, we add a shadow to it.

Create a Copy of the Title 01 Clip

1 Click the **Available Media** button to switch to the **Available Media** view, if it's not already active.

2 **Right-click** the **Title 01** clip in the **Available Media** view to bring up the contextual menu.

3 Select **Duplicate** from the contextual menu.

4 Select the duplicate clip, **Title 01 Copy**, in the **Available Media** view and **right-click** on the clip.

5 From the contextual menu select **Rename**.

6 Rename the copy **Drop Shadow**.

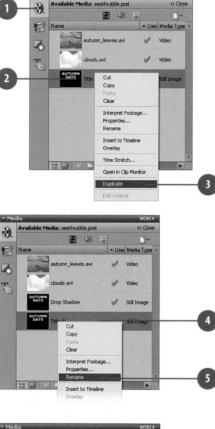

Place the Shadow Clip on the Timeline

1 Drag the **Drop Shadow** title clip from the **Available Media** view and drop it onto the **Video 2** track on the Timeline.

2 Grab the tail end of the clip and trim it so that it is the same length/duration as the other clips on the Timeline.

Did You Know?

You need to create a separate clip for shadows. You may be saying to yourself, "Hey, why didn't we just add a drop shadow to the title we already have?" Consider this: Had we used the Titler's drop shadow capabilities for the **Title 01** clip (the one with the sky now floating in it), the **clouds.avi** clip would show through the drop shadow as well. This is due to the fact that the Track Matte Key effect works by allowing the second clip to appear through the matte's white space. And since there's just a little white in the drop shadow, a bit of the clip shows through. By using a second clip (a copy of the first **Title 01** clip), we get a nice, clean drop shadow and retain our crisp "see-through" title. For the shadow to work, it must be on the right track, and this would be behind (below) both the **Title 01** track on the **Video 4 track** and the **clouds.avi** clip on the **Video 3** track.

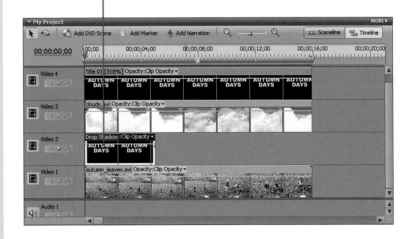

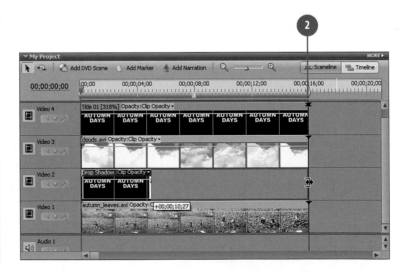

Create the Drop Shadow

 Double-click on the **Drop Shadow** clip on the **Video 2** track to access the **Titler**.

 Click the **Color Properties** button to access the **Color Properties** dialog box.

 On the **Color Properties** dialog box, add a drop shadow to the text by clicking the **Drop Shadow** check box.

 Set the following drop shadow parameters:

- ◆ **Angle: 140**

- ◆ **Distance: 20**

- ◆ **Softness: 40**

 Click **OK**.

TIP *For these settings, you can type the numbers in directly, or use your mouse to slide across and adjust them that way. For the* **Angle** *setting, you can use the knob control if you choose. Also, feel free to adjust these settings as you see fit. You can see the changes you make in the* **Titler** *in real time. (Move the* **Color Properties** *dialog box out of the way to see the* **Titler**, *if necessary.)*

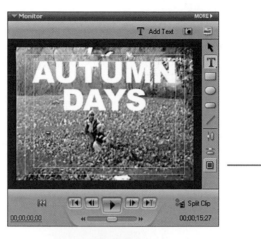

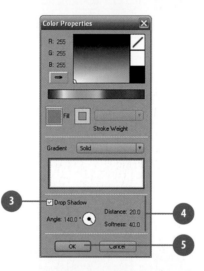

The Title text with the drop shadow added.

Adding Some Theme Music

The final, and necessary, touch to a good opening credits sequence is to have some music playing "under." On the DVD that accompanies this book we've provided you with just the thing, a mellow little tune called **jazz-theme.wav**. This is a a small sample from the SmartSound Quicktracks collection (**www.smartsound.com**). We'll add this to the **Audio 1** track and adjust the volume a bit so that it's not too overpowering, and our sequence is complete.

Add a Little Music for the Final Touch

1 Click the **Get Media from** button on the **Media** panel to access the **Get Media from** view, if it's not already active.

2 Select **DVD, Digital Camera, Mobile Phone, Hard Drive Camcorder, Card Reader**.

3 When the **Media Downloader** displays, click the **Advanced Dialog** button to switch to Advanced mode.

4 Select the **jazz-theme.wav** clip for this project.

5 Click the **Get Media** button. Premiere Elements copies the **jazz-theme.wav** clip from the DVD onto your hard drive and adds it to the Available Media list for this project.

6 From the **Media** panel, drag and drop the **jazz-theme.wav** clip onto the **Audio 1** track on the **Timeline**.

7 Grab the tail end of the **jazz-theme.wav** clip and resize it so that it matches the length of the video clips.

8 In the **Properties** panel, adjust the overall volume of the clip by typing **-12** dB (note the minus sign) in the **Clip Volume** control of **Volume** effect.

9 Click the **Fade Out** button for the **Volume** property.

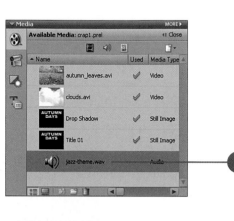

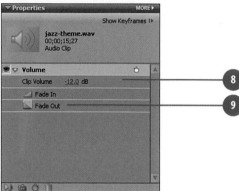

Adding a "Fade Out" to All Video and Title Clips ▶

We want to have a gentle "fade to black" for all of our video clips (and title clips) at the end. Premiere Elements provides us with a very simple way to do this. On each clip's **Properties** panel there is a **Fade Out** button. We'll click each of the clips in the video tracks one by one and click their **Fade Out** button and this project is complete!

Fade Out All of the Clips on the Video Tracks

1 Click the **Title 01** clip on the **Video 4** track.

2 In the **Properties** panel for the **Title 01** clip, click the **Fade Out** button.

3 Click on the **clouds.avi** clip on the **Video 3** track.

4 In the **Properties** panel for the **clouds.avi** clip, click the **Fade Out** button.

5 Click on the **Drop Shadow** clip on the **Video 2** track.

6 Again, in the **Properties** panel for the **Drop Shadow** clip, click the **Fade Out** button.

7 Finally, click on the **autumn_leaves.avi** clip on the **Video 1** track.

8 As before, in the **Properties** panel for the **autumn_leaves.avi** clip, click the **Fade Out** button.

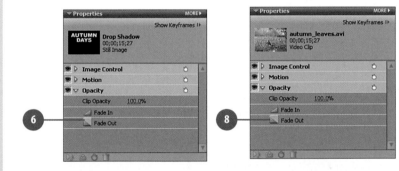

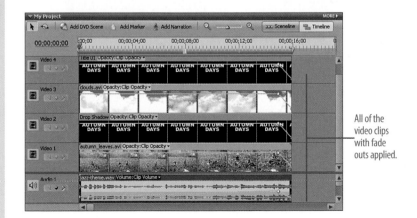

All of the video clips with fade outs applied.

Making Adjustments, Rendering, and Exporting

Before you finish this project, make any final tweaks as needed, and you are ready to save, render, and make your movie.

Finishing the Project

1 Once you have played back your clip and made the necessary adjustments, press the **ENTER** key on your keyboard to render your project.

2 Press **CTRL-S** to save your project (you can select **File, Save** from the menu). Of course, you should be doing this all the time while creating this or any other project in Premiere Elements.

3 Finally, export your work as an AVI file. To export the clip, select **File, Export, Movie**.

TIP *You can optionally bring this clip into a larger project, show it on your computer, upload it to an Internet video sharing site, or burn it to a DVD.*

As the project renders, Premiere Elements provides you with status information, including estimated time to complete and a progress bar.

The finished project running in Windows Media Player, showing the full See-Through title effect with drop shadow, superimposed over the background video.

The Retro Title Effect

MEDIA:

retro-footage.avi
shag-party.mp3

2

COMPLEXITY:	Simple	Moderate	**Complex**
SKILL LEVEL:	Novice	Intermediate	**Advanced**
MATERIALS:	**None**	Some Props	Greenscreen

Introduction

Titles tend to be underutilized to a degree in many video productions, which is unfortunate. Aside from conveying essential information, titles can set the tone, add style and fun to a video, and let the video editor show off a bit. This chapter will explore the use of motion, color, fonts, and music to create a retro '60s look. This title technique can be a lot of fun to put together and can quickly turn an ordinary picnic, family reunion, or other subject into a cool "happening" with a real '60s-style flair.

There's a lot to learn in this chapter, and a lot to do. But once you get the handle on this technique (and don't have to keep referring to this book for instructions on how to do it), you'll see how surprisingly quick and easy it really is to apply this title effect, and variations of it, whenever you want.

You'll find that the skills and knowledge that you learn in creating this simple (but cool, baby!) effect will be something that you'll be able to apply on a variety of projects in a number of different ways. Using keyframes, motion effects, and mattes—as well as understanding the basic size and shape of the screen and techniques such as timing and synchronization—are essential skills for any video editor seeking to create enjoyable, watchable, and interesting movies.

What You'll Do

Install the Fonts for this Project

Add the Video Clip to the Timeline

Modify the Clip to Give it a "Cinematic 60's" Feel

Create the First Still

Understand Aspect Ratio and Garbage Mattes

Create the Second Still

Create the Third Still

Create "Credits" for Each Still

Animate the First Actor's Still and Credits

Understand Motion and Keyframes

Animate the Second Actor's Still and Credits

Animate the Third Actor's Still and Credits

Create an Opening Title

Create a Title to Set the Scene

Add a Little "Retro" Music to the Project

Make Adjustments, Render, and Export

Installing the Fonts for this Project

For the "retro" look of the Retro Titles Effect, we need '60's-style typefaces. In a later task, we'll also be adding some '60's-style music. The fonts we're using are fonts that were created by Ben Balvanz, a pioneer in the field of electronic type design. The two fonts, *Alba* and *Chick*, have a distinctive 1960's feel and will help give this project the retro look we're shooting for. We'll use the *Alba* font for the actor's credits and the *Chick* font for the opening and closing titles.

Install the Two Fonts

1 From the Windows **Start** button, select **Control Panel**.

2 On the **Control Panel**, select **Appearance and Themes**.

> **NOTE** *These steps and illustrations refer to the default setup of Windows XP. If you have Windows XP in "Classic View," select* **Fonts** *from the Control Panel at this time.*

3 From the **See Also** box on the left side of the screen, select **Fonts**.

4 When the **Fonts** folder opens, select **File, Install New Font**.

5 On the **Add Fonts** dialog box, use the **Drives** drop down to locate your DVD drive.

> **TIP** *Be sure the DVD supplied with this book is in your DVD drive.*

6 Navigate to the **Extras** folder on the DVD, then to the **Fonts** folder.

7 The *Alba (True Type)* font and the *Chick (True Type)* fonts will show up in the list of fonts. Select these two fonts and click **OK**.

> **NOTE** *After the fonts have been installed, close the* **Fonts** *folder and close the* **Appearance and Themes** *window.*

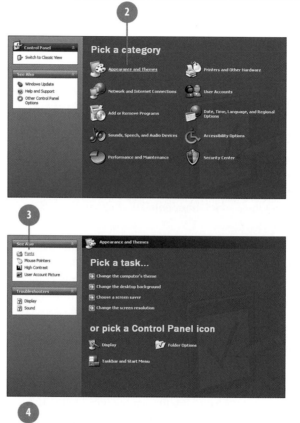

Adding the Video Clip to the Timeline

The first step in creating this effect is the same basic step for virtually all of the projects in this book: go get your media clips and place them on the Timeline. For this project, the video clip is **retro-footage.avi**. We'll be taking stills ("freeze frames") taken directly from this video that we later will manipulate to show just a very narrow area, concentrating almost exclusively on the subject and cutting out most of the background.

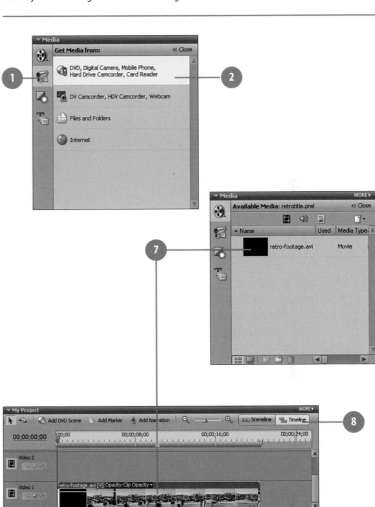

Add the Video Clip to the Timeline

1. Start Premiere Elements and create a new project called **retrotitle**.

2. Click the **Get Media from** button on the **Media** panel to access the **Get Media from** view, if it's not already active.

3. Select **DVD, Digital Camera, Mobile Phone, Hard Drive Camcorder, Card Reader**.

4. When the **Media Downloader** displays, click the **Advanced Dialog** button to switch to Advanced mode.

5. Select the **retro-footage.avi** clip.

6. Click the **Get Media** button. Premiere Elements copies the **retro-footage.avi** clip from the DVD onto your hard drive and adds it to the Available Media list for this project.

7. Select the **retro-footage.avi** clip on the **Media** panel and drag and drop it onto the **Timeline** in the **Video 1** track. Be sure to line up the start of the **retro-footage.avi** clip with the beginning of the **Video 1** track.

    TIP *If you're in **Sceneline** view, drop the **retro-footage.avi** clip onto the first scene box. Premiere Elements will place it on the **Video 1** track.*

8. Click the **Timeline** button on the **My Project** panel to switch to **Timeline** view, if it's not already the active view.

    NOTE *We need to switch to **Timeline** view because for this project we are working with multiple clips on multiple video tracks.*

Modifying the Clip to Give it a "Cinematic '60's" Feel

With technologies and concepts such as "HD" and "24p," the holy grail of digital video is the transformation of video into film, or more precisely, the *look* of film. While most solutions involve expensive cameras and software, as well as special filming techniques, we can create an acceptable approximation by simply taking some of the **Image Control** settings for the clip and deliberately pushing them outside the normal range. Also, by adding a bit of "noise" (in some applications this is actually called *film noise*), we can also help to soften the harsher lines of video and create the illusion of the somewhat softer look of film.

Brighten the Clip

1️⃣ Click the **retro-footage.avi** clip on the **Video 1** track to select it.

2️⃣ In the **Properties** panel for the **retro-footage.avi** clip, click the triangle next to **Image Control** to reveal the effect's controls.

3️⃣ Set the following new settings:

◆ **Brightness: 20.0**

◆ **Contrast: 80.0**

◆ **Hue: 10.0°**

◆ **Saturation: 200.0**

TIP *Scrub the **Current Time Indicator** (CTI) on the Timeline to a point in the clip past the black, so that you can see the changes in the clip as you make them.*

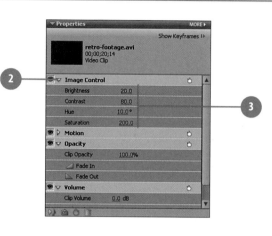

Add a Little Noise

1️⃣ Click the **Effects and Transitions** button on the **Media** panel to switch to the **Effects and Transitions** view.

2️⃣ In the **Effects and Transitions** view, type **noise** in the text box.

3️⃣ Drag and drop the **Noise** effect onto the **retro-footage.avi** clip on the **Video 1** track on the **Timeline**.

TIP *The **Noise** effect might not be visible at first. To see it, you may need to scroll down.*

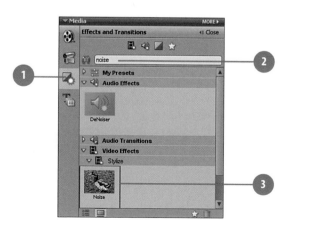

4 In the **Properties** panel for the **retro-footage.avi** clip, click the triangle next to **Noise** to reveal the effect's controls.

> **TIP** *You may need to close one of the other effects or scroll down the list of effects, to find the **Noise** effect.*

5 Set the **Amount of Noise** to **10.0%**. Leave all other settings "as is."

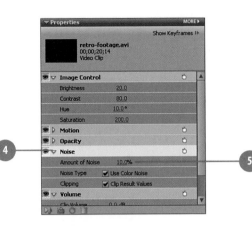

Did You Know?

There's more to creating a "film look."
This was a very simplified version of what is a very complicated process involving a lot more than what was covered in these last couple of pages. But you did get a taste for not only the power of the built-in color effects in Premiere Elements, but also—and more importantly—the ability of color in film and video to set a mood. We're using color almost exclusively to suggest film, and to suggest the super-saturated, bright colors of 1960's Technicolor® films in particular. However, there are other software products and plug-ins available that are made specifically for achieving that "film look" with video.

The **retro-footage.avi** clip, as it appears normally.

The **retro-footage.avi** clip, with a '60s film look, courtesy of a little noise and a little image manipulation.

Understanding Aspect Ratio and Garbage Mattes

The unfortunately-named set of mattes known as, collectively, **garbage mattes**, serve an important purpose within Premiere Elements: they let you hide stuff you don't want, basically the "garbage."

For the purposes of this project, we're using the Four-Point Garbage Matte to simultaneously crop our stills and create the black background we want. Premiere Elements also has an Eight-Point Garbage Matte and a Sixteen-Point Garbage Matte available.

The Coordinates on the Screen

The standard video signal in North America and Japan —that is, the non-letterbox, not-high definition signal—is 480 by 720. This is known as the *aspect ratio*.

These numbers are used when positioning items on the screen as coordinates. Specifically, the location of any item on the screen can be defined by its "*x*" (horizontal) and "*y*" (vertical) coordinates. For an NTSC signal (the television standard in the United States and elsewhere in the world), the horizontal length (left and right) is 720, and the vertical length (up and down) is 480.

As shown in the previous illustration in Cartesian terms (*x,y*), the four corners of the television screen (as well as the Premiere Elements Monitor panel), for an NTSC signal would be expressed as *0,0* for the upper left corner; *720,0* for the upper right; *0, 480* for the lower left; and *720,480* for the lower right.

Controlling the Garbage Matte

The Four-Point Garbage Matte's controls are listed on the Properties panel in order, from the top two corners to the bottom two corners. Each corner, such as "Bottom Left," shows the coordinate for the *x*-axis first, followed by the coordinate for the *y*-axis. You can also view the controls "by side." As shown below, the Left side controls are at the top and bottom, while the right side controls are in the middle.

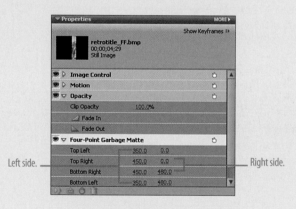

You can also control the size and shape of a garbage matte by grabbing the garbage handles and dragging them to a new position, or by entering new sets of *x,y* coordinates in the Properties panel, or a combination of the two methods. In the illustration on the next page, the handles can be seen in each of the four corners after the title of the **Four-Point Garbage Matte** effect in the **Properties** panel has been clicked.

How to Use the Matte

Click on the **Four-Point Garbage Matte** name here in the Properties panel...

...and handles appear in each corner of the image in the **Monitor** panel.

Grab the handles one at a time to adjust the location of that handle's *x,y* point, which is reflected on the matte's controls on the **Properties** panel.

The **Four-Point Garbage Matte** is adjusted here so that both the lower left and lower right corners now sit on the bottom of the screen (notice that the *x* coordinate for both "bottoms" is at *480*). The result is shown in the illustration to the right.

Finally, the **Four-Point Garbage Matte** is adjusted so that the rectangle is even (with a width of *100*) and reaches both the top (*0*) and the bottom (*480*). The result is shown in the illustration to the right.

Creating the First Still

In this task, we'll create a still, or "freeze frame," from the video, resize it to add "focus," and recolor it to add "coolness." Each of our "retro" stills will have its own bright color so that as it appears on the screen it makes its own unique statement. We'll be using shades of orange, magenta, and green for our stills.

Use Premiere Elements' Freeze Frame Feature to Create the Still

1 Move the **CTI** 10 seconds into our clip, to **00;00;10;00**. This is the frame that we'll use as our first still.

2 Click the **Freeze Frame** button on the **Monitor** panel to access the **Freeze Frame** dialog box.

3 On the **Freeze Frame** dialog box, click the **Insert in Movie** button.

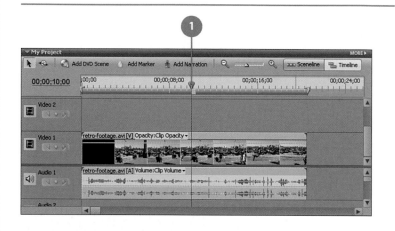

Did You Know?

Choose any color for your next project.
It doesn't matter which colors you choose for your stills in your next project. You can "colorize" each still in a different shade of blue, for example. Or, you can make each one a primary color: red, yellow, and blue. For a 4th of July video, you could colorize each clip red, white, and blue. For a Holiday clip, perhaps reds and greens.

Crop the Image Using the Garbage Matte

1 Click the **Effects and Transitions** button on the **Media** panel to switch to the **Effects and Transitions** view, if it's not already active.

2 In the **Effects and Transitions** view, type **four** in the text box.

3 Drag the **Four-Point Garbage Matte** effect and drop it onto the **retro-title_FF.bmp** clip on the **Video 1** track on the Timeline.

4 Click the triangle next to **Four-Point Garbage Matte** on the **Properties** panel to reveal the effect's controls.

5 Make the following adjustments to the **Four Point Garbage Matte**.

- ◆ **Top Left:**   350.0   0.0
- ◆ **Top Right:**   450.0   0.0
- ◆ **Bottom Right:** 450.0   480.0
- ◆ **Bottom Left:**   350.0   480.0

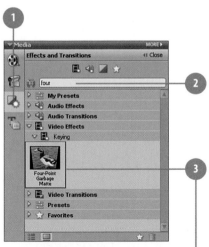

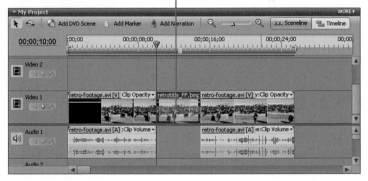

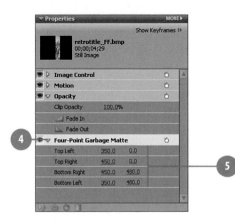

2

Color the Image Using the Color Balance (RGB) Effect

1 Click the **Effects and Transitions** button on the **Media** panel to switch to the **Effects and Transitions** view, if necessary.

2 In the **Effects and Transitions** view of the **Media** panel, type **rgb** in the text box.

3 Drag the **Color Balance (RGB)** effect and drop it onto the **retro-title_FF.bmp** clip on the **Video 1** track on the **Timeline**.

4 In the **Properties** panel for the **retro-title_FF.bmp**, click the triangle next to **Color Balance (RGB)** to reveal the effect's controls.

> **NOTE** *You may need to close one of the other effect's controls by clicking the triangle, or scroll down to see the **Color Balance (RGB)** controls.*

5 Make the following changes to the **Color Balance (RGB)** effect:

- ◆ **Red: 200**
- ◆ **Green: 40**
- ◆ **Blue: 30**

> **TIP** *You can optionally click the **Setup** button and use the sliders on the **Color Balance Settings** dialog box.*

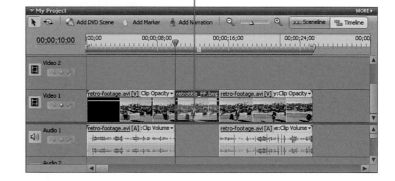

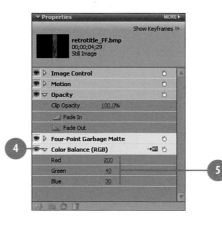

Creating the Second Still

Now that we have our first snapshot cropped and colorized, let's continue along the clip and find a good frame for our second actor and take our next snapshot. The procedure for taking the snapshot, creating the shape with the **Four-Point Garbage Matte**, and colorizing the clip is exactly the same as for the first snapshot. The difference will be in the location of the matte and in the color that we choose (since we want each actor to have his or her own unique color).

Create the Snapshot

1. Move the **CTI** eight seconds to **00;00;18;00**. This is the frame that we'll use as our second still "photograph."

2. Click the **Freeze Frame** button on the **Monitor** panel to access the **Freeze Frame** dialog box.

3. On the **Freeze Frame** dialog box, click the **Insert in Movie** button.

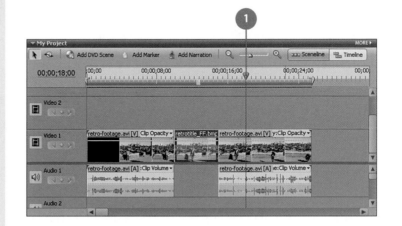

Did You Know?

You can paint by numbers.
RGB refers to **R**ed, **G**reen, and **B**lue, a standard color format for online use. It uses two of the three primary colors on the color wheel, Red and Blue. Green is a combination of Yellow (the third primary color) and Blue. By mixing these colors much as you would paint, you can create virtually any color you can imagine. You "mix" your colors with the **Color Balance (RGB)** effect by changing the number for each color, from 0 to 200.

Modify the Shape

1 Click the **Effects and Transitions** button on the **Media** panel to switch to the **Effects and Transitions** view, if necessary.

2 In the **Effects and Transitions** view, type **four** in the text box.

3 Drag the **Four-Point Garbage Matte** effect and drop it onto the **retro-title_FF_1.bmp** clip on the **Video 1** track (this is the *second* still clip on the Timeline).

4 Click the triangle next to **Four-Point Garbage Matte** on the **Properties** panel to reveal the effect's controls.

5 Make the following adjustments to the **Four Point Garbage Matte**.

- ◆ **Top Left:**   275.0   0.0
- ◆ **Top Right:**   375.0   0.0
- ◆ **Bottom Right:** 375.0   480.0
- ◆ **Bottom Left:** 275.0   480.0

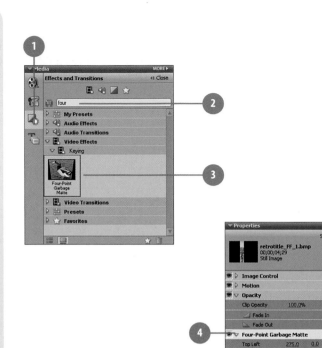

Modify the Color

1 In the **Effects and Transitions** view of the **Media** panel, type **rgb** in the text box.

2 Drag the **Color Balance (RGB)** effect and drop it onto the **retro-title_FF_1.bmp** clip (the *second* freeze frame you created) on the **Video 1** track on the **Timeline**.

3 In the **Properties** panel, click the triangle next to **Color Balance (RGB)** to reveal the effect's controls.

4 Make the following changes to the **Color Balance (RGB)** effect.

- ◆ **Red: 200**
- ◆ **Green: 30**
- ◆ **Blue: 130**

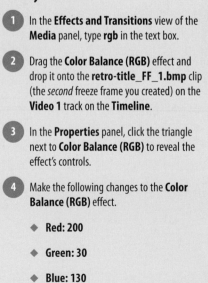

Creating the Third Still

We're now ready to create our third, and final, actor's snapshot. We'll create this one just as before, and apply the **Four-Point Garbage Matte** and the **Color Balance (RGB)** effects as before, as well. After we have our clips in place, we'll create the "credits" that will accompany each clip, and start the animation of all of these elements.

Create the Final Snapshot

① Once again, move the **CTI**, this time twenty-six seconds in to **00;00;26;00**. This is the frame that we'll use as our final still picture.

② Click the **Freeze Frame** button on the **Monitor** panel to access the **Freeze Frame** dialog box.

③ On the **Freeze Frame** dialog box, click the **Insert in Movie** button.

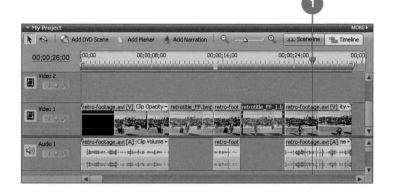

Modify the Shape

1. If necessary, click the **Effects and Transitions** button on the **Media** panel to switch to the **Effects and Transitions** view.

2. In the **Effects and Transitions** view, type **four** in the text box.

3. Drag the **Four-Point Garbage Matte** effect and drop it onto the **retro-title_FF_2.bmp** clip on the **Video 1** track (the *third* still).

4. On the **Properties** panel, click the triangle next to **Four-Point Garbage Matte**.

5. Make the following adjustments to the **Four Point Garbage Matte**.

   - **Top Left:**   325.0   0.0

   - **Top Right:**   425.0   0.0

   - **Bottom Right:** 425.0   480.0

   - **Bottom Left:**   325.0   480.0

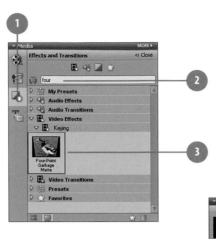

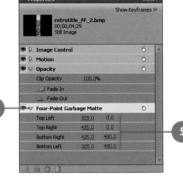

Modify the Color

1. In the **Effects and Transitions** view of the **Media** panel, type **rgb** in the text box.

2. Drag the **Color Balance (RGB)** effect and drop it onto the **retro-title_FF_2.bmp** clip (the *third* freeze frame you created.) on the **Video 1** track on the Timeline.

3. In the **Properties** panel, click the triangle next to **Color Balance (RGB)** to reveal the effect's controls.

4. Make the following changes to the **Color Balance (RGB)** effect.

   - **Red: 50**

   - **Green: 200**

   - **Blue: 50**

Creating "Credits" for Each Still

Create "Credits" for the First Actor

1 Move the **CTI** to **00;00;10;00**, which is the beginning of the **retrotitle_FF.bmp** clip in the **Video 1** track on the **Timeline**.

2 On the **Monitor** panel, click the **Add Text** button.

3 In the **Properties** panel, change the font to **Alba**.

4 Change the font size to **48**.

5 Click the **Right Align Text** button to change the alignment to right-aligned.

6 Drag your mouse across the **Add Type** text in the **Titler** and type **Miles W as "Sketch"** to replace it.

7 Move you cursor after **as** and before **"Sketch"** and press the **ENTER** key on your keyboard so that your text looks like the text in the illustration to the right.

8 Click the **Selection Tool** (the arrow).

9 Grab the text box and drag it so that it is on the left side of the screen.

Now that we have created all of our still images, we need the identifying credits to match. We'll create these in Premiere Elements **Titler**. Once we have all of our pieces in place, we'll be ready to animate them using the **Motion** effect on the **Properties** panel, which we'll begin to do in the upcoming tasks.

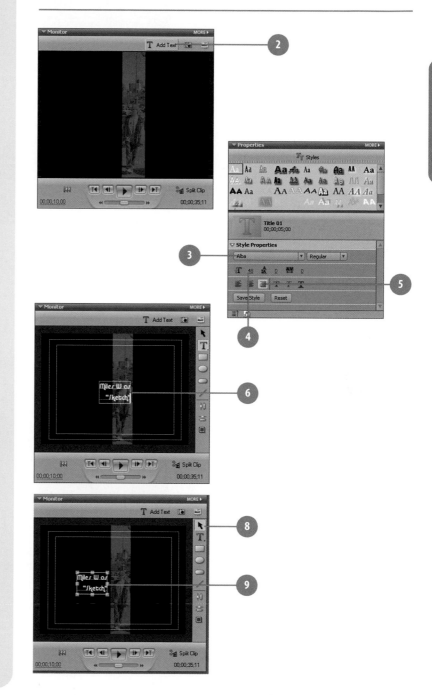

2

Create "Credits" for the Second Actor

1 Move the **CTI** to **00;00;18;00**, the beginning of the **retrotitle_FF_1.bmp** clip in the **Video 1** track on the **Timeline**.

2 On the **Monitor** panel, click the **Add Text** button.

3 In the **Properties** panel, change the font to **Alba,** the font size to **48**, and the alignment to *left*-**aligned**.

4 Drag your mouse across the **Add Type** text in the Titler and type **Viola Barkley as "Sing"** to replace it.

5 Move you cursor after **Barkley** and before **as** and press the **ENTER** key so that your text looks like the text in the illustration.

6 Click the **Selection Tool** (the arrow) and move the text box so that it is on the lower right side of the screen, next to the actor.

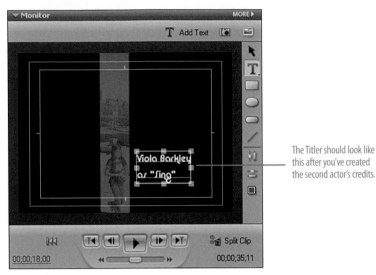

The Titler should look like this after you've created the second actor's credits.

Create "Credits" for the Third Actor

1 Move the **CTI** to the beginning of the third clip, **retrotitle_FF_2.bmp**, at **00;00;26;00**.

2 Click the **Add Text** button on the **Monitor**.

3 In the **Properties** panel, change the font to **Alba, 48**, *right*-**aligned**.

4 Drag your mouse across the **Add Type** text in the **Titler** and type **Joey Donuts as "Ben Ten."**

5 Move you cursor after **Donuts** and before **as** and press **ENTER**.

6 Click the **Selection Tool** and move the text box so that it is on the lower right side of the screen, near the actor (as shown in the illustration to the right).

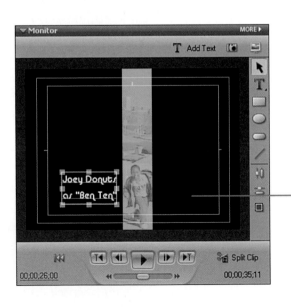

The Titler should look like this after you've created the final actor's credits.

Animating the First Actor's Still and Credits

We'll now start animating all of the clips we've created so that they move in and out of our audience's frame of vision while the music plays. To do so, we'll use one of Premiere Elements' most powerful effects features, the **Motion** effect. By the way, the **Motion** effect is one of Premiere Elements' *fixed effects*, meaning that the effect is available for all clips and doesn't need to be applied to a clip first from the **Effects and Transitions** panel.

Using the Motion Effect

1 On the **Timeline**, move the **CTI** to **00;00;10;00**, whish is the start of the **retro-title_FF.bmp** clip**.**

2 Click on the **retro-title_FF.bmp** and in the **Properties** panel, click **Show Keyframes**.

3 Click the **triangle** next to **Motion**.

4 Click the **Toggle animation** button for **Motion**.

5 Move the **CTI** (either on the **Properties** panel of the **Timeline**) to **00;00;14;28**.

6 Change the **Position** to **360 725**.

> **TIMESAVER** *Premiere Elements automatically places a keyframe here at the change in* **Position**.

7 Move the **CTI** to the halfway point, at **00;00;12;15**.

8 Change the **Position** here to **360 240**.

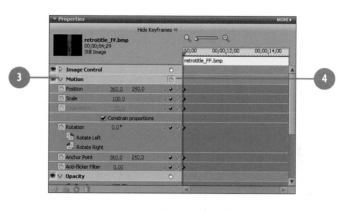

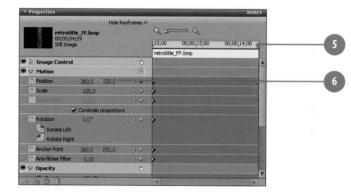

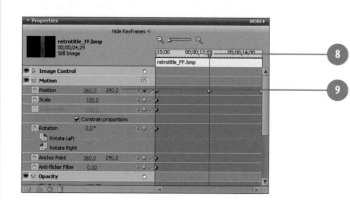

Did You Know?

You can control time.

By placing a keyframe at a point in the middle of the clip's timeline, you are controlling exactly how much time the **retro-title_FF.bmp** clip stays on screen before it starts to move. Therefore, since the clip is 5 seconds long, for the first 2.5 seconds the **retro-title_FF.bmp** clip will remain "frozen." After 2.5 seconds, the clip will rapidly depart the "stage," so to speak, following the path you set.

Understanding Motion and Keyframes

A key part of creating the Retro Titles Effect is the use of motion. Motion is one of the effects in Premiere Elements that you can control with **keyframes**. Video clips are made up of frames. *Keyframes* are the key points in a clip where something significant, or "key," happens, such as when a video clip changes size, speed, direction, or opacity, for example, or when an audio clip changes volume.

The Motion Effect

For the purposes of this effect, we want to create motion—in other words, we want to *animate*—both the actors' stills and the credits. To do this, we are using Premiere Elements' **Motion** effect, which is a default effect for every visual media on the Timeline, including video clips, stills, and titles.

To animate a clip, you first set a start point (assigning the *x,y* coordinates as explained earlier in this chapter), an end point (again assigning the *x,y* coordinates), and one or as many middle points as are needed. Each point is defined using a keyframe and each keyframe marks the frame where a change takes place.

You don't need to set keyframes or set the *x,y* coordinates for every frame in a clip, however. Premiere Elements takes care of the "in between" changes for you. This is known as *tweening*, a term that comes from the animation (cartooning) world (as does the term keyframe).

Using the **Motion** effect, you can control the position of any clip over time, as well as its scale (size) and scale width (proportionally or not; that is, with or without distorting it), and even rotate it (as well as set its rotation anchor point), which by default is in the center of the screen.

Motion and speed is set by the keyframe's position in the **Properties** panel timeline for the clip. The default motion type is "Linear" and "Auto Bezier," which are the temporal (time) and spatial (space) types, respectively. These can be changed by right-clicking on a keyframe and selecting a different temporal or spatial type. The contextual menu that appears when you right-click also contains options for copying, cutting, and pasting keyframes.

Selected keyframes in the **Properties** panel timeline are blue. Unselected keyframes are gray. Many of the temporal keyframes have their own shape. For example, Linear is a triangle while Auto Bezier is a circle.

You can navigate from keyframe to keyframe using the "go to next" keyframes buttons; one button moves the **CTI** one keyframes to the right (forward), the other one keyframes to the left (backward). Note that these are interactive buttons that "light up" when the **CTI** is on a keyframe, showing which action you can take. The center (round) button is for adding or removing keyframes. Keyframes are also added automatically anytime you make a change to a setting.

For example, if you have a keyframe that has the clip starting in the lower left corner of the screen and a keyframe that has the clip ending in the upper right corner, Premiere Elements will "tween" (in other words, or provide us with) all of the changes to the clip for the intervening frames across the screen.

Controlling the Timing of a Clip

In the preceding example, the speed at which the clip travels diagonally across the screen is uniform for the given duration of the clip. If we want to speed up or slow down how the clip moves at any point, we can add additional keyframes. How far apart or close together these keyframes are controls how fast or slow the clip plays.

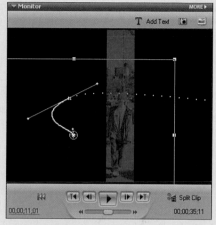

You can control the motion and timing of a clip using a combination of dragging the clip in the **Monitor** panel to define the motion, and setting keyframes and entering numeric values in the **Properties** panel to define the timing.

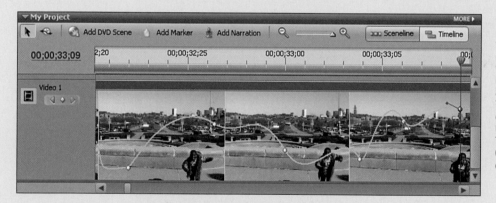

You can also view and manipulate keyframes right on the Timeline. Keyframes are gold when selected and gray when not. You navigate from keyframe to keyframe and add and delete keyframes in the Timeline the same way that you do in the **Properties** panel. Using keyframes on the Timeline is best suited for Opacity changes and Volume changes (for audio clips).

For example, if near the end of the clip we were to add another keyframe at the middle of the screen, then the clip will be take a relatively long time to move from the left corner to the center of the screen, after which it would rocket from the center to the upper right.

If, on the other hand, we set this third keyframe very near the end of the clip and very near the upper right corner, the clip would rocket immediately to the upper right, and then take a relatively long time to go from that point to the end frame in the upper corner.

Animate the Credits for the First Actor

1 Move the **CTI** to **00;00;14;05**, where the top edge of the **retrotitle_FF.bmp** clip just passes the bottom of the **Title 01** clip, as shown in the illustration.

2 Click the **Title 01** clip, the credits for the first actor, in the **Video 2** track on the Timeline.

3 In the **Properties** panel, click the **triangle** next to **Motion**.

> **IMPORTANT** *Be sure you click just once on the Title 01 clip. This will ensure that we are working with the clip as a media clip. If you double-click, you'll open the Titler, and you will be working with the clip as a title.*

4 Click the **Toggle animation** button.

> **NOTE** *If the keyframes work area is not displayed (as it is in the illustration), click the click Show Keyframes button.*

5 On the **Properties** panel or on the **Timeline**, move the **CTI** to the end of the **Title 01** clip, **00;00;14;29**.

6 Change the **Position** here to **940 240**.

> **TIMESAVER** *Premiere Elements automatically places a keyframe here to mark the change in Position.*

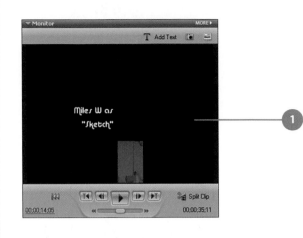

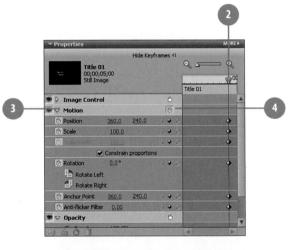

Animating the Second Actor's Still and Credits

In this task, we'll animate the second actor's freeze frame as well as her credits. We'll be using the same keyframing technique with the **Motion** effect as we did with the first actor's freeze frame and credits.

Animate the Second Actor's Still

1. On the **Timeline**, move the **CTI** to **00;00;18;00**, which is the start of the **retro-title_FF_1.bmp** clip.

2. Click on the **retro-title_FF_1.bmp**.

3. In the **Properties** panel for the clip, click the triangle next to **Motion**.

4. Click the **Toggle animation** button.

5. Move the **CTI** to **00;00;22;28**.

6. Change the **Position** to **360 -245**.

7. Move the CTI to **00;00;20;15**.

8. Change the **Position** here to **360 240**.

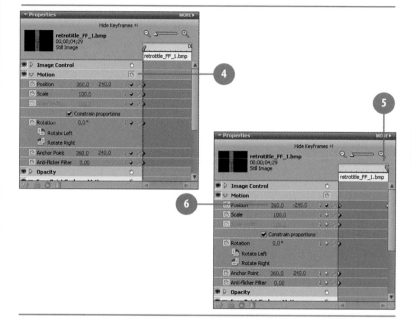

Animate the Second Actor's Credits

1. On the **Timeline**, click the **Title 02** clip, the credits for the second actor, in the **Video 2** track.

   IMPORTANT *Be sure to click just once to ensure that we are working with the clip as a media clip and not as a text clip in the **Titler**.*

2. In the **Properties** panel, click the triangle next to **Motion**.

3. Move the **CTI** until the bottom edge of the **retro-title_FF_1.bmp** clip is just above the **Title 02** clip, as shown in the illustration (at about **00;00;21;12**).

4. Click the **Toggle animation** button.

5. Move the **CTI** to the end of the **Title 02** clip, at **00;00;22;29**.

6. Change the **Position** to **-225 240**.

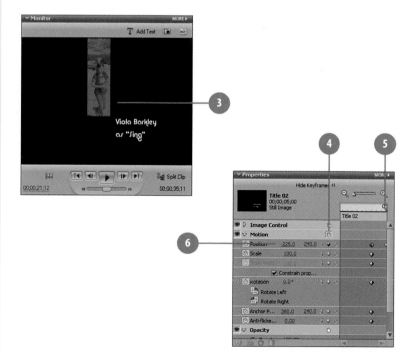

Animating the Third Actor's Still and Credits

Finally, you'll animate the third actor's still and credits with the **Motion** effect and keyframes, just as you did with the first and second actor's stills and credits.

Animate the Third Actor's Still

1. On the **Timeline**, move the **CTI** to **00;00;26;00**, which is the start of the **retro-title_FF_2.bmp** clip.

2. Click on the **retro-title_FF_2.bmp**.

3. In the **Properties** panel for the clip, click the triangle next to **Motion**.

4. Click the **Toggle animation** button.

5. Move the **CTI** to the end of the clip, at **00;00;30;28**.

6. Change the **Position** to **360   725**.

7. On the **Timeline**, move the **CTI** to the halfway point, at **00;00;28;15**.

8. Change the **Position** here to **360   240**.

Animate the Second Actor's Credits

1. On the **Timeline** in the **Video 2** track, click the **Title 03** clip, the third actor's credits.

2. In the **Properties** panel, click the triangle next to **Motion**.

3. Move the **CTI** until the top edge of the **retro-title_FF_2.bmp** clip is just below the bottom of the **Title 02** clip, as shown in the illustration (at about **00;00;30;15**).

4. Click the **Toggle animation** button.

5. Move the **CTI** to the end of the **Title 03** clip, at **00;00;30;29**.

6. Change the **Position** to **990   240**.

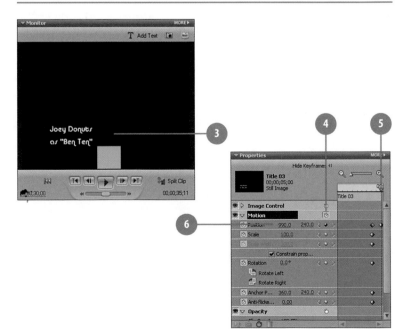

Creating an Opening Title

To finish up the project and create the full "movie credits" effect, we'll create a couple of quick additional titles using the Premiere Elements **Titler**. The first is an opening title for our movie, which we'll call "The Crazy Caper." We'll create the title using a particularly '60s-looking font called *Chick*, created by Ben Balvanz. We'll add a gradient fill to the font for added grooviness.

Add a '60s-Style Opening Title

1. Press the **HOME** key on your keyboard to return the **CTI** to the beginning of the **Timeline** tracks.

2. Click the **Add Text** button on the **Monitor** panel.

3. Change the font to **Chick**.

4. Change the font size to **72**.

5. Click the **Center Text** button to change the alignment to center-aligned.

6. Type **the crazy caper** to replace the **Add Text** text (you may need drag your mouse across the **Add Text** text first to select it).

    TIP *Be sure to press the **ENTER** key on your keyboard after **crazy** and before **caper**.*

7. Click the **Vertical Center** button.

8. Click the **Horizontal Center** button.

9. Click the **Color Properties** button.

10. On the **Color Properties** dialog box, select **Linear Gradient** from the **Gradient** drop down menu.

11. Click the first color button.

12. Set the first color to R: **50**, G: **250**, B: **200**.

13. Click the second color button.

14. Set the second color to R: **200**, G: **250**, B: **50.**

15. Click **OK.**

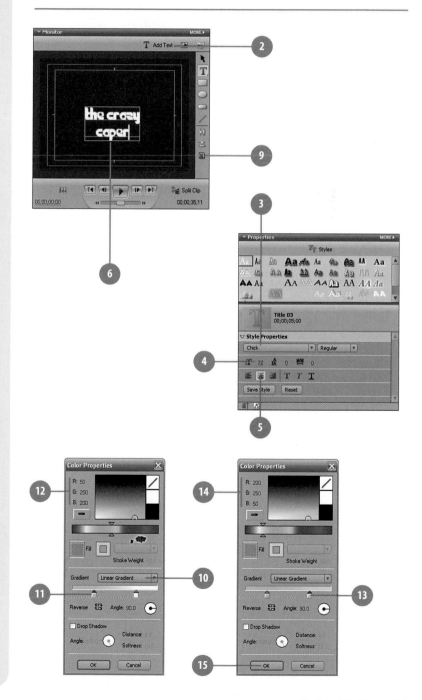

Add a Transition to the Opening Title

 On the **Timeline**, select the end (tail) of the **Title 04** opening title clip and drag it until it meets the **Title 01** clip on the **Video 2** track, as shown in the illustration.

② Click the **Effects and Transitions** button on the **Media** panel to switch to the **Effects and Transitions** view.

③ In the **Effects and Transitions** view, type **random blocks** in the text box.

④ Drag the **Random Blocks** transition and drop it onto the front (head) of the **Title 04** clip on the **Video 2** track on **the Timeline**.

⑤ Select the **Random Blocks** transition again, and drag and drop it this time onto the tail (end) of the **Title 04** title clip.

TIP *To apply the transition to the end of the opening title clip, hold down the **CTRL** key on your key board.*

⑥ Finally, in the **Properties** panel for the **Title 04** clip, select the triangle next to **Opacity** and then click the **Fade Out** button.

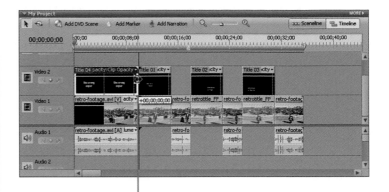

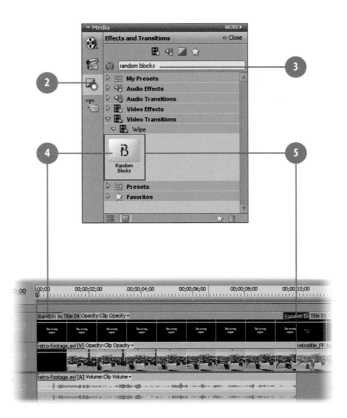

Creating a Title to Set the Scene

This is the final clip for this project: the scene-setting title that will appear at the end of the movie, just before the movie fades out. We're setting our caper in Rome, Italy, circa 1966, so we need to create a title to communicate this. We also need to create a "freeze frame" for the last image of our video by taking one last snapshot and adding it to the end of the clip. The "freeze frame" image will also be used as the back drop for our end title.

Add a '60s-style Scene-Setting Title

1. Press the **End** key on your keyboard to send the **CTI** to end of the Timeline.

2. Click the **Add Text** button on the **Monitor** panel.

3. Change the font to **Chick**.

4. Change the font size to **72**.

5. Click the **Center Text** button to change the alignment to center-aligned.

6. Type **rome, italy** to replace the **Add Text** text (you may need drag your mouse across the **Add Text** text first to select it). Press the **ENTER** key on your keyboard and type **1966**.

7. Click the **Vertical Center** button.

8. Click the **Horizontal Center** button.

9. Click the **Color Properties** button.

10. On the **Color Properties** dialog box, enter the following value for the color:
    - ◆ **R: 250**
    - ◆ **G: 100**
    - ◆ **B: 230**

11. Create a drop shadow by clicking the **Drop Shadow** check box and then setting the following:
    - ◆ **Angle: 130**
    - ◆ **Distance: 10**
    - ◆ **Softness: 10**

12. Click **OK**.

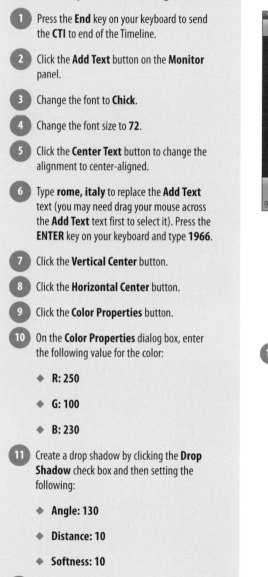
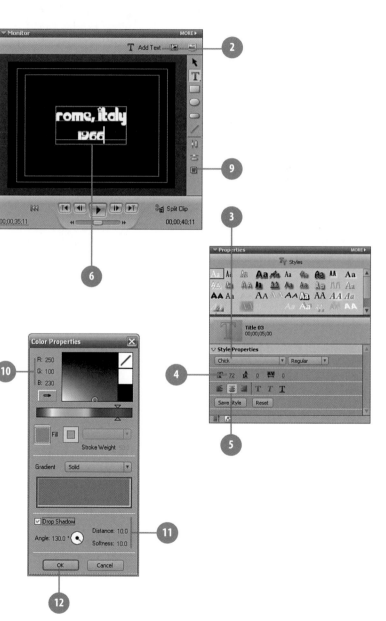

2

Add a Final Freeze Frame and a Transition for the Closing Title

1 Move the **CTI** to **00;00;35;10**.

2 On the **Monitor** panel, click the **Freeze Frame** button.

3 On the **Freeze Frame** dialog box, click **Insert in Movie**.

4 Move the **Title 05** clip from the **Video 1** track to the **Video 2** track, directly above the **retrotitle_FF_3.bmp** clip, as shown in the illustration.

5 Click the **Effects and Transitions** button on the **Media** panel to switch to the **Effects and Transitions** view, if necessary.

6 In the **Effects and Transitions** panel, type **swirl** in the text box.

7 Drag the **Swirl** video transition and drop it onto the front (head) of the **Title 05** clip on the **Video 2** track on the Timeline.

8 In the **Properties** panel for the **Title 05** clip, click the triangle next to **Opacity** and then click the **Fade Out** button.

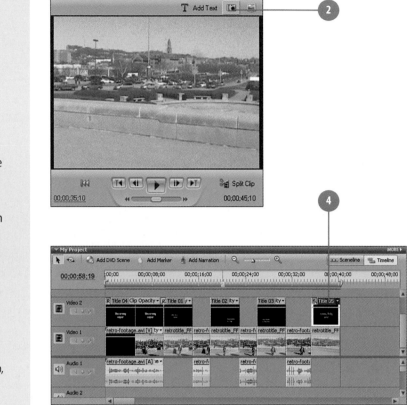

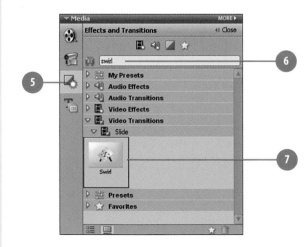

Adding a Little "Retro" Music to the Timeline

For this effect to really work, we need just the right music. A bit of instrumental music by a quintessential '60s group such as *Herb Alpert and the Tijuana Brass* or *Sergio Mendes and Brazil '66* would be perfect. Nonetheless, on the DVD supplied with this book, we've given you the next best thing: a little retro-lounge music that we believe works just as well. This music clip is supplied to us by UniqueTracks (**www.uniquetracks.com**). In this step, we'll load the clip, add it to an audio track, and we're done!

Add Little Lounge Music to the Movie

1 Press the **HOME** key on your keyboard to return the **CTI** to the beginning of the Timeline tracks.

2 Click the **Get Media from** button on the **Media** panel to access the **Get Media from** view, if it's not already active.

3 Select **DVD, Digital Camera, Mobile Phone, Hard Drive Camcorder, Card Reader**.

4 When the **Media Downloader** displays, click the **Advanced Dialog** button to switch to Advanced mode.

5 Select the **shag-party.mp3** clip.

6 Click the **Get Media** button. Premiere Elements copies the **shag-party.mp3** clip from the DVD onto your hard drive and adds it to the Available Media list for this project.

7 Select the **shag-party.mp3** clip on the **Media** panel and drag and drop it onto the **Timeline** in the **Audio 2** track.

> **NOTE** *Make sure that the shag-party.mp3 clip starts at the very beginning of the Timeline and matches the start of the video clips.*

8 In the **Properties** panel, click the triangle next to **Volume** to reveal the effect's controls, if necessary, and then click the **Fade Out** button.

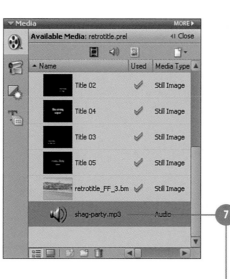

Making Adjustments, Rendering, and Exporting

Well, you've done it! All of the pieces are in place and fully animated, your music track is ready, and you have your '60s-style opening and closing credits. Test your production by pressing the **Spacebar** to see how it all fits together. If it's not quite right tweak the timing (move the keyframes around a bit, or add a couple of new ones here or there as needed, shorten the soundtrack, and so on) until it's just right. Then, press the **ENTER** key on your keyboard to render (apply all effects and transitions to the clips) your project.

Finishing the Project

1. After you have played back your project and made the necessary adjustments, press the **ENTER** key on your keyboard to render your project.

2. Press **CTRL-S** to save your project (or you can select **File, Save** from the menu).

3. Finally, export your work as an AVI file. To export the clip, select **File, Export, Movie**.

    NOTE *Premiere Elements will first render the project (everything on the Timeline and all of the effects and transitions) and then create the .avi file. By default, the .avi file will have the same name as your project, **retrotitle.avi**, but you can change that if you prefer.*

    IMPORTANT *Rendering can take a while, depending upon the speed of your computer and the number of frames that need rendering.*

    TIP *You can optionally bring this clip into a larger project, show it on your computer, upload it to an Internet video sharing site, or burn it to a DVD.*

The completed "'60's" clip, in all its retro glory, playing in Windows Media player.

The Star Wars Opening Sequence Effect

MEDIA:

jedifont.ttf
starfield.jpg
starwarstheme.wav

3

COMPLEXITY:	Simple	Moderate	Complex
SKILL LEVEL:	Novice	Intermediate	Advanced
MATERIALS:	None	Some Props	Greenscreen

Introduction

Fascination with George Lucas' Star Wars® trilogies continues decade after decade, and will never really leave us. In this chapter, you will learn how to create your own vanishing logo and epic "scrolling story" just like you've come to know and love from the Star Wars movies. Now, we can't promise that your movies will produce the same goosebumps among your friends and family, but the look is very convincing.

No special equipment or additional software is needed to create this effect, but on the DVD supplied with this book you will find a starfield background (complete with a supernova!) provided courtesy of the National Aeronautics and Space Administration (NASA). Also on the DVD is a font you might want to use (although it's not completely necessary as any modern looking sans serif font will work), called *jedifont.ttf*. (There are instructions in this chapter for installing it in your Windows Fonts directory in case you're not sure how.) Finally, the DVD includes a .WAV sample file, *starwarstheme.wav*, from the John Williams score for the film series. Remember, this is intended as a sample *only* to give your work that air of authenticity and is not intended for distribution with any project from which you intend to make money.

Now, although we've supplied you with a convincing starfield, think outside the galaxy on this. You can superimpose your Star Warsian title across any background, including stills and video clips from the videos that you took; they don't need to be from "outer space" necessarily. In addition, while nothing beats the Star Wars theme, feel free to change that out and add your favorite music. As long as it has punch, it will work just fine, and will make the title sequence truly your own.

What You'll Do

Add the Starry Background

Create Your "Long Ago" Text

Install the Jedi Font

Build Your "Star Wars" Logo

Animate Your Logo

Prepare the Scrolling Text

Transform the Shape of the Scrolling Text

Animate the Scrolling Text

Make the Scrolling Text Scroll

Add the Star Wars Theme Music

Synchronize Audio and Video

Make Adjustments, Render, and Export

Adding the Starry Background

You can't have a proper Star Wars opening sequence without a starfield background for the titles and text to display against. Our starfield is brought to you courtesy of National Aeronautics and Space Administration, or NASA. If this one doesn't suit your tastes, visit the NASA website (**www.nasa.gov/home**) and search for more. They have hundreds of still images and video clips that you can use that are perfect for any science—and science fiction—projects.

Load the Star Clip into the Project

1. Start Premiere Elements and create a new project called **starwarstitle**.

2. Click the **Get Media from** button on the **Media** panel to access the **Get Media from** view, if it's not already active.

3. Select **DVD, Digital Camera, Mobile Phone, Hard Drive Camcorder, Card Reader**.

4. When the **Media Downloader** displays, click the **Advanced Dialog** button to switch to Advanced mode.

5. Select the **starfield.jpg** clip.

6. Click the **Get Media** button. Premiere Elements copies the **starfield.jpg** clip from the DVD onto your hard drive and adds it to the **Available Media** list for this project.

7. Drag the **starfield.jpg** clip onto the **Video 1** track on the Timeline so that the head (front) of the clip is at the very beginning of the track.

    TIP If you are in **Sceneline** view, just drop the clip onto the first scene placeholder (as shown in the illustration).

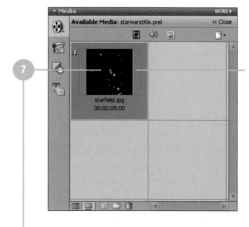

The **starfield.jpg** clip added to the project.

8. For this project, we'll need to be in **Timeline** view because we are working with multiple clips on multiple video tracks. So, if the **My Project** panel is not already in **Timeline** view, click the **Timeline** button (shown below) to switch.

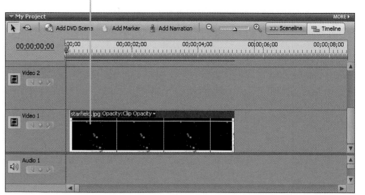

Creating Your "Long Ago" Text

All of the Star Wars movies begin with the now universally recognizable, "Long ago, in a galaxy far, far away..." The beauty of this opening text is how it sets an almost fairytale-like tone in just seven simple words (with "far" repeated), reminiscent of the equally well-known "happily ever after." You can use this exact phrase, unmodified, because we live in a galaxy far, far away from somewhere. And "long ago" is such a relative term. So, the phrase works well with virtually any video clip that you want to use it with. You can also easily modify the phrase to suit the movie you're putting together, as we do here with, "A short time ago, on vacation far, far away..."

Create the Opening Text

1. Click the **Add Text** button on the **Monitor** window.

2. Right-click on the default **Add Text** box and select **Cut** from the contextual menu.

3. Click the **Text** key in the Titler, if it isn't already selected.

4. Starting in the upper left corner of the screen, **drag a box** across the entire screen, down to the lower right corner, as shown in the illustration. Be sure to stay within the safe margins for titles.

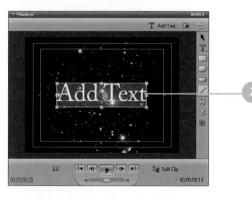

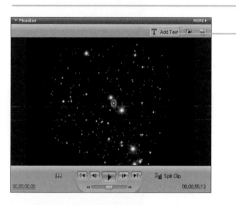

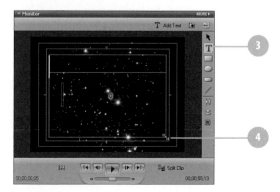

Did You Know?

You can play it safe with margins.
Your computer screen can show text and graphics right to the edge of your screen. Therefore, displaying movies online in a media player won't be a problem. But playing it on a television screen is another story. A television screen will clip the image a bit at the edges, especially text. Whenever you create text and titles, be sure to use safe text margins. To display the safe text margins, click the **MORE** button on the **Monitor** panel and select **Safe Title Margins**. Optionally, you can display the **Safe Action Margins** as well.

3

Type and Style the Text

1 Type the following text: **A short time ago, on vacation far far away...** (including the ellipses).

2 Press **CTRL-A** on your keyboard to select all the text you just typed.

3 **Right-click** and from the contextual menu that displays, select **Font, Arial Narrow, Bold**.

4 Change the size from the default 100 to **35**.

> **TIP** *The text all needs to fit on one line. If you are creating different text than the text we're using here and it doesn't quite fit on one line, just reduce the font size a bit more.*

5 Set the justification to centered by clicking the **Center Text** button.

Did You Know?

All of your fonts are here, and out there, too...
All of the fonts that you have installed on your Windows system, including TrueType and OpenType fonts, will be available for you to select from and use in your projects here in the Premiere Elements **Titler**. In addition, there are thousands of free fonts available on the Web that can add a unique look to your titles. One excellent source is Blambot (**www.blambot.com**), a site for comic book artists and fans. There are plenty of other font sites out there, too. Just search on "fonts," or "free fonts" using your favorite Internet search engine.

6. Resize the text box by clicking the **Selection Tool** button:

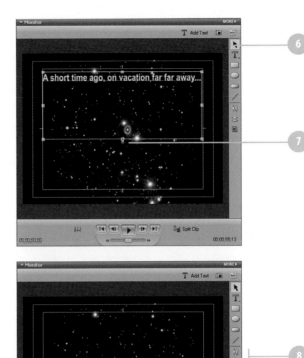

7. Grab the bottom handing of the box and make the box evenly surround the text by dragging it up, as shown in the illustration.

8. Reposition the text so that it sits in the center of the screen by clicking the two "centering" buttons:

   ◆ Click the **Vertical Center** button.

   ◆ Click the **Horizontal Center** button.

9. Premiere Elements should have automatically placed the new title on the Timeline. If not, drag and drop the title you just created from the **Media** panel to the **Video 2** track, on the Timeline so that the head (front) of the clip is at the very beginning of the track.

Installing the Jedi Font

Installing fonts is easy in Windows XP. You have two options. You can either drag and drop the font from its current location (on the DVD supplied with this book), or you can follow the installation feature built into Windows. Either way, you'll need to temporarily jump out of Premiere Elements for just a second; in other words, you'll need to save your work and exit Premiere Elements. The reason we need to exit is that in order for Premiere Elements (or any program) to see newly-installed fonts, the program needs to restart.

Install the Jedi Font into the Windows Fonts Folder

1 Exit Premiere Elements by selecting **File, Exit**. If your are prompted to save your changes before closing, click **Yes**.

2 Using Windows Explorer, navigate to the Fonts folder, typically **C:\Windows\Fonts**.

3 When the Fonts folder opens, select **File, Install New Font**.

4 On the **Add Fonts** dialog box, use the **Drives** drop down to locate your DVD drive.

> **TIP** Be sure the DVD supplied with this book is in your DVD drive.

5 Navigate to the **Extras** folder, then **Fonts**.

6 The *Star Jedi Hollow (True Type)* font will show up in the list of fonts. When it does, select it and click **OK**. The font will be installed.

7 Restart Premiere Elements and select the **starwarstitle** project (it should be at the top of the list of projects. The font will now be ready to use.

Did You Know?

Simply dragging and dropping the font into the Fonts folder does the job. You have at your disposal an alternative, and a bit quicker, method if you want to use it. Exit Premiere Elements. Using Windows Explorer, navigate to the **Fonts** folder on the DVD supplied with this book. Open another instance of Windows Explorer and navigate to **C:\Windows\Fonts**. Select the **jedifont.ttf** font from the DVD and drag and drop it into the Windows Fonts folder.

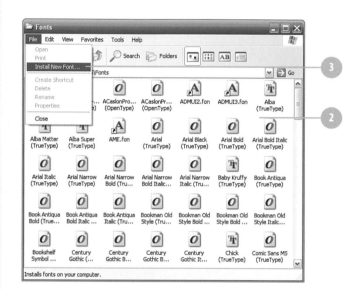

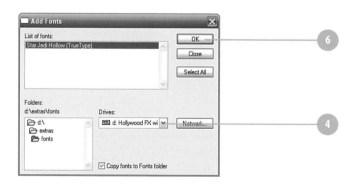

As the font is installed, you'll see progress bars appear briefly in a dialog box like this, if all goes well.

Building Your "Star Wars" Logo

Every Star Wars movie had its instantly recognizable opening logo, and every good parody (or *homage*) should have it, too. Creating the logo is straight-forward. You'll use the **Titler** to enter the text. Here we are using "Snow Wars." In the future, when working on your projects, remember to keep your "logo" short and sweet. Your "logo" should echo the Star Wars logo in terms of word length, such as "School Wars," "Beach Wars," "Tennis Wars," "BBQ Wars," and so on. You don't even need "Star" or "Wars" in the title; for example, "Spelling Bee." Just be sure you use the font from this chapter. The font is so recognizable that people will understand the reference right away. In addition, the logo behaves a certain way (static and bigger than full screen for the first few seconds, then drifting out to vanish in deep outer space). By following these few simple rules, everyone will understand the reference.

Setup Your Logo in the Titler

 With the **Current Time Indicator** (**CTI**) at the home position (the very beginning of the Timeline), click the **Add Text** button on the **Monitor** panel.

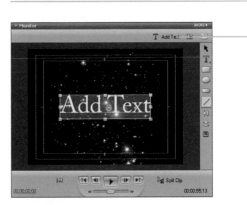

The Add Text default text is automatically selected. Type over it with this text:

> **snow**
> **wars**

TIP *Type the name in lower case. Be sure to press the **Enter** key on your keyboard after the first word so that each word is on its own line.*

Highlight the text you just typed by dragging your mouse across it, or by pressing **CTRL-A** on your keyboard.

Right-click on the text and from the contextual menu, select the **Star Jedi Hollow** font.

TIP *Depending on the number of fonts installed on your computer, you may have to select **More** at the top of each list of fonts to navigate to the **Star Jedi Hollow** font.*

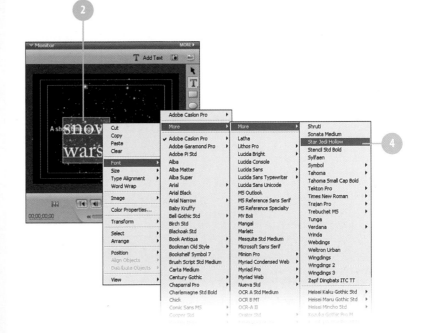

3

Adjust and Stylize the Logo

1 We need to adjust the size of the text until it nearly fills the screen. To do so, on the **Properties** panel, enter these settings:

- ◆ **Font Size: 333**

- ◆ **Leading: -218**

2 Adjust the text justification by clicking the **Center Text** button.

3 Center the two words on the screen this way:

- ◆ Click the **Vertical Center** button.

- ◆ Click the **Horizontal Center** button.

4 Click the **Color Properties** button.

5 Select a yellow color by enter these settings:

- ◆ **R: 255**

- ◆ **G: 255**

- ◆ **B: 0**

6 Click **OK**.

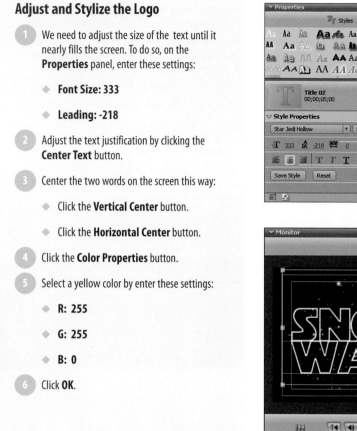

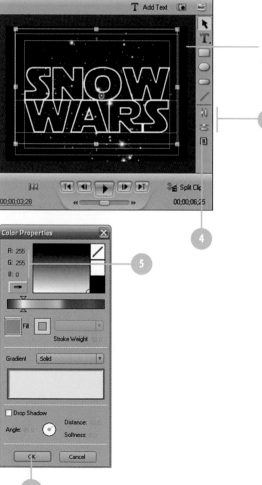

The Snow Wars logo, centered and with the correct font.

Relocate the Snow Wars Logo

1 Finally, move the Snow Wars title clip to its proper location on the Timeline. To do, first select the **Snow Wars** clip.

TIMESAVER *When moving and aligning clips, use the **CTI** has a guide. For example, in this case you could first move the **CTI** to the tail end of the "Short time ago" title clip so that it's at position* **00;00;05;00**.

2 Next, drag the **Snow Wars** title clip so that the *head* (front) of the clip aligns with the *tail* (end) of the two other clips.

Did You Know?

Turning Snap on makes your job easier.
Make sure you have the "Snap" function turned on in Premiere Elements. This helps whenever you are aligning clips to each other, or clips to the **CTI**. There are three ways to activate the Snap function. One is to select it from the Timeline: **MORE, Snap**. The second way is to select it from the Premiere Elements menu: **Timeline, Snap**. The third and final way is to use the shortcut key: press the "**S**" key on your keyboard to turn Snap on or off.

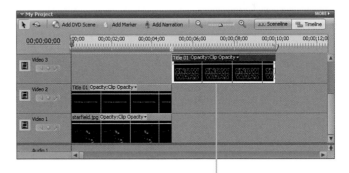

The Snow Wars logo, now in its new position.

Animating Your Logo

Now that you've created your own version of the Star Wars logo, you need to animate it to give it that cinematic touch. In the Star Wars movies, the logo waits on the screen for just a second as the music begins to swell. Once we're fully engaged, the logo drifts out of the way into outer space, to let the scrolling text tell the story. In this section, you'll learn how to animate the logo using a built-in Premiere Elements "Preset" effect, which we'll have to tweak slightly. You'll learn how to adjust the settings on a keyframe as an introduction to the concept of keyframes, which are used extensively in other chapters in this book. For this task, we apply keyframes and then make small adjustments to the keyframes to get the effect we want.

Make Your Logo Zoom Off Into Space

1. Select the **Snow Wars logo** in the **Video 3** track on the Timeline.

2. Press the **Page Up** or **Page Down** key as needed to move to the head (start) of the clip.

3. In the **Properties** panel for the **Snow Wars logo**, click the **Show Keyframes** button to reveal the workspace for adding keyframes, as shown in the illustration.

   Show Keyframes

   TIP *After you click it, the **Show Keyframes** button becomes the **Hide Keyframes** button.*

4. In the **Properties** panel, click the triangle next to **Motion** to reveal the effect's controls.

5. Set the **Scale** to **125.0**.

6. Click the **Toggle animation** button (shown below) to turn on the animation functionality of Premiere Elements.

   TIP *Premiere Elements automatically places a keyframe at this point.*

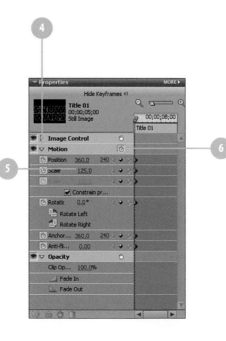

7 Move the **CTI** to the end of the clip by pressing the **Page Down** key on your keyboard.

8 Set the **Scale** to **0.0**.

TIP *Premiere Elements automatically places another keyframe at this point.*

9 We now have a logo that starts at 125% and fades away to nothing. However, we want the Snow Wars logo to pause on screen at 125% for a few seconds, so let's jump back to the beginning of the clip and "insert" a pause. Press the **Page Up** key.

10 To insert the pause, drag the CTI to the **00;00;08;00** point.

11 Set the **Scale** to **125.0**.

TIP *Again, Premiere Elements automatically places a keyframe at this point.*

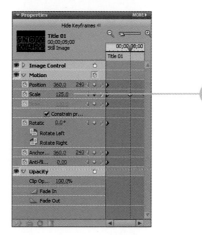

Did You Know?

The difference between Render and Realtime. You can optionally render your project at anytime, for example after applying an effect such as a **Motion** effect. When you apply an effect, Premiere Elements shows you a realtime representation of the effect. This representation allows you to see somewhat how the effect will look which lets you try different effects and tweak their settings. It's not until you *render*, however, by pressing the **ENTER** key that you will see how the effect truly looks. To show you that a clip has effects applied but not rendered, Premiere Elements places a thin red line above any clip waiting for rendering.

Preparing Your Scrolling Text

Now that you have your opening text and your logo prepared, your next step is to create your scrolling text. In the Star Wars movies, this text is used to set time, place, and mood, as well as to introduce a few key characters for the movie. In the text provided for this chapter, we've stuck to that format. To save time, we have provided you the text that you can cut and paste into the Premiere Elements Titler.

Create Your Text

1 Move the **CTI** to the end of the Snow Wars logo clip by pressing the **Page Down** key on your keyboard.

2 Once again, click the **Add Text** button on the **Monitor** panel.

3 **Drag** the new title clip you just created from the Video 1 track up to the **gray area above the Video 3 track**. A new **Video 4** track will be created automatically.

> **TIP** *If you have Premiere Elements configured with more than three video tracks, simply drag the clip to the existing* **Video 4** *track.*

4 **Right-click** on the default **Add Text** title, and from the contextual menu, select **Cut**.

5 Click the **Text** key in the Titler workspace.

6 Starting in the upper left corner of the screen, **drag a box** across the entire screen, down to the lower right corner, being careful to stay within the safe margins for titles.

7 On the **Properties** panel for the text box you just drew, set the following font properties:

- ◆ **Arial Narrow**

- ◆ **Bold**

- ◆ Set the size to **22**

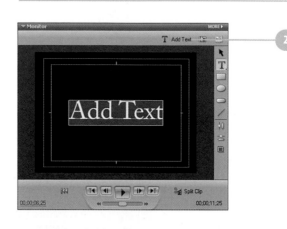

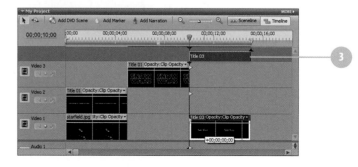

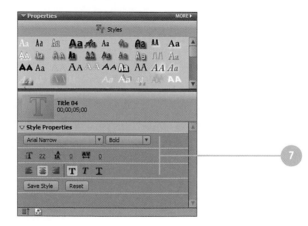

Import the Scrolling Text

1 Jump out to Windows Explorer and navigate to the DVD supplied with this book.

2 Navigate to **Extras** folder.

3 **Double-click** on the file, **starwarstext.txt**.

NOTE *If you don't have the file association for text files to be open by Windows Notepad, right-click on the file instead, and from the contextual menu, select* **Open With** *and then select* **Notepad**.

4 Select **Edit, Select All** from the Notepad menu, or press **CTRL-A** on your keyboard.

5 Select **Edit, Copy** from the Notepad menu, or press **CTRL-C**.

6 Return to Premiere Elements.

7 **Right-click** on the empty text box you created and from the contextual menu select **Paste**.

NOTE *The text from the* **starwarstext.txt** *file you copied should appear. If not, repeat the steps above.*

8 Use the **selection tool** (the arrow) to expand the text box so that all of the scrolling text is visible at the same time.

9 Click the **Center Text** button so that the text will be centered.

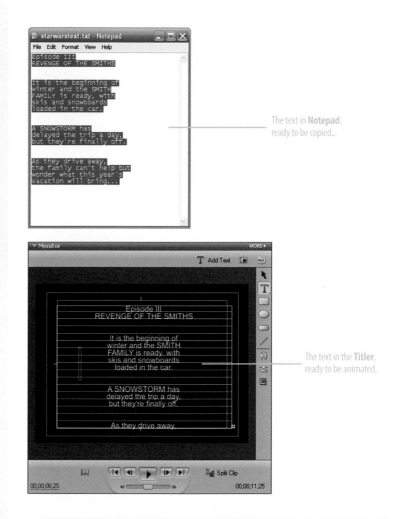

The text in **Notepad**, ready to be copied...

The text in the **Titler**, ready to be animated.

3

Did You Know?

Three choices of paragraph alignment are available in the Titler. Premiere Elements has three paragraph alignment styles: left, right, and center. Die-hard Star Wars fans will know that the scrolling text is fully justified both to the left *and* to the right. However, Premiere Elements doesn't have a "fully justified" setting. Instead, we'll use centered, which, once the text is animated to drift into outer space, will be a convincing compromise.

Creating the Perfect Star Wars Scrolling Text

All Star Wars Movies Follow These Scrolling Text Rules

When you create your own scrolling text in the future, keep in mind these three basic rules and your Star Wars text will look right and be easy to read. First, your text should only have three paragraphs, and each paragraph should only contain about 25 words. Second—and this is very important for legibility—be sure that you have no more than five words per line. Remember, this is text that is not only scrolling but is on a 65 degree plane as well. Third, your scrolling text should start with a short, *catchy* title in all capital letters (you could even include an "Episode" number as well, if you wanted), such as what we used here, "Episode III: REVENGE OF THE SMITHS." And fourth, your final paragraph should always end with an ellipsis, those three little dots that say so much: ...

Color the text

1. Your final step in creating your scrolling text (prior to animating the text and reshaping it) is to give it that gold color. To do so, click the **Color Properties** button.

2. Then, just as you did when you created your Snow Wars logo, drag the color selector to select a bright yellow or type the following color values:

   ◆ **R: 255**

   ◆ **G: 255**

   ◆ **B: 0**.

3. Click **OK**.

Did You Know?

For more efficient writing and editing, use a word processor such as Microsoft Word. Why not benefit from not only your knowledge of your favorite word processor, but also its built-in spellchecker and other tools anytime you need to create longer text? Here's how: First, write your scrolling text in your word processor until you get it just right. Then, use the word processor's thesaurus and spell checker to finish the passage. Finally, select the text (use the mouse or the shortcut keys **CTRL-A**) and copy it to the clipboard (**CTRL-C**). Back in Premiere Elements, press **CTRL-V** to paste the text into a text box and you're ready to go.

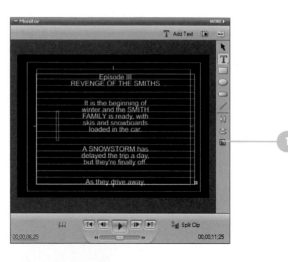

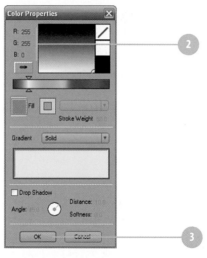

The contents of the scrolling text, in the correct font and color, ready to be transformed and animated.

Transforming the Shape of the Scrolling Text

Now that we have our "scrolling text" created and looking the way we want, we next need to create the appropriate shape of the text block for when it actually scrolls across the screen. What we want is for the text to start off close to the screen and to gradually fade back into space, with the text shrinking progressively smaller (and harder to read). We'll do this using a video effect to transform the text so that it has the right shape and is on the right plane for when it floats back into the vanishing point in space.

Change the Perspective

1. Switch to the **Effects and Transitions** view on the **Media** panel by clicking the **Effects and Transitions** button.

2. On the **Effects and Transitions** panel, type **Basic** to bring up the **Basic 3D** video effect.

3. Select the **Basic 3D** effect from the Perspective Video Effects and drop it onto the **Title 03** title clip (the clip containing the "Episode III: Revenge of the Smiths" text) on the **Video 4** track.

4. In the **Properties** panel for **Title 03**, click the triangle next to the **Basic 3D** control to view the effect's controls.

    TIP *You won't see your changes in the Monitor panel unless the **CTI** is positioned somewhere on the Title 03 clip. So, if the **CTI** is elsewhere on the Timeline, move it over the clip.*

5. Adjust the **Tilt** and **Distance** settings:

    ◆ **Tilt: -65**

    ◆ **Distance to Image: -30**

    NOTE *Leave the other controls—Swivel, Specular Highlight, and Preview—at their default settings.*

The scrolling text, "tilted."

Change the Speed

① **Right-click** on the **Title 03** clip and select **Time Stretch** from the contextual menu, as shown in the illustration.

TIP *If a short menu displays, this is the* ***Properties*** *contextual menu. Simply right-click a second time, and the correct contextual menu will appear, from which you can select* ***Time Stretch***.

TIMESAVER *You can optionally click the clip and then press* ***CTRL-R*** *on your keyboard to access the* ***Time Stretch*** *dialog box.*

② On the **Time Stretch** dialog box, click on the **link (chain) icon** until it "breaks" to disconnect the speed from the duration.

③ Double-click the **Speed** and type **6.25**.

④ Double-click on **Duration** and type **00;00;40;00.**

⑤ Click **OK.**

TIP *We have now increased the amount of time that this clip displays from the default of 5 seconds to a full 40 seconds, and decreased the speed from 100% (standard speed) to a more easy-to-read 6.25%.*

The broken chain, indicating that Speed and Duration have been unlinked.

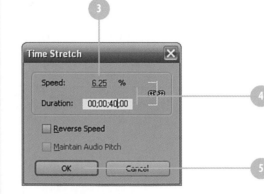

Animating the Scrolling Text

Now that your scrolling text looks like it should, let's get it to behave correctly. To animate the appearance of the text scrolling off into space and getting smaller as it reaches the vanishing point, we are using the same technique that we used with the "Snow Wars" logo, and we'll again be making adjustments using keyframes.

Add the Effect and Adjust the Keyframes

1 Select **Title 03**, the scrolling text on the **Video 4** track on the Timeline.

2 Press the **Page Up** or **Page Down** key as needed to move to the head (start) of the clip.

3 In the **Properties** panel for the **scrolling text**, click the **Show Keyframes** button to reveal the workspace for keyframes, if it's not already showing.

> **TIP** *You may see the **Hide Keyframes** button, instead, if the **Show Keyframes** button was clicked previously.*

4 In the **Properties** panel, click the triangle next to **Motion** to reveal the effect's controls.

5 Set the **Scale** to **200.0**.

6 Click the **Toggle animation** button to turn on the animation functionality of Premiere Elements.

> **TIP** *Premiere Elements automatically places a keyframe at this point.*

7 Move the **CTI** to the end of the clip by pressing the **Page Down** key.

8 Set the **Scale** to **0.0**.

> **TIP** *Premiere Elements automatically places another keyframe at this point.*

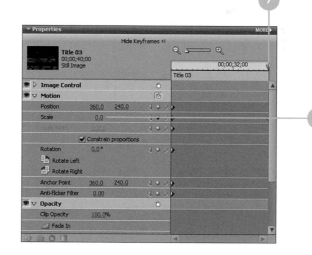

Making the Scrolling Text Scroll ▶

If you press the **Spacebar** at this point, you'd be disappointed to see that your scrolling text, after all this work, doesn't actually scroll. This is because, while we have the right shape and the text is slowly getting smaller over time and so on, the text is only moving in space, it isn't actually scrolling. Do we need to apply some mysterious, little-known effect from the Premiere Elements bag of tricks to get this to work? Do we then need to tweak it in sophisticated ways? Not at all. All we need to do at this point is tell Premiere Elements that we want this text to roll, as it's called, tweak two simple settings, and we'll be, well, ready to roll.

Make the Text "Roll" Text

1. Double click **Title 03**, the **scrolling text** in the **Video 4** track on the Timeline to open the text in the Titler.

2. Click the **Roll/Crawl Options** button to open the **Roll/Crawl Options** dialog box.

3. In the **Roll/Crawl Options** dialog box, select **Roll**.

4. In the **Timing (Frames)** area, click both of these boxes:

   ◆ **Start Off Screen**

   ◆ **End Off Screen**

   TIP *When you click* **Start Off Screen**, **Preroll** *is disabled, and when you click* **End Off Screen**, **Postroll** *is disabled.*

5. Click **OK**.

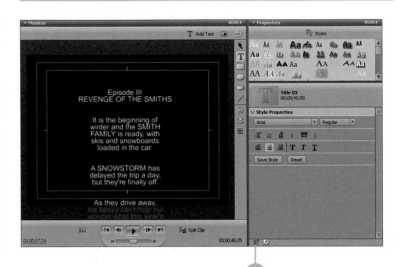

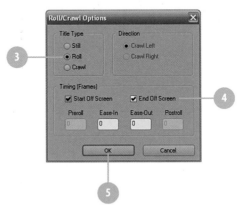

Adding the Star Wars Theme Music

You certainly can't have a Star Wars opening without the crescendo of the John Williams' theme. On the DVD supplied with this book, we have a .wav file with that famous theme music for you to use with your projects. That said, however, for your movie you can certainly use any heroic (or silly) music at your disposal and it will work just fine.

Add the Music to the Timeline

1. Click the **Get Media from** button on the **Media** panel to access the **Get Media from** view, if it's not already active.

2. Select **DVD, Digital Camera, Mobile Phone, Hard Drive Camcorder, Card Reader**.

3. When the **Media Downloader** displays, click the **Advanced Dialog** button to switch to Advanced mode.

4. Select the **starwarstheme.wav** clip.

5. Click the **Get Media** button. Premiere Elements copies the **starwarstheme.wav** clip from the DVD onto your hard drive and adds it to the **Available Media** list for this project.

6. Drag the **starwarstheme.wav** clip from the **Available Media** view of the **Media** panel to the **Audio 1** track on the Timeline, so that the head (front) of the clip is at the very beginning of the track (as shown in the illustration).

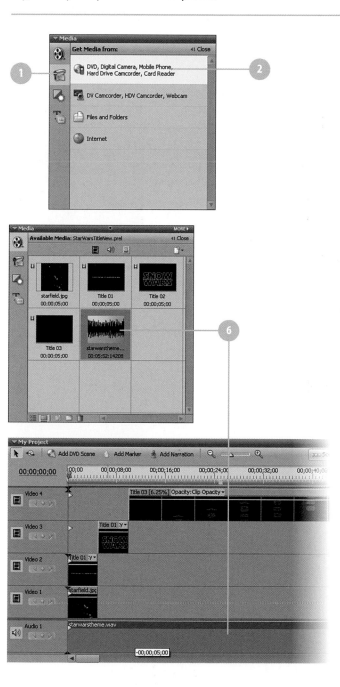

3

Synchronizing Audio and Video

As you look at the Timeline, you can see that the clips all end at different times. We'll want to adjust this so that the ends of the longer clips all stop at close to the same time. In addition, we'll want to adjust the clips so that the movie fades out at the end and so that the "big bang" of the Star Wars theme occurs just when the Star Wars logo first appears on the screen. That adjustment is known as *syncing* the audio and video.

Syncing the Audio Track

1   To adjust the soundtrack, first press the \ (backslash) key to view your entire project.

2   Drag the **starwars.wav** clip in the **Audio 1** track until the head of the clip aligns with the head of the **Snow Wars logo** clip in the **Video 3** track. This will give us the "boom" of the music just as the logo appears on the screen.

3   Drag the **CTI** to 50 seconds into the project (**00;00;50;00** on the Timeline).

   TIMESAVER *You can type* **00;00;50;00** *directly in the timecode area and the* **CTI** *will jump to exactly that point in the Timeline.*

4   With only the **starwars.wav** clip selected, press the **Split Clip** button on the **Monitor** panel.

5   The "split" clip, the half of the original audio clip now on the right (beyond the **00;00;50;00** point), should automatically be selected. (If not, select it now).

6   **Right-click** on the clip and select **Cut** to delete it. (We only need the *first* 50 seconds of the Star Wars theme for our project.)

   TIP *If necessary, press the* \ **(backslash)** *key again to view your entire project.*

7   Select the **starwars.wav** clip again and on the **Properties** panel, under the **Volume** control, click the purple **Fade Out** button.

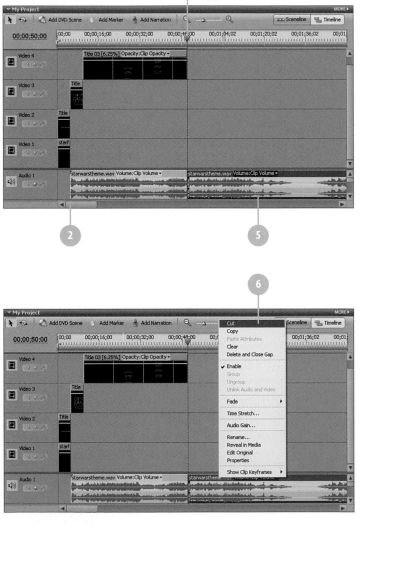

Make Final Tweaks to the Starfield Clip and the Opening Text Clip

1 The **starfield.jpg** clip is too short for the length of our movie. To lengthen it, grab the tail end of the starfield clip and trim the clip out until it matches the length of the soundtrack clip (**00;00;50;00** on the Timeline).

2 With that clip still selected, click the **Fade Out** button in the **Opacity** control in the **Properties** panel.

3 Select the **Title 01** clip on the **Video 2** track. (This is the title clip that has the text, "A short time ago, on vacation far far away....).

4 On the **Properties** panel for this clip, apply a **Fade Out** to its **Opacity**.

5 Finally, so that the scrolling text appears at the right time in relation to both the Snow Wars logo disappearing into space and synchronizing with the Star Wars theme, **drag** the **Title 03 clip** in the **Video 4** track so that the head (start) of the clip lines up with the head of the Snow Wars logo clip.

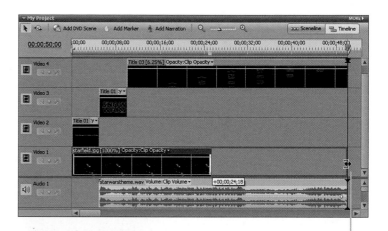

3

Making Adjustments, Rendering, and Exporting

Play your movie by pressing the **Spacebar** and make sure everything looks good. You may want to adjust the audio a bit, tweak this or that. For example, you might want to have the opening "A short time ago..." text to appear on screen for a longer time. Remember, however, that changes you make to any given element in this project may cause another element to be out of sync. Once everything is just as you want it, you're ready to share the results, either as a video file or on tape or DVD.

Finishing the Project

1. After you have played back your clip and made the necessary adjustments, press the **ENTER** key on your keyboard to render your project.

2. Press **CTRL-S** to save your project (or you can select **File, Save** from the menu).

3. Finally, export your work as an AVI file. To export the clip, select **File, Export, Movie**.

   TIP *You can optionally bring this clip into a larger project, show it on your computer, upload it to an Internet video sharing site, or burn it to a DVD.*

   IMPORTANT *After you select to export your movie, Premiere Elements will first render the entire project (even if you just rendered it yourself). You may have between 1,000 and 2,000 frames and, depending on your computer, it may take anywhere from 15 minutes to over an hour to render. This particular project, because of the scrolling text, can take especially long to render.*

Rendering and exporting your video can take awhile. You can always cancel and go back and finish later. Premiere Elements will pick up where it left off.

Once the video has been exported, sit back and enjoy the show!

The Passing of Time Effect

MEDIA:

parkscene.avi
SmartSound - Underwater
- Ascent [00;31;24].wav

4

COMPLEXITY:	Simple	Moderate	Complex
SKILL LEVEL:	Novice	Intermediate	Advanced
MATERIALS:	None	Some Props	Greenscreen

What You'll Do

Add the Clip to the Timeline

Break the Clip into Individual Scenes

Remove Time (Frames) from the Clip

Add a Cross Dissolve Between Clips

Adjust the Transitions in the Properties Panel

Use SmartSound® Quicktracks™ with Premiere Elements 3

Select the Music for the Soundtrack

Mix in the Music Track

Make Adjustments, Render, and Export

Introduction

There are many times when you are telling story that you'd like, in an onscreen timeframe of a few seconds, to indicate that a much longer period of time has gone by. This can be easily accomplished using the Passing of Time effect. This effect capitalizes on some of the skills you already have if you've been using Premiere Elements for awhile (or are familiar with another non-linear editor).

It also capitalizes on "best practices" within the software. That is, when you take a longer clip and cut it into smaller clips, and move those smaller clips or delete sections out of those clips, as well as manipulate each clip separately, you are following best practices for nonlinear video editing. In this chapter, we'll be adding transitions at the beginning of these clips so that they dissolve in and out from clip to clip.

For the passage of time to be convincing we will really be doing two things. First, we'll remove some time from the clip. How? It sounds like we have magic powers, but actually we are just deleting frames from the clip to remove transitional frames. For example, if someone crosses the room, we could leave the first part of the clip and the last part, but delete all the frames in the middle of the clip of the actual walk across the room. In this way, the actor is first at one end of the room and then suddenly they appear at the opposite end. By splitting the clip in two and applying a transition between the two clips, the actor slowly vanishes (dissolves) from the left side of the room while slowly appearing at the other end.

This effect works well any time you want to show the passage of time; for example, when a girl is waiting by the phone for her boyfriend to call. She can be looking at the phone. Standing behind the couch. Off in the kitchen. And back sitting on the couch, phone on her lap. By deleting all of the frames where she's in motion from location to location, and by adding a dissolve between clips, you can effectively communicate the sense of time passing.

Adding the Clip to the Timeline

Your first task in working on any project, even if that project is simply creating a short video segment, is to create a new Premiere Elements project and give it a descriptive name. Your next step is to bring in the media files you'll be using for the project. For this project, we will work with, and make modifications to, a single video clip, **parkscene.avi**.

Load the Video Clip into Premiere Elements

 1 Start Premiere Elements and create a new project called **passingtime**.

 2 Click the **Get Media from** button on the **Media** panel to access the **Get Media from** view, if it's not already active.

 3 Select **DVD, Digital Camera, Mobile Phone, Hard Drive Camcorder, Card Reader**.

 4 When the **Media Downloader** displays, click the **Advanced Dialog** button to switch to Advanced mode.

 5 Select the **parkscene.avi** clip for this project.

 6 Click the **Get Media** button. Premiere Elements copies the **parkscene.avi** clip from the DVD onto your hard drive and adds it to the Available Media list for this project.

 7 Click on the **parkscene.avi** clip on the **Media** panel and drag on drop it onto the **Timeline** in the **Video 1** track.

> **IMPORTANT** *Be sure to line up the head (start) of the **parkscene.avi** clip with the front of the **Video 1** track.*

> **TIP** *If you're in **Sceneline** view, drop it onto the first scene box. Premiere Elements will place it on the **Video 1** track.*

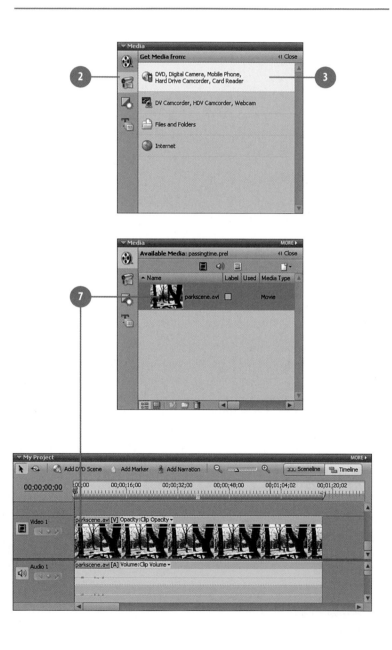

Marking the Individual Scenes

As it is, **parkscene.avi** is a nice, but ordinary, 90 second clip (00;01;30;00) that shows a woman walking thoughtfully through a park. In the tasks that follow, however, we will begin transforming this ordinary clip into something a bit extraordinary. We'll start by breaking this long clip into six individual scenes. Once we have our scenes defined, we'll work to make changes to each of the scenes so that they reflect fairly dramatic changes in time. We want to mark each place in the clip where we want to add a transition. To add a transition, we'll need to split the clip at that point. The **parkscene.avi** clip begins with our actress in the park taking pictures. We want a few seconds of this scene so we'll create our first clip to be 17 seconds long, to the point just where she's beginning to stand up after taking the shot.

Finding and Marking the Scenes in the Clip to Identify Six Shorter Clips

 We first want to want to mark the scene of the actress walking from where she took the picture at the start of the clip, to where she stood by the tree. To do so, move the **Current Time Indicator**, or **CTI**, to the **00;00;17;00** point 17 seconds into the clip. This will mark both the end of the "picture taking" clip and the start of the "walking to the tree" clip.

> **NOTE** *You'll need the **My Project** panel to be in **Timeline** view, if it isn't already. To switch to **Timeline** view, click the **Timeline** button (shown below) in the right corner of the **My Project** panel.*

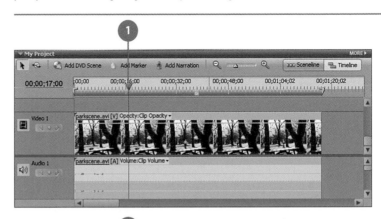

At the **00;00;17;00** point, click the **Add Marker** button (shown below) to place a marker.

 Move the **CTI** to the **00;00;52;00** point.

> **TIMESAVER** *You can optionally drag the **CTI** with your mouse (known as "scrubbing"), press the **Spacebar** to play and pause the **CTI**, or type the timecode directly in the timecode area at the upper left of the **Timeline** view.*

> **TIMESAVER** *If you stop just after or just before **00;00;52;00**, use the **left arrow** or **right arrow** keys on your keyboard to "zero in" on the right frame, as needed.*

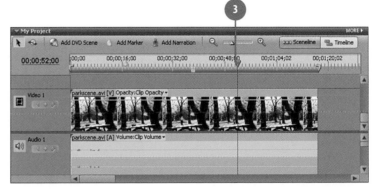

4

Click the **Add Marker** button to place a marker at this spot (**00;00;52;00**).

 Move the **CTI** to the **00;00;59;00** position.

 Click the **Add Marker** button to place a third marker at this spot (**00;00;59;00**).

 Move the **CTI** to the **00;01;02;00** position and place a marker here using the **Add Marker** button.

 Add two additional markers, at these positions:

◆ **00;01;08;00**

◆ **00;01;16;00**

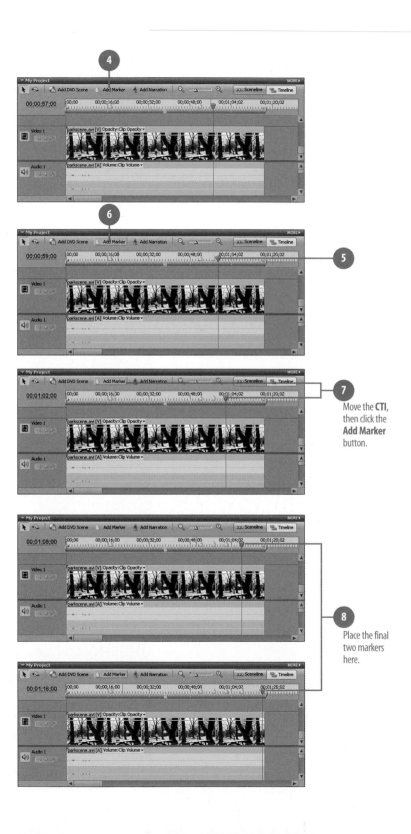

Move the **CTI**, then click the **Add Marker** button.

Place the final two markers here.

Removing Time (Frames) from the Clip

In this step, we will remove a fairly large number of frames by deleting segments from the clip. When you view the clip after these deletions have been made, the clip will appear quite choppy, and the actor will appear to jump from location to location. What we now have is a series of *jump cuts*. A jump cut is created when, as you will do in this task, you remove some or most of the middle of a clip resulting in the actor (and even some of the objects) appearing to jump about from their starting location at the beginning of the clip to their new location at the end of the clip. You will have removed, in short, the transition frames (the walking in this case) that showed how the actor moved naturally between the two locations.

Splitting the Clips

1 Press the **Home** key on your keyboard to return the **CTI** to the beginning of the **parkscene** clip.

> **TIMESAVER** *If the full clip is not visible, press the backslash key, \, on your keyboard to view the full project.*

2 While holding down the **CTRL** key on your keyboard, press the **right arrow** key to jump to the first marker.

3 Click the **Split Clip** button on the Monitor panel to split the clip at this point (**00;00;17;00**).

4 Press **CTRL-right arrow** again to jump to the next marker.

5 Click the **Split Clip** button again to split the clip here (**00;00;52;00**).

6 Press **CTRL-right arrow** to jump to each of the remaining markers and split the clip at each marker using the **Split Clip** tool, as described in the preceding steps:

- ◆ **00;00;59;00**
- ◆ **00;01;02;00**
- ◆ **00;01;08;00**
- ◆ **00;01;16;00**

> **IMPORTANT** *You should end up with seven (7) smaller clips after making a total of six (6) cuts using the **Split Clip** tool.*

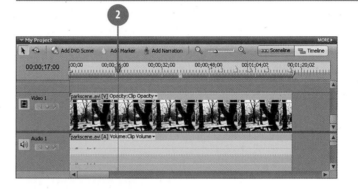

Notice this section is now a new, separate, clip.

Remove Frames from the Larger Clip by Cutting Smaller Clips

1 Return the **CTI** to the beginning (head) of the clip by press the **Home** key on your keyboard.

2 Jump to the first marker by pressing **CTRL-right arrow** on your keyboard.

3 Click to select the second clip on the **Video 1** track (it starts on **00;00;17;02** and ends **00;00;51;29**) in the sequence.

4 Press **Shift-Delete** on your keyboard to delete the selected clip.

5 We want to keep the next clip, so jump over it to the ***third* clip** (of the remaining clips) by pressing **CTRL-right arrow** on your keyboard **two times**.

6 Click to select the third clip (it starts on **00;00;59;00** and ends **00;01;01;29**) and press **Shift-Delete** to delete it.

7 Finally, jump to the ***fifth* marker** by again pressing **CTRL-right arrow** on your keyboard **two times**.

8 Click to select the fourth clip (of the remaining clips). It starts on **00;01;08;01** and ends **00;01;15;29**) and press **Shift-Delete** to delete it.

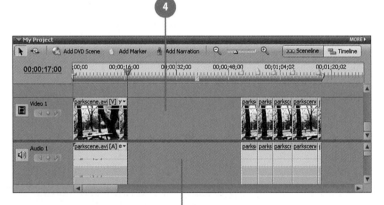

When you press **Shift-Delete**, the clip will be cut, as shown above, leaving a gap. The gap is critical for now, so that we can use the markers we placed.

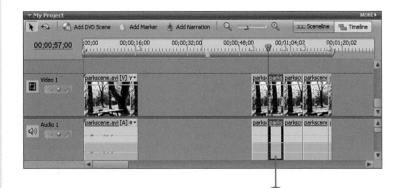

Delete the Gaps

1 Now that we've deleted the clips we won't be using to create our jump cuts, let's close up the gaps we created in the process. To do so, **right-click** on the gap between the third and fourth clips and select **Delete and Close Gaps**.

2 **Right-click** on the gap between the second and third clips and again select **Delete and Close Gaps**.

3 Do the same for the large gap between the first and second clips.

Did You Know?

Let it rip(ple).
Pressing **Shift-Delete** on the keyboard with a clip selected deletes the clip and leaves the gap "as is." We need to leave the gap at this point in order to use the markers we placed. If you want to use a "ripple delete" on a project, simply use the Delete key by itself. Using the **Delete** key deletes the clip and slides everything to the right of the deleted clip to fill the gap created by the deleted clip. This is known as a "ripple edit" because the clips "ripple" in to fill the space.

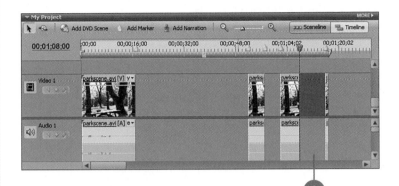

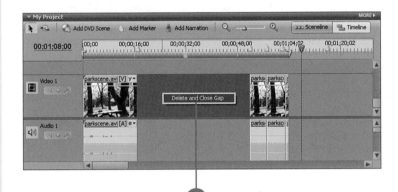

Disjointed Jumps

Disorientating Audiences is Sometimes Deliberate

The Jump Cut can have a disconcerting effect. For you film history buffs, this sort of thing was once done deliberately in films as one part of a technique to deliberately remind the audience that they were watching a movie, thus not allowing them to enter into the "world" the film was representing. The technique was known as *verfremdungseffekt* and was also known as the *V-effect* for short. The V-effect actually uses a number of different techniques, only one of which is the jump cut. Recent examples of this technique can be seen in the television series, *Homicide: Life on the Street*, the movie *Domino*, and the film, *V for Vendetta*, which used the letter "V" heavily throughout (both as a capital V and as the Roman numeral five) dabbled in the V-effect as well, specifically in the final scene.

Adding a Cross Dissolve Between Clips

As already mentioned, our clips, while showing somewhat startling and unnatural jumps in time, are too jumpy to represent any passage of time. Left as is they look like we were either going for a very different effect or have made a mistake, or in filmmaking terms, a gaffe. To transform our video into an almost dream-like visualization of time passing, all we need to do know is add one of the most respected transitions in film, the dissolve (the cut and the fade being the other two important transitions used in film).

Applying a Dissolve

1 Click the **Effects and Transitions** button on the **Media** panel to switch to the **Effects and Transitions** view.

2 In the text box on the **Effects and Transitions** view, type **cross**.

3 Drag and drop the **Cross Dissolve** onto the **Timeline** between the first and second clips.

Did You Know?

It takes just a second....

The default duration for transitions in Premiere Elements is 30 frames, or one second (shown in timecode format as **00;00;01;00**). Since there are 30 frames in each second, the Cross Dissolve by default fades out the last 15 frames on the first clip and fades in the first 15 frames on the second clip. However, you can change this duration to be any amount you want. To do so select **Edit, Preferences, General**. Find the Video **Transition Default Duration frames** field and type in the number of frames you prefer as the default. You can also access this field using the **MORE** menu from the **Effects and Transitions** view on the **Media** panel.

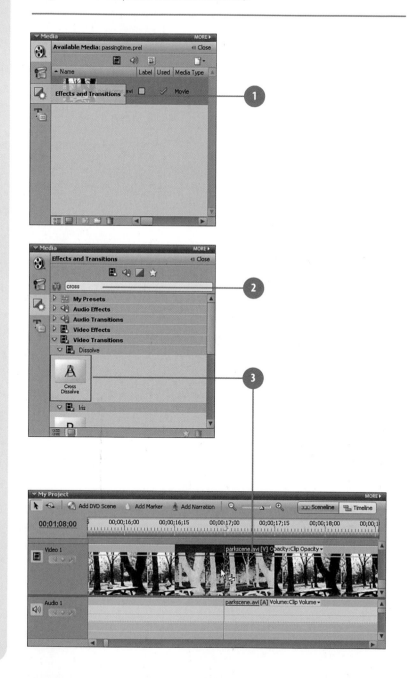

4 Add the second transition:

◆ Select the **Cross Dissolve** transition again.

◆ Drag and drop it between the second and third clips.

5 Finally, add the third transition:

◆ Select the **Cross Dissolve** transition one more time.

◆ Drag and drop it between the third clip and the fourth clip.

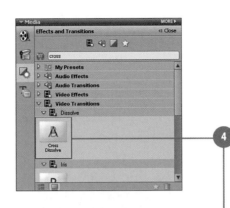

Did You Know?

You can quickly switch between Timeline view and Sceneline view to suit the task. While some functions in Premiere Elements work better when in **Timeline** view, such as working with multiple tracks, choosing whether to work in Timeline or **Sceneline** view is mostly a matter of personal taste. When applying the Cross Dissolve transition for this project, for example, either view works fine and give you different kinds of feedback as you work.

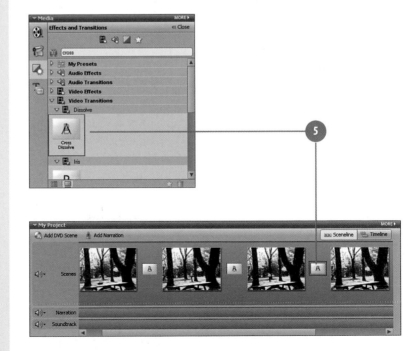

4

Adjusting the Transitions in the Properties Panel

Because we want to exaggerate the transitions between clips a bit, we want the transition to last longer on the first clip of the two clips we apply the transition to. To do so, we'll use the Properties panel for each of the transitions to control how the transitions behave. By extending all of the frames of the transitions to the first clip in each transition and increasing the duration of the dissolve, we can increase the dramatic effect to make it seem more dreamlike. The clips will also overlap more obviously, and the actor in the scene will appear to be in two places at once: dissolving out of one location while simultaneously dissolving into another location.

Change the Default Behavior for the First Cross Dissolve

1 To access the **Properties** panel for the transition, select the **Cross Dissolve** between the first and second clips on the Timeline.

2 On the **Properties** panel for the transition, select the triangle on the drop down menu for **Alignment**.

3 From the **Alignment** drop down menu, select **End at Cut**.

> **NOTE** *Selecting End at Cut, instead of the transition's default Center at Cut will cause the Cross Dissolve transition to overlap all of the frames using the first clip.*

4 Change the **Duration** of this transition to **7 seconds**, or **00;00;07;00**.

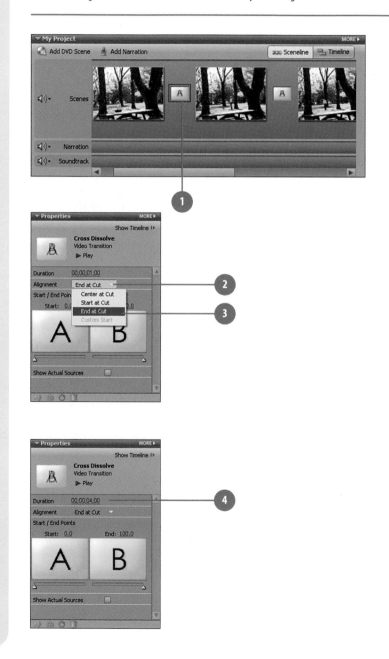

Change the Default Behavior for the Second and Third Dissolves

 Modify the second dissolve:

◆ Select the **Cross Dissolve** between the second and third clips on the Timeline.

◆ On the **Properties** panel for this transition, select the triangle on the drop down menu for **Alignment**.

◆ From the **Alignment** drop down menu, select **End at Cut**.

◆ Change the **Duration** of this transition to **4 seconds: 00;00;04;00**.

TIP *You may find that it's easier to select each of the transitions if you switch to **Sceneline** view on the Timeline. Additionally, if you adjust the Timeline by dragging the top of the **Timeline** panel down, you'll see that the size of the scenes shrink until you can eventually see all of the scenes and transitions in the project.*

2 Modify the third dissolve:

◆ Select the **Cross Dissolve** between the third and fourth clips on the Timeline.

◆ On the **Properties** panel for this transition, select the triangle on the drop down menu for **Alignment**.

◆ Leave the Alignment at **Center at Cut**.

◆ Change the **Duration** of this transition to **3 seconds, or 00;00;03;00**.

NOTE *The Alignment automatically changes from Center at Cut to Custom Start once you set the Duration to 3 seconds.*

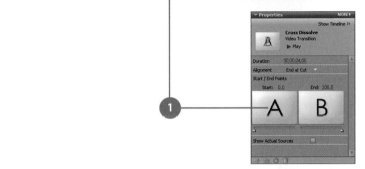

Using SmartSound® Quicktracks™ with Premiere Elements 3

Quicktracks is an interesting product from the people at SmartSound that allows you to use both the songs that come bundled with the product right off the QuickTracks CD, as well as the hundreds of songs that come on the additional music CDs available from the company and available for download from directly from the company's Web site.

The music provided with Quicktracks and on the additional music CDs is very similar to the music you'll hear on commercials, corporate presentations, and multimedia and Flash presentations on the Web. What's unique about Quicktracks is that you can choose not just a given tune, but variations on that tune. For example, if you select the music selection called "It's Cool" from the list of tracks available with Quicktracks (which SmartSound describes as "Way cool, easy feel jazz with trumpet, sax, piano, bass and drums"), you'll be able to select from a number of variations on the theme, including:

◆ Cool

◆ Sly

◆ Miles

◆ Bluesy

Installing Quicktracks

Quicktracks is a software product that was designed as a plug-in to work with Adobe Premiere Pro. As such, it looks for and installs into the Plug-ins folder for Premiere Pro. If you don't have Premiere Pro, Quicktracks discovers this during the installation process and prompts you to choose an alternative folder in which to install Quicktracks. Choose **C:\Program Files\Adobe\ Premiere Elements 3.0 \Plug-ins\en_US**. (Choose the appropriate folder below Plug-ins if en_US does not apply.) If the installation should finish without prompting you for a folder, after installation use the Windows Search feature and search for **Importer Quicktracks.prm**. Then copy it into the Premiere Elements Plug-ins folder (the full path is listed above).

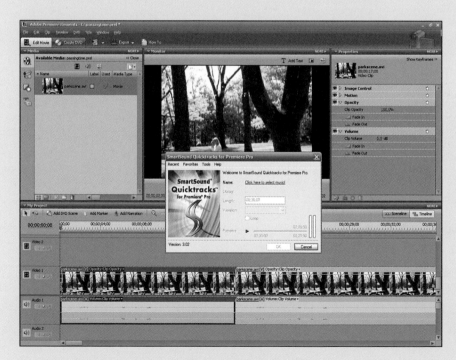

Starting Quicktracks

Using Quicktracks in Premiere Elements 3 is simply a matter of starting Premiere Elements (if you installed Quicktracks while Premiere Elements was running, close Premiere Elements and start it up again). Access the **Available Media** tab on the **Media** panel. Click on the **New Item** button (shown at right). The menu that appears will now include "SmartSound."

Select SmartSound and the SmartSound Quicktracks for Premiere Pro window displays:

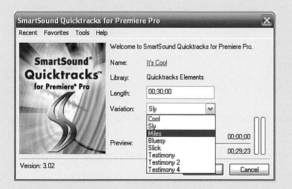

Using Quicktracks

To choose a song from Quicktracks, click the "Click here to select music!" link next to **Name** field. When you click the prompt, the SmartSound Maestro window appears, shown below, where you can choose the song you want.

You can also:

◆ Search for music (on your hard drive as well as on SmartSound's Website).

◆ Sort and filter the music by category, style, and "intensity."

◆ Listen to selections of the music to help you choose the music that best fits the project you're working on.

Some of the music that comes with Quicktracks is ready to use, and some requires you to purchase the music. You can purchase music on the spot over the Internet, which lets you get right back to your project with just a minor interruption. After you select your music, it's copied to your hard drive ready for editing in Premiere Elements just like any other media.

Select the Music for the Soundtrack

To enhance the mood of this clip, we'll add music to our project. If you have installed the trial version of SmartSound Quicktracks, you will be able to select the song we'll be using directly from the Quicktracks window from within Premiere Elements. If for some reason you won't be using Quicktracks, we have supplied you with the same track, generated from QuickTracks, on the DVD that came with this book.

Select the Music and

1 Click the **Available Media** button on the **Media** panel to switch to the Available Media view.

2 On the **Available Media** view, click the **New Item** button.

3 From the **New Item** drop down menu, select **SmartSound**.

> **IMPORTANT** *The SmartSound option only appears if you have installed SmartSound Quicktracks on your computer. If you don't have the Quicktracks software installed on your system, skip to the **Mixing in the Music Track** task on page **80** and continue from there.*

4 On the SmartSound Quicktracks for Premiere Pro window, click the link in the Name field, **Click here to select music!**

5 On the SmartSound Maestro window, select **Owned by me** from the **Find Music** column.

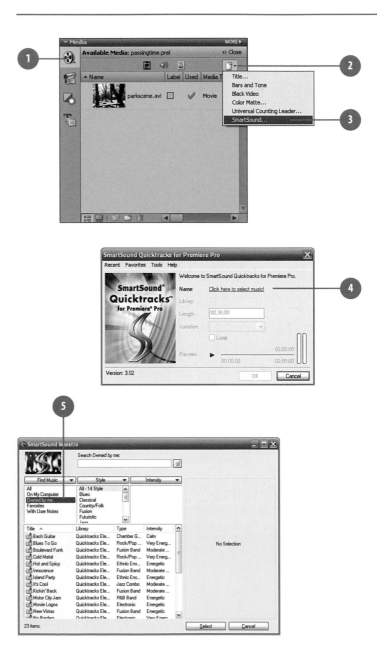

6 Select **New Age/Easy** from the **Style** column.

7 Select **Underwater** from the track list.

8 Click **Select**.

9 On the SmartSound Quicktracks for Premiere Pro window, select **Ascent** from the **Variation** list.

10 Click the **Loop** check box.

11 Click **OK** and you'll be prompted to save the file.

12 Save the music file to a location on your hard drive and click **OK**.

TIP *The Quicktracks music file,* **SmartSound - Underwater - Ascent [00;31;24].wav,** *has been added to your list of media for this project.*

IMPORTANT *If Quicktracks has also added* **SmartSound - Underwater - Ascent [00;31;24].wav** *to the Timeline, you may need to move it to the* **Audio 2** *track. If so, do that now and adjust the clip so that it is aligned with the beginning of the* **Audio 2** *track, as shown in the illustration on page* **78**. *In addition, if the insertion of the music track created gaps, simply* **right-click** *on each gap and select* **Delete and Close Gap** *when it appears.*

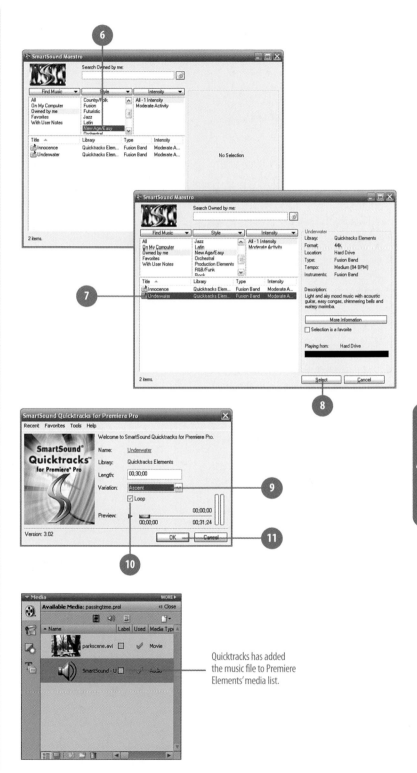

Quicktracks has added the music file to Premiere Elements' media list.

Mixing in the Music Track ▶

Add the Music to the Project's Soundtrack

① If you don't have Quicktracks installed, this music track is also on the DVD supplied with this book. To retrieve it, click the **Get Media from** button on the **Media** panel to access the **Get Media from** view, if it's not already active.

② Select **DVD, Digital Camera, Mobile Phone, Hard Drive Camcorder, Card Reader**.

③ When the **Media Downloader** displays, click the **Advanced Dialog** button to switch to Advanced mode.

④ Select the **SmartSound - Underwater - Ascent [00;31;24].wav** clip for this project.

⑤ Click the **Get Media** button. Premiere Elements copies the **SmartSound - Underwater - Ascent [00;31;24].wav** clip from the DVD onto your hard drive and adds it to the Available Media list for this project.

⑥ Drag and drop the **SmartSound - Underwater - Ascent [00;31;24].wav** clip from the **Media** panel on to the **Audio 2** track. Be sure to line up the head of the music clip with the start of the **Audio 2** track.

⑦ As is, this track is too loud for our project. We won't be able to hear the ambient sounds in the **parkscene.avi** clip. To correct this, on the **Properties** panel for the **SmartSound - Underwater - Ascent [00;31;24].wav** clip, adjust the clip so that the volume is at or near **negative 10 decibels (-10 dB)**.

Now that we've selected the track that best fits our project, we will add it to the **Audio 2** track and manipulate it slightly so that the volume of this music track doesn't overwhelm our clip. As it is right now, it's a bit too loud.

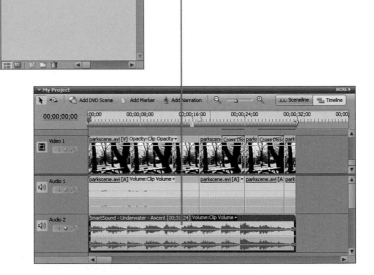

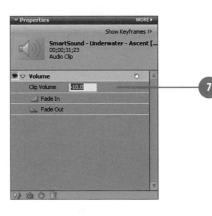

TIP *You can also adjust the volume using the rubberband on the* **SmartSound - Underwater - Ascent [00;31;24].wav** *clip by dragging the rubberband lower in the clip. Note that as you drag the rubberband, Premiere Elements gives you feedback as to the decibel level (db) that track is at:*

8 Click on **Fade In** on the **Properties** panel. This way, the music track will gently begin playing from silence at first.

TIP *You might want to apply a* **Fade In** *to the first video clip in the* **Video 1** *track and a* **Fade Out** *to the last video clip in the* **Video 1** *track. This will create a nice fade up from black and fade down to black for the project.*

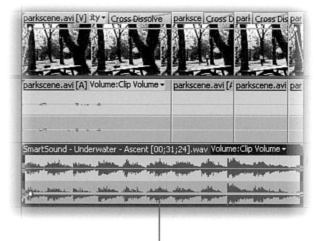

The finished tracks. Notice the location of the yellow rubberband on the bottom audio track and how it ramps up at the beginning of the clip, graphically showing the audio "fade in."

Making Adjustments, Rendering, and Exporting

Well, you've done it: another special effects production completed! Test your production by pressing the **Spacebar** to see how it all fits together. If it's not quite right, tweak things a bit until it's to your liking, such as the timing of the dissolves or the relative loudness or softness of the music track. Then, press the **ENTER** key on your keyboard to render (apply all effects and transitions to the clips) your project and you're ready to export the finished movie for all to see!

Finishing the Project

1   Once you have played back your clip and made the necessary adjustments, press the **ENTER** key on your keyboard to render your project.

2   Press **CTRL-S** to save your project (you can select **File, Save** from the menu).

3   Finally, export your work as an AVI file. To export the clip, select **File, Export, Movie**.

TIP *You can optionally bring this clip into a larger project, show it on your computer, upload it to an Internet video sharing site, or burn it to a DVD.*

The finished movie, playing in Windows Media player.

The Fast Times Effect

MEDIA:

manypeople.avi
oneperson.avi
moreanimated.wav

5

COMPLEXITY:	Simple	Moderate	Complex
SKILL LEVEL:	Novice	Intermediate	Advanced
MATERIALS:	None	Some Props	Greenscreen

What You'll Do

Add the Two Video Clips to the Project

Increase the Speed of the Background Clip

Add the Green Screen to the Foreground Clip

Learn How Two Controls Help the Green Screen Key Filter Out the Green

Match the Appearance of the Two Clips

Add the Soundtrack

Make Adjustments, Render, and Export

Introduction

The Fast Times Effect is perfect to show the world rushing by your subject as he or she moves in normal time, thereby communicating a world of information about the character and story. For example, you could direct the actors playing a couple on the verge of a breakup to move further and further apart on a bench at an airport in "real time," looking at everything but each other, while all the world traveling to their destinations hurries past them in a frenzied blur. The dramatic effect of everyone else in the world moving in fast motion emphasizes the emotion the couple is feeling in the moment.

The Fast Times Effect can be used, as well, whenever you need your main character to move with superhuman speed. In this case, your background clip would be kept at normal speed and the clip of the main character, filmed in normal speed, would be sped up to "super speed" and overlaid on top of the normal-moving background. Think "Dash" from *The Incredibles*.

Playing with time by experimenting with the Time Stretch function in Premiere Elements can yield a range of results that may be useful in different projects. Keep in mind that although the effect can be very dramatic (as demonstrated in this chapter), it can also be used very subtly. For example, in a normal scene you could use the Fast Times Effect for just a second or two as two people pass by on a crowded city street and have an internal moment of "haven't we met before, maybe in another lifetime....?" And then the scene returns to full speed. To add to the drama, you could even slow down the two actors a bit. For the most part, you are only limited on how you can apply this effect by your imagination.

Adding the Two Video Clips to the Project

In this project, we'll be using two clips. One is of the subject of the piece, the actor who is moving in "real time." The other clip is the "rest of the world." This clip is the one that we will be speeding up. In fact, the original clip is almost three minutes long. We'll be speeding this up so that it matches the "real time" clip and will be, then, merely 10 seconds. Three minutes of action condensed down into ten seconds. This will be one fast-moving crowd!

Import the Two Clips

1 Start Premiere Elements and create a new project called **fasttimes**.

2 Click **OK**.

3 Click the **Get Media from** button on the **Media** panel to access the **Get Media from** view, if it's not already active.

4 Select **DVD, Digital Camera, Mobile Phone, Hard Drive Camcorder, Card Reader**.

5 When the **Media Downloader** displays, click the **Advanced Dialog** button to switch to Advanced mode.

6 Select the following clips:

- ◆ **manypeople.avi**

- ◆ **oneperson.avi**

7 Click the **Get Media** button. Premiere Elements copies the clips from the DVD onto your hard drive and adds it to the Available Media list for this project.

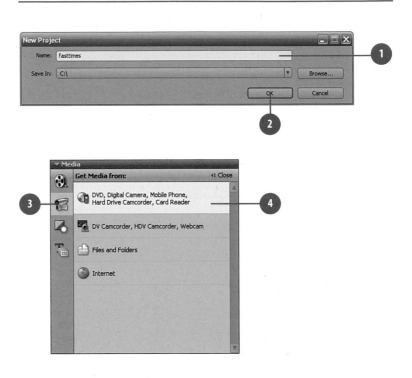

Acquiring A Greenscreen for Your Projects

Web Sources for Greenscreens

After you've mastered this technique, you'll want to use it with your own clips. Creating greenscreen clips requires a greenscreen (or bluescreen) for the background. While any solid green surface will work for a greenscreen or bluescreen, such as a sheet, for best results get yourself an industry-approved greenscreen. If you search on "greenscreen" using your favorite Web search engine, you'll find a lot of different makes and models to choose from. Through-out this book, we've been using greenscreens and stands and other equipment from **www.chroma-key.com**. They supply a variety of blue- and greenscreens, portable and studio stands, and even greenscreen paint.

Add the "Background" Clip to the Timeline

1 Drag the **manypeople.avi** clip from the **Available Media** view of the **Media** panel and drop it onto the **Timeline** in the **Video 1** track. Be sure to line up the start (head) of the **manypeople.avi** clip with the beginning of the **Video 1** track.

TIP *If you're in **Sceneline** view, drop the **manypeople.avi clip** onto the first scene box. Premiere Elements will place it on the **Video 1** track.*

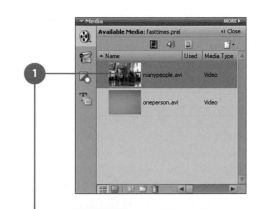

Add the "Foreground" Clip to the Timeline

1 Click the **Timeline** button on the **My Project** panel to switch to **Timeline** view, if it's not already the active view.

NOTE *We need to switch to **Timeline** view because we are working with multiple video clips and need to view multiple video tracks.*

2 Drag the **oneperson.avi** clip from the **Media** panel and drop it onto the **Timeline** in the **Video 2** track. Again, be sure to line up the head of the **oneperson.avi** clip with the beginning of the **Video 2** track.

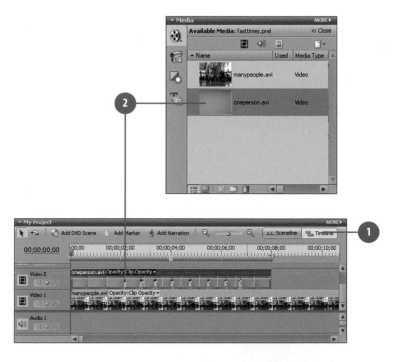

5

Increasing the Speed of the Background Clip

In this task, we will "super speed" the clip of the crowd in the background to achieve the effect of time rushing past. The foreground clip, which shows the actor walking across the screen at normal speed, is about 8 seconds long. The background clip—which shows the world rushing (or until we increase the speed, meandering) by—is roughly 3 *minutes* long. To make the two clips work better together in terms of duration, and to speed up the background clip, we'll use the **Time Stretch** function in Premiere Elements to speed up the crowd and condense three minutes of meandering into ten seconds of purposeful action.

Change the Speed of the manypeople.avi Clip

1. Press the **backslash** (\) key on your keyboard to view all of the clips on the Timeline.

2. On the Timeline, **right-click** the **manypeople.avi** clip in the **Video 1** track.

3. From the contextual menu, select **Time Stretch**.

4. On the **Time Stretch** dialog box, set the **Speed** to **1700%**.

5. Click **OK**.

Did You Know?

Increasing a clip's speed shortens its duration (and vice versa). You can use the **Time Stretch** dialog box to change the speed of a clip, which simultaneously affects its *duration* (how long the clip plays). Making the clip play faster decreases its duration (by playing faster, it finishes sooner). The inverse is true, as well. Making a clip slower increases its duration (it plays slower, so it takes longer to finish). In other words, as nonintuitive though it may seem at first, when adjusting a clip's speed, up is down and down is up. For example, increasing the **Speed** of a clip to 200% will slow the clip to *half* its normal speed, and decreasing the **Speed** to 50% will *increase* the clip to *twice* its normal speed.

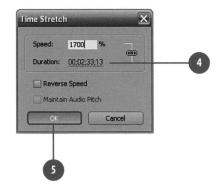

Add a Fade Out and Adjust the Timing

① Press the **backslash** (\) key on your keyboard again to zoom in on the clips on the Timeline.

② With the **manypeople.avi** clip selected, go to the **Properties** panel for the clip and , if necessary, click the triangle next to **Opacity** to reveal the effect's controls.

③ Click the **Fade Out** button to add a fade to black at the en of this clip.

④ Adjust the fade (because this clip is accelerated) by dragging the first keyframe of the fade out back so that it lines up with the tail (end) of the **oneperson.avi** clip in the **Video 2** track (see the illustration), at **00;00;08;00**.

TIP *The yellow popup box will show you the timecode as you move the keyframe. Just watch as the number decreases and approaches **00;00;08;00**, and stop when it reaches that number.*

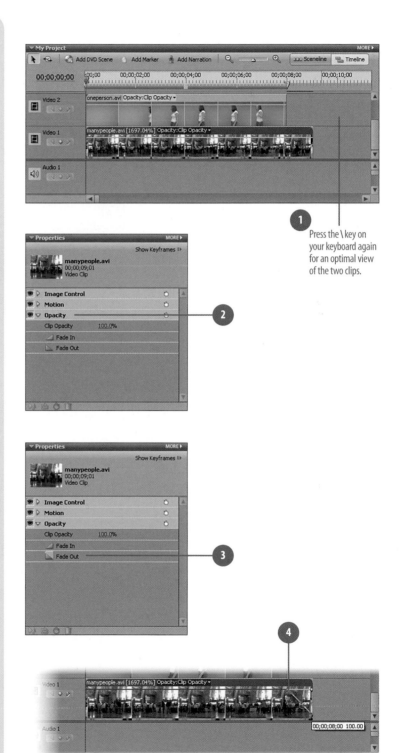

Press the \ key on your keyboard again for an optimal view of the two clips.

Applying the Green Screen Key to the Foreground Clip

The foreground clip, **oneperson.avi**, was filmed against a greenscreen. In order for the background clip of the fast-moving crowd to appear behind the actor is this project, we need to remove—or "key out"—the green background behind her. We'll do that using the **Green Screen Key**.

Apply the Green Screen Key

1 Click the **Effects and Transitions** button on the **Media** panel to switch to the **Effects and Transitions** view.

2 In the **Effects and Transitions** view, type **green** in the text field.

3 Drag the **Green Screen Key** from the Keying effects in the Video Effects list and and drop it onto the **oneperson.avi** clip on the **Video 2** track.

4 In the **Properties** panel, click the triangle next to the **Green Screen Key** to view the effect's controls.

Did You Know?

If the background in your clip is not one solid green color, use the Chroma Key instead.
The Green Screen Key, like the Blue Screen Key, in Adobe Premiere Elements works for one particular color only. If the green in your background is not the exact shade of green that the Green Screen Key expects to find (or if, due to light and shadows, there are multiple shades of green), you may not achieve the results you want, in terms of the background being removed. In that case, use the Chroma Key instead. If your greenscreen material was crease-free and lit correctly, the Chroma Key has a "Similarity" control that enables you to tweak the key giving you a better chance of success. For touchy keying problems, use the Chroma Key!

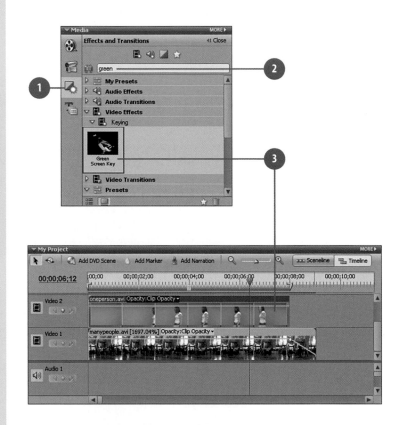

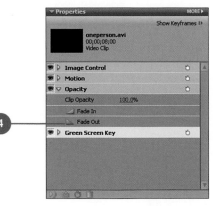

TIP *If the **oneperson.avi** clip is not currently displayed in the **Monitor** window, move the **CTI** along the **Timeline** until it does.*

5 On the **Properties** panel, set the following **Green Screen Key** properties:

- ◆ **Threshold**: **33.0%**

- ◆ **Cutoff**: **33.0%**

6 From the **Smoothing** drop down menu, select **High**.

NOTE *Leave the **Mask Only** check box unchecked. However, if you want to see a silhouette of the actor in white against the background clip, check this box temporarily to see how your Green Screen Key is working.*

How Two Controls Help the Green Screen Key Filter Out the Green

Working with the Green Screen Key

When you first apply the Green Screen Key to a clip, you rarely get a perfect result. What you typically see is the first "layer" of green removed from the background of the greenscreen clip, revealing the hazy background behind the clip. The background itself is revealed as if behind a curtain. As you tweak the two key settings for the Green Screen Key—**Threshold** and **Cutoff**—you'll gradually see the background emerge and the foreground become brighter and

more pronounced. Tweaking too far causes the figure in the foreground to deteriorate, allowing some of the background to bleed through. Typically, the **Threshold** and **Cutoff** settings are the same and when you find the right settings for the clip, the scene looks natural, with little, if any, evidence that a greenscreen was used. For more on greenscreens, the Green Screen Key, the Non-Red Key, and the Chroma Key, refer to **Chapter 16: The Enchanted Elf Effect** in the section, "Troubleshooting a Greenscreen Project."

The original clip, prior to applying the Green Screen Key.

The original clip, with the Green Screen Key applied. Here, the **Threshold** is at its default 100% setting and the **Cutoff** is at 0%. Notice how the background appears to be hidden behind a sheer, gray curtain.

The clip, with the Green Screen Key applied, and the **Threshold** at 50% and the **Cutoff** is still at 0%. The background image is showing through much better as more of the green is removed, but the actor's image is too faded.

The clip, with the Green Screen Key applied, and the **Threshold** at 25% and **Cutoff** at 25%. Notice the degradation that has begun.

Matching the Appearance of the Two Clips

The two sample video clips for this project, **oneperson.avi** and **manypeople.avi**, were filmed at different locations, at different times of day, and under uniquely different lighting conditions. (One was filmed on a sunny day in greenscreen studio-slash-garage at about noon, the other on an overcast day inside a train terminal about 4:00 in the afternoon.) When you are using your own clips—or perhaps a royalty-free clip as the background—you may run into similar color and lighting mismatches, either great or small. Fortunately, these are usually fairly easy to fix with some minimal tweaking of one or both of the clips' Image Control settings.

Adjusting the Image Control Settings as Needed

1 Click the **oneperson.avi** clip on the **Video 2** track.

2 In the **Properties** panel for the clip, click the triangle next to **Image Control** to view the effect's controls.

3 Set the following **Image Control** properties:

◆ **Brightness**: **-1.0**

◆ **Contrast**: **95.0**

◆ **Hue**: **-1.0°**

◆ **Saturation**: **95.0**

Did You Know?

All clips are different, at least to some degree. Keep in mind that the settings in Step 3 above are specifically for the two clips used in this project. When you are working on your next greenscreen project, look at how the clips are working together on the screen and make adjustments as necessary—use your own judgement. Maybe the Hue needs to be +1.0°. Maybe the Saturation needs to be increased, the Contrast decreased. Experiment until you like what you see. For this task, it's a little bit art, and a little bit science.

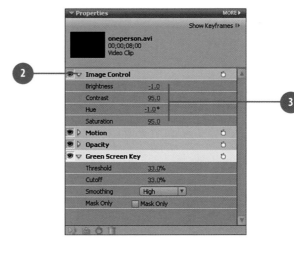

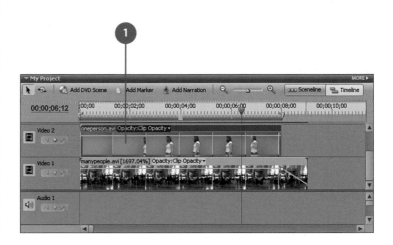

5

Adding the Soundtrack

Music sets the mood, and for this clip we're adding a music clip aptly entitled, **moreanimated.wav**. Ohio has brought us great music, including Chrissie Hynde of the Pretenders, Dwight Yoakum, and Devo. *More Animated Than Most* is a song from another Ohio band, Montgomery Greene, and it adds to the mood of the clip by providing a rock and roll beat and some ironic lyrics to the scene we're creating.

Select the Song and Add it To the Timeline

1 Click the **Get Media from** button on the **Media** panel to access the **Get Media from** view, if it's not already active.

2 Select **DVD, Digital Camera, Mobile Phone, Hard Drive Camcorder, Card Reader**.

3 When the **Media Downloader** displays, click the **Advanced Dialog** button to switch to Advanced mode.

4 Select the **moreanimated.wav** clip.

5 Click the **Get Media** button. Premiere Elements copies the **moreanimated.wav** clip from the DVD onto your hard drive and adds it to the Available Media list for this project.

6 Drag the **moreanimated.wav** clip from the **Media** panel and drop it onto the **Timeline** in the **Audio 1** track. Be sure to line up the start (head) of the **moreanimated.wav** clip with the beginning of the **Audio 1** track.

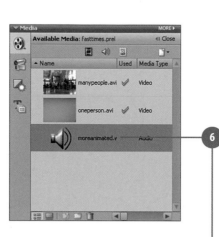

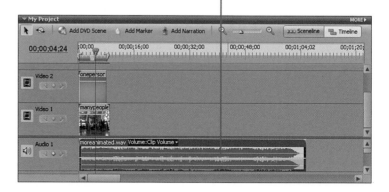

Adjust the Song's Length to Match Movie

 Move the **CTI** 17 seconds in, to **00;00;17;00**.

> **TIMESAVER** *You may want to press the backslash (\) key on your keyboard to view all of the clips on the Timeline in full.*

2 Drag the end of the **moreanimated.wav** clip and trim it back until it meets the **CTI** at **00;00;17;00**.

3 In the **Properties** panel for the moreanimated clip, click on the **Fade Out** button under **Volume**.

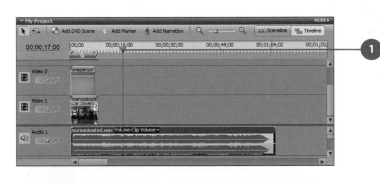

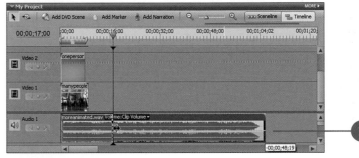

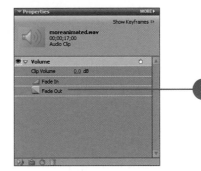

More Montgomery Greene

MG CDs Are Available

If you like what you hear on the clip included for this project, there's good news. Although the band is no more, their CDs live on. Their CDs include *Secondary Wish List* (2000), *Polar Camp Audience* (2001), *Attack Culture* (2003), and *Ready By the Next Symbol* (2004). To order a CD, or for more information, contact Kyle Melton at **montgomerygreene@yahoo.com**. By the way, the other two Montgomery Greene songs on the DVD supplied with this book are also from *Ready By the Next Symbol*. They are *What Size Should I Be?* (whatsize.mp3) and *The Popular Secret* (popular.mp3).

5

Making Adjustments, Rendering, and Exporting

Before you call this project finished, you may want to make some final adjustments to the clips as needed, based on your own personal style. After which, you're ready to save, render, and make your movie.

Finishing the Project

1. After you have played back your clip and made the necessary adjustments, press the **ENTER** key on your keyboard to render your project.

2. Press **CTRL-S** to save your project (or you can select **File, Save** from the menu).

3. Finally, export your work as an AVI file. To export the clip, select **File, Export, Movie**.

   TIP *You can optionally bring this clip into a larger project, show it on your computer, upload it to an Internet video sharing site, or burn it to a DVD.*

The finished project running in Windows Media Player.

The Reverse Action Effect

MEDIA:

running.avi
cartoon_bonk.wav
cartoon_stagger.wav
cartoon_music.wav

6

COMPLEXITY:	Simple	Moderate	Complex
SKILL LEVEL:	Novice	Intermediate	Advanced
MATERIALS:	None	Some Props	Greenscreen

Introduction

The Reverse Action Effect is one of the easiest and quickest effects to do in Premiere Elements. (You can apply the effect in less time than it took you to read that last sentence.) Nonetheless, it has the potential to be one of the most powerful and dramatic effects in your effects arsenal, as well. This effect can be used to turn a perfectly fine, enjoyable clip into a comedy classic, as we'll demonstrate in this chapter.

You can use the Reverse Action Effect for dramatic and comic purposes, and you can apply it to virtually any clip with almost guaranteed interesting results. You've seen it used when a Jedi, having had his light saber dangerously knocked from his hand, uses the "force" to pull it back to him (actually what you're watching is the light saber rolling or falling away played back in reverse). Or a six-million-dollar man "leaping" up great heights (again, what you're seeing is the actor leaping down, played in reverse).

You can use this effect, too, to show your son leap "out" of a pool, your daughter slide "up" the slide, or a friend extract a candy bar out of his mouth and reassemble it back into its wrapper. Because the effect is found on the Time Stretch dialog box (which is used to speed up and slow down clips), reversing clips while at the same time changing their speed or duration are natural effect "companions."

What You'll Do

Add Your Clip to the Timeline

Select a Section of the Clip to Reverse

Know Where You Are In Time

Copy & Paste the New Selection

Double Up the Clips

Reverse the "B" Clips for a "Back and Forth" Effect

Find Another Selection to Reverse

Triple the Clips

Add Cartoon Sound Effects to the Action

Add a Touch of Silly Music

Add a Still Image at the End of the Movie

Make Adjustments, Render, and Export

Adding Your Clip to the Timeline

We have provided you with a sample clip, **running.avi**, on the the DVD supplied with this book. Once you master this technique, you can apply it to any clip you have available. You want to use a clip with a good amount of action, such as someone sliding into second base (so you can show them sliding *away* from the base back into a standing position) or slipping off the parallel bars (so you can show them slipping back on), or pouring water over their head at the pool (so you can show the water being sucked back up into the pail)—anything that will look interesting or comical in reverse.

Add a Good Clip to the Timeline

1. Start Premiere Elements and create a new project called **reverseaction**.

2. Click the **Get Media from** button on the **Media** panel to access the **Get Media from** view, if it's not already active.

3. Select **DVD, Digital Camera, Mobile Phone, Hard Drive Camcorder, Card Reader**.

4. When the **Media Downloader** displays, click the **Advanced Dialog** button to switch to Advanced mode.

5. Select the **running.avi** clip for this project.

6. Click the **Get Media** button. Premiere Elements copies the **running.avi** clip from the DVD onto your hard drive and adds it to the Available Media list for this project.

7. Select the **running.avi** clip on the **Media** panel and drag and drop it onto the **Timeline** in the **Video 1** track. Be sure to line up the head of the clip with the start of the track (00;00;00;00).

   TIP *If you are in Sceneline view, just drop the clip onto the first scene placeholder (as shown in the illustration).*

8. For this project, we'll need to be in **Timeline** view because we are working with multiple clips on multiple video tracks. So, if the **My Project** panel is not already in **Timeline** view, click the **Timeline** button to switch.

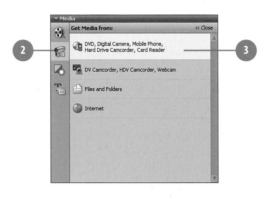

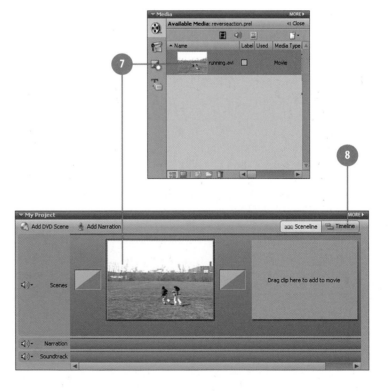

Selecting a Section of the Clip to Reverse

Find a Good Section of the Clip to Reverse

1 Move the **CTI** to the **4 second** mark (**00;00;04;00**) on the Timeline.

TIMESAVER *You can type* **00;00;04;00** *directly on the timecode area in the upper left corner of the* **My Project** *panel to jump there.*

2 Click the **Split Clip** button on the Monitor panel to split the **running.avi** clip at this point.

3 Scrub the **CTI** a bit further to the **5 second, 5 frames** position (**00;00;05;05**).

4 Click the **Split Clip** button again to split the **running.avi** clip at this point as well, creating a sub-clip.

Did You Know?

Jogging is good for you.
On professional editing equipment, editors move back and forth a frame at a time using a device called a "jog wheel." If you have a scroll wheel on your mouse, you can simulate the jog wheel on the **Monitor** panel. Just click anywhere in the **Monitor** panel and then roll your scroll wheel up and down to move the clip back and forth. Now you're jogging like the pros! This is a great way, as you're exploring for a good clip to apply the reverse effect to, to see exactly what the reverse effect will look like at any given point. By the way, the "jog wheel" technique does not work on the Timeline. On the Timeline, the scroll wheel moves you back and forth along the Timeline instead.

While you can apply the reverse effect to an entire clip, we'll be applying the reverse effect to only a small portion of this clip. Actually, we'll be applying the effect to two different small sections of this clip. For this first reversal, we're just looking for an interesting point in the clip where a slight change in the action happens. The first moment where this seems to occur is when the girl first catches up to the boy, at about the 4 second mark (00;00;04;00).

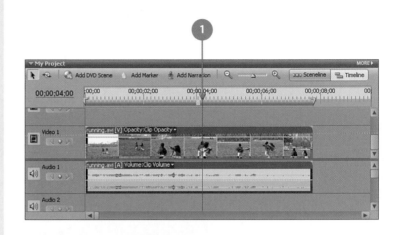

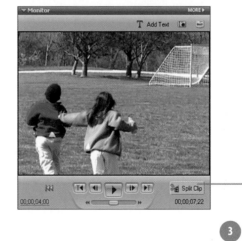

6

Knowing Where You Are in Time

Premiere Elements gives you two ways to determine exactly where you are in a clip or in a project. In fact, you can tell where you are not only down to the exact second, but to the exact frame. The **Monitor** panel and the **Timeline** both provide you with the timecode as you play or scrub your way through a clip, while the **Timeline** also gives you a ruler for the precise placement of clips and for the selection of

cutting and trimming points. Both the **Monitor** panel and the **Timeline** on the **My Project** panel use the same timecode system of hours, minutes, seconds, and frames, represented as *hh;mm;ss;ff*.

In the illustration, the frame in the **Monitor** panel is the initial frame in the sixth second of the clip. (Each second of your video contains approximately 30 frames.) Notice that on the right of the **Monitor** panel you can see the full length of the project. In this case, because we only have one clip currently loaded for the project, both the length of the project and the length of the clip are the same.

The timecode on the **Timeline** is showing the same location in the clip (notice the location of the **CTI** on the **Timeline**). If you look at the image directly under the **CTI**, you'll see that it doesn't match the image in the **Monitor** panel. This shows you that the visual clues that Premiere Elements gives you on the **Timeline** are only approximations of the content and are not meant to be used for editing. You should only edit watching the **Monitor** panel. By the way, If you look at the timeruler, it also shows you the same hours, minutes, seconds, and frames.

The timecode appears here on the **Monitor**...

The measurements on the ruler change as you zoom in and out. Here, the short notches indicate four-frame increments, while the longer notches indicate 2-second increments.

...and here by the timeruler on the **Timeline**.

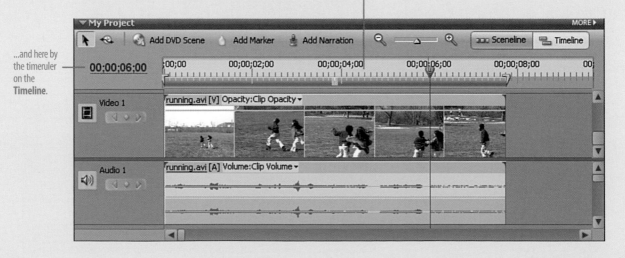

98

Copying and Pasting the New Selection

Copy & Paste

1 Using your mouse, select the clip you just created (the middle clip that starts at **00;00;04;00**).

> **TIP** *You could also right-click on the clip and select **Copy** from the contextual menu, or select **Edit**, **Copy** from the main menu.*

2 Press **CTRL-C** on your keyboard to copy it.

3 Press **CTRL-*SHIFT*-V** on your keyboard or **Edit, Paste Insert** on the main menu to insert the copied clip into place on the Timeline.

> **IMPORTANT** *Be careful not to use the **CTRL-V** key combination here. This will overlay the clip at the **CTI** point, which will erase anything that's already there when we drop in, or paste, this clip. Effectively, it's a copy and replace. We want to do a copy and add, so we need to insert our new copy onto the Timeline, nudging everything else out of the way a bit and that's done using **CTRL-SHIFT-V** If you accidentally used **CTRL-V**, use **CTRL-Z** to undo it, then try again.*

Now that you have a suitable clip (or sub-clip, so to speak) created on the Timeline, we'll next need to make a copy of it as our next step in creating a movie using the **Reverse Action** effect. It's important that we insert the copy, rather than overlay it. So, we'll be using **CTRL-*SHIFT*-V**, not simply **CTRL-V**.

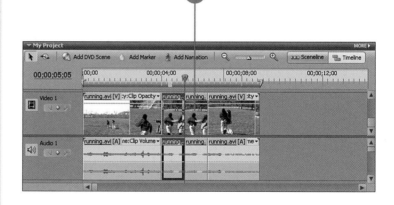

Doubling Up the Clips

For this project, we want to create a "back and forth" motion, and to do that, we'll need two copies of each clip, two in the forward direction and two in the reverse direction. To keep things organized, we'll rename each of the clips. The "A" clips will be our forward (normal) clips, and the "B" clips will be our backwards clips. So we'll end up with A1 and B1, and A2 and B2.

Adding Two and Two Together

 1 Select both of the sub-clips by pressing the **SHIFT** key on your keyboard and then clicking on the copy clip. You should now have two clips selected, as shown in the illustration.

2 Press **Ctrl-C** on your keyboard.

3 Press the **Page Down** key on your keyboard to move to the end of the second clip (at **00;00;06;10**).

4 Press **CTRL-SHIFT-V** on your keyboard to insert the copied clips into place on the Timeline.

> **IMPORTANT** *Be sure that you use the* **CTRL-SHIFT-V** *keys on your keyboard. Pressing just SHIFT-V will overwrite the clips to the left on the Timeline. CTRL-SHIFT-V inserts the clips.*

5 Deselect all clips. We are now going to rename each of these clips, one by one, so that we have clips named A1, B1, and A2, B2.

6 **Right-click** on the first clip in this group and select **Rename** from the contextual menu.

7 Enter **A1** in the **Rename** dialog box and click **OK**.

8 Right-click on the second clip and select **Rename** from the contextual menu and name this clip **B1**.

9 Right-click on the third clip is this group, select **Rename**, and rename this clip **A2**.

10 Finally, right-click on the fourth clip, select **Rename**, and rename this clip **B2**.

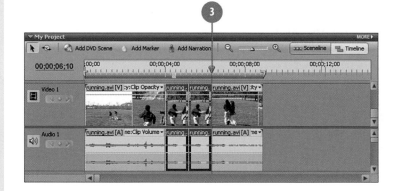

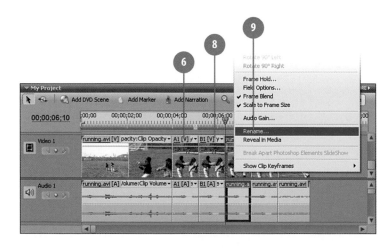

Reversing the "B" Clips for a "Back and Forth" Effect

Now that we have our copies (to apply the **Reverse Action** effect to) and our originals (preserving the forward motion), we can apply the **Reverse Action** effect. Actually, you will not find a "Reverse Action" effect or anything like it in the **Effects and Transitions** panel. The **Reverse Speed** function is actually hidden in the **Time Stretch** dialog box. The **Time Stretch** dialog box is available by right-clicking the clip itself, and selecting **Time Stretch**, or by selecting **Clip**, **Time Stretch** from the Premiere Elements menu.

Apply the Reverse Effect

1 **Right-click** on the **B1** clip, and from the contextual menu, select **Time Stretch**.

2 From the **Time Stretch** dialog box, click the **Reverse Speed** check box and click **OK**.

3 **Right-click** on the **B2** clip, and select **Time Stretch.** Click the **Reverse Speed** check box and click **OK**.

4 If you want to optionally maintain the sound "as is," **right-click** the **B1** clip again and from the contextual menu, select **Time Stretch**.

5 From the **Time Stretch** dialog box, click **Maintain Audio Pitch** and click **OK**.

6 Do the same for the **B2** clip.

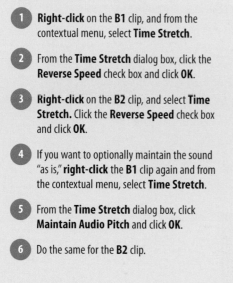

For both of the **B1** and **B2** clips, right-click and select **Time Stretch** to access the **Reverse Speed** option on the **Time Stretch** dialog box.

Did You Know?

You can keep the sound moving forward.
One problem with reversing action (or adjusting speed) is that the sound also gets modified. If you choose to leave the sound unaltered using the **Maintain Audio Pitch** check box, keep in mind that doing so will put lip movement out of sync with speech. Also, if you choose to speed up your footage but keep the soundtrack "normal," the video of the clip will finish before the audio, thereby "clipping" the audio. For example, a child saying, "Dad, watch me slide down the slide!" in the unaltered clip may become, *"Dad, watch…!"* in the altered version. Or, for that matter (in reverse), *"!…hctaw ,daD".*

Go back and click the **Maintain Audio Pitch** check box if you want the sound to remain unaffected by the change in direction.

6

Finding the Next Selection to Reverse

For this task, we will again "cut out" another sub-clip from our main clip, **running.avi**, to create the source for one more reverse action clip. We'll create with this clip even more of the "back and forth" that we gave the first set of clips, by creating additional copies of the clip.

Find the Another Section of the Clip to Reverse

1 Move your **CTI** to just after the **10 second** mark (**00;00;10;03**). We'll use this as the start of our last reverse clip.

2 Click the **Split Clip** button on the **Monitor** panel to split the **running.avi** clip again at this point.

3 Press the **Right Arrow** key on your keyboard to move the **CTI** over a bit further to **00;00;10;08**.

4 Click the **Split Clip** button again to create a new sub-clip.

Tripling the Clips

This step may look a bit complicated, but it's only because you're laying down multiple copies of a clip on the Timeline all at once. Remember, there's strength in numbers. You'll copy the clip once and then "paste-insert" five copies of the original clip in a row right across the track. After that, we'll rename these tracks to make it easy to apply the Reverse effect to the correct clips.

Triple Threat

1 Using your mouse, select the clip you just created (the clip that starts at **00;00;10;03**) and press **CTRL-C** on your keyboard.

2 Press **CTRL-SHIFT-V** on your keyboard **five** times to insert **five** copies of the clip onto the Timeline.

> **IMPORTANT** *Remember to press the* ***CTRL-SHIFT-V*** *key combination (not CTRL-V) so that you insert each copy without overwriting the clips that are already there.*

> **NOTE** *When you are done, you should have six copies of the clip in a row on the Timeline, starting at* ***00;00;10;03*** *and ending at* ***00;00;11;03***, *as shown in the illustration.*

Rename the Clips

1 **Right-click** on the first clip is this group, select **Rename** from the contextual menu, rename the clip **C1**, and click **OK**.

2 **Right-click** on the second clip, select **Rename** from the contextual menu, and rename this clip **D1**.

3 Using this same technique, rename the third and fourth clips **C2** and **D2**, respectively.

4 Finally, rename the fifth and the sixth clips **C3** and **D3**, respectively.

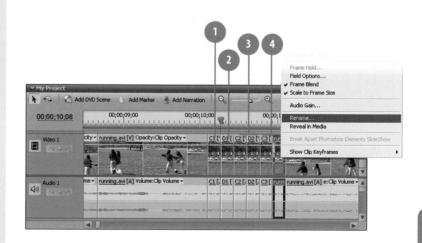

6

Reversing Every Other Clip

By combining two clips back-to-back (or in this case, back-to-back-to-back), with every other clip reversed, you can create a kind of "funniest home videos" type of look. This is a nice touch to show someone tripping and getting immediately back up again, for example. Or, as in our earlier example, jumping into a pool and jumping right back out again.

Reverse the D1, D2, and D3 Clips

1. **Right-click** on the **D1** clip and from the contextual menu, select **Time Stretch**.

2. On the **Time Stretch** dialog box, do this:

   ◆ Click the **Reverse Speed** check box.

   ◆ Click the **Maintain Audio Pitch** check box.

   ◆ Click **OK**.

3. **Right-click** on the **D2** clip and from the contextual menu, select **Time Stretch** and again click the **Reverse Speed** check box, the **Maintain Audio Pitch** check box, and click **OK**.

4. Finally, **right-click** on the **D3** clip and repeat the same process as described above.

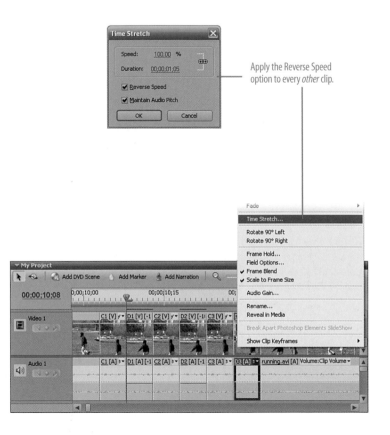

Apply the Reverse Speed option to every *other* clip.

Adding Cartoon Sound Effects to the Action

What's a good "reverse action" clip without a cartoon-ish sound effect or two thrown in for good measure? On the DVD that accompanies this book, we've provided you with just the right clips, **cartoon_bonk.wav** and **cartoon_stagger.wav**.

Add Sound Effects

1 Click the **Get Media from** button on the **Media** panel to access the **Get Media from** view, if it's not already active.

2 Select **DVD, Digital Camera, Mobile Phone, Hard Drive Camcorder, Card Reader**.

3 When the **Media Downloader** displays, click the **Advanced Dialog** button to switch to Advanced mode.

4 Select the following clips for this project:

◆ **cartoon_bonk.wav**

◆ **cartoon_stagger.wav**

5 Click the **Get Media** button.

6 Drag and drop the **cartoon_bonk.wav** clip from the **Media** panel onto the **Audio 2** track in the **Timeline** directly under the **B1** clip, being careful to line it up with the start of the **B1** clip.

7 Drag and drop the **cartoon_bonk.wav** clip *a second time* onto the **Audio 2** track directly under the **B2** clip, being careful to line it up with the start of the **B2** clip.

8 Drag and drop the **cartoon_stagger.wav** clip onto the **Audio 2** track directly under the video clip, **C1**, being careful to line it up with the start of the **C1** clip.

> **TIP** *To easily drop the sound effects clips on the right spot, "scrub" first with your **CTI** along the **runners.avi** clip to the point where you want to drop the sound effect. This will give you an easy guide for lining up the sound clip with the video clip.*

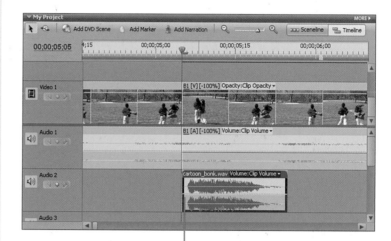

Drag and drop the sound effect file, **cartoon_bonk.wav**, directly under clip **B1** and again under clip **B2**.

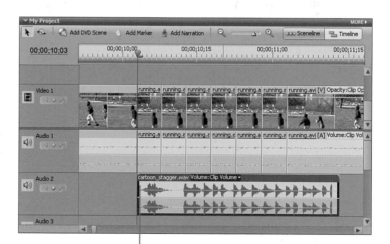

Drag and drop the sound effect file, **cartoon_stagger.wav**, directly under track **C1**, lining up the start of the sound effect clip with the start of the **C1** clip (as shown).

6

Adding a Touch of Silly Music

Finally, a bit of music to finish this project. Remember, these last two steps (funny sound effects and music) apply only if you are constructing a humorous clip. If you are using the **Reverse Action** effect for other purposes—such as creating various cinematic illusions for action, adventure, or sci-fi projects—then leave off the funny sounds and music and replace them with the sounds and music appropriate to your project. On the DVD that accompanied this book, we've provided you with a selection courtesy of the SmartSound folks. It's an edited version of their clip, *Fetch the Bone*, from their *Comedy* CD, available on their website, **www.smartsound.com**.

Add Some Music

1 Click the **Get Media from** button on the **Media** panel to access the **Get Media from** view, if it's not already active.

2 Select **DVD, Digital Camera, Mobile Phone, Hard Drive Camcorder, Card Reader**.

3 When the **Media Downloader** displays, click the **Advanced Dialog** button to switch to Advanced mode.

4 Select the **cartoon_music.wav** clip.

5 Click the **Get Media** button.

6 Select the **cartoon_music.wav** clip on the **Media** panel and drag and drop it onto the **Timeline** in the **Audio 3** track.

> **IMPORTANT** *Be sure that you drag the* **cartoon_music.wav** *clip so that the head (start) of the clip is right up against the very start of the* **Audio 3** *track.*

7 In the **Properties** panel for the **cartoon_music.wav** clip, click the **Fade Out** button for **Clip Volume**.

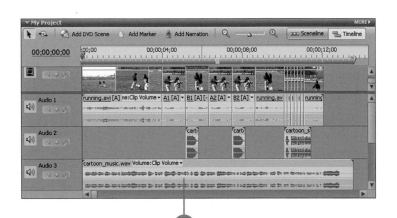

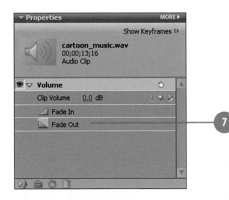

Adding a Still Image at the End of the Movie

Rather than just end the movie suddenly when the action ends, think about ending some of your movies with a "freeze frame." This effect is very easy to achieve. You just take a snapshot using the freeze frame function of Premiere Elements. You can then lengthen or shorten the snapshot as need to change the duration of the clip to have it stay on screen.

Add a Still Frame for Effect

① With the **CTI**, navigate to position **00;00;12;01** on the Timeline.

② In the **Monitor** panel, click the **Freeze Frame** button to save the frame as a still picture.

③ Click **Insert in Movie**.

④ The freeze frame will be inserted in place, on the **Video 1** track on the Timeline. Unfortunately, the music track will be split there, and moved over.

⑤ Adjust the orphaned **cartoon_music.wav** clip by dragging it and returning it to its proper place at the end of the music track, as shown in the illustration.

Did You Know?

You should always deinterlace when exporting. The **Freeze Frame** dialog box has an **Export** button enabling you to export any still you capture in a variety of formats (GIF, BMP, JPEG, and so on). Whenever you export a still image from a video file, it's always a good idea to deinterlace the image—in other words, remove the lines. A video image is made up of alternating scan lines. When you save a snapshot from a video clip, you are basically saving only one half of the information available, or one set of the alternating lines. Select the **Settings** button on the **Export Frame** dialog box before you save your picture. The **Export Frame Settings** dialog box displays. Select the **Keyframe and Rendering** option. You'll find a check box there for **Deinterlace Video Footage**. Click it and then continue saving your snapshot.

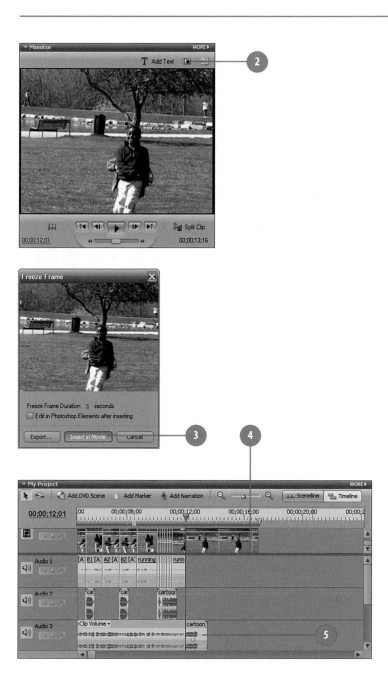

6

Making Adjustments, Rendering, and Exporting

Render your project by pressing **ENTER** to see if everything is working as expected. If not, now's the time to make adjustments and tweaks as needed, such as adding a Fade Out to the freeze frame at the end. Once you're ready, you can export your clip, and subsequently either share it as is, or bring it into a bigger project and keep on working on that project.

Finishing the Project

1 Once you have played back your clip and made the necessary adjustments, press the **ENTER** key on your keyboard to render your project.

2 Press **CTRL-S** to save your project (you can select **File, Save** from the menu).

3 Finally, export your work as an AVI file. To export the clip, select **File, Export, Movie**.

4 You can optionally bring this clip into a larger project, show it on your computer, upload it to an Internet video sharing site, or burn it to a DVD.

The completed movie playing in the
Windows Media Player.

The Pencil Sketch Effect

MEDIA:
pencil_house.avi
drawingpaper.bmp

7

COMPLEXITY:	Simple	Moderate	Complex
SKILL LEVEL:	Novice	Intermediate	Advanced
MATERIALS:	None	Some Props	Greenscreen

Introduction

The Pencil Sketch Effect is an "artistic" effect that, like the Watercolor Effect, can be used for dramatic changes at the end of a movie or scene, or at the beginning of a production. You can also use this effect to create a postcard or greeting card type of effect with your videos.

For example, at the start of a vacation video, you could open with a "pencil sketch" version of the beach house or hotel you stayed at, dissolve to the "true picture" and then cut to the live action of you and your family bursting out of the front door. Or, you can end a clip about your trusty family dog sitting by the fireplace by dissolving into the Pencil Sketch Effect while in full motion, apply a bit of slow motion to the clip, and finally finish in freeze frame. If the clip is *in memoriam* for a pet that has passed on, you could then superimpose the pet's name and birth date and date of death for a tasteful way to close a tribute video.

Premiere Elements does not actually have an effect called "Pencil Sketch" (or anything like it). To create this effect, you'll take advantage of a couple of built-in video effects in Premiere Elements, and tweak them to achieve a close approximation of the look of pencil on paper.

What You'll Do

Add Your Clip to the Timeline

Apply the Sharpen Effect

Apply the Extract Effect

Add a "Paper" Background

Apply the Paper Texture to the "Drawing"

Make Adjustments, Render, and Export

Adding Your Clip to the Timeline

Your first step will be to choose an appropriate clip. While you can apply the **Pencil Sketch** effect to virtually any clip, keep in mind that the effect can carry a positive emotional punch, too, and is best used when you want to create a sentimental mood. If you want to experiment with this effect before trying it with your own clips, we've provided you with a sample clip to use on the DVD that accompanies this book. It's called **pencil_house.avi**.

Add Your Clip to the Timeline

1. Start Premiere Elements and create a new project called **pencilsketch**.

2. Click the **Get Media from** button on the **Media** panel to access the **Get Media from** view, if it's not already active.

3. Select **DVD, Digital Camera, Mobile Phone, Hard Drive Camcorder, Card Reader**.

4. When the **Media Downloader** displays, click the **Advanced Dialog** button to switch to Advanced mode.

5. Select the **pencil_house.avi** clip.

6. Click the **Get Media** button. Premiere Elements copies the **pencil_house.avi** clip from the DVD onto your hard drive and adds it to the Available Media list for this project.

7. From the **Media** panel, select **pencil_house.avi** and drag it to the **Timeline** onto the **Video 1** track so that the head (front) of the clip is at the very beginning of the track.

    TIP *If you are in* **Sceneline** *view, just drop the clip onto the first scene placeholder.*

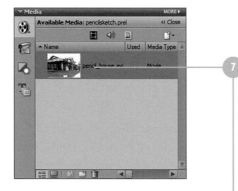

Applying the Sharpen Effect

As the first step in transforming a regular video clip into a "pencil sketch" version, we want to bring out the lines in the video. Then, when we later remove the color from the clip, these lines will stand out much like the marks made when drawing with pencil. Bringing out the lines in the video clip is achieved by applying the **Sharpen** effect, one of Premiere Elements' built-in video effects.

Sharpening the Lines

1. Switch to the **Effects and Transitions** view on the **Media** panel by clicking the **Effects and Transitions** button.

2. Type **sharpen** in the **text box** on the **Effects and Transitions** view.

3. Select the **Sharpen** effect from the **Blur & Sharpen** subfolder of the **Video Effects** folder and drag and drop it onto the **pencil_house.avi** clip on the **Video 1** track on the Timeline.

4. On the **Properties** panel for the **pencil_house.avi** clip, click the **triangle** next to **Sharpen** to reveal the effect's controls.

5. Enter **333** for the **Sharpen Amount** under the **Sharpen** effect .

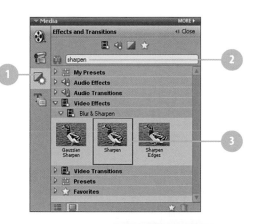

The original clip.

The clip after the Sharpen effect has been applied.

Applying the Extract Effect

The next step in the transformation process for this clip from a normal, everyday video clip to simulated pencil sketch is to eliminate the color properties. This is done by applying the Extract effect, another one of Premiere Elements' built-in effects. By eliminating (extracting) the color from the clip, you are left with only the sharpened outlines of the images in the clip.

Extract the Colors

1. Switch to the **Effects and Transitions** view on the **Media** panel, if it's not already visible, by clicking the **Effects and Transitions** button.

2. Type **extract** in the **text box** on the **Effects and Transitions** view of the **Media** view.

3. Select the **Extract** effect from the **Adjust** subfolder of the **Video Effects** folder and drag and drop it onto the **pencil_house.avi** clip on the **Video 1** track on the Timeline.

4. On the **Properties** panel for the **pencil_house.avi** clip, click the **triangle** next to the **Extract** effect to reveal the effect's controls.

5. Select the **Setup** button for the **Extract** effect.

6. On the **Extract Settings** dialog box, click the **Invert** check box.

7. Click **OK** to apply the change and close the **Extract Settings** dialog box.

Adjust the Extract Effect Settings

1 Back on the **Properties** panel, make the following changes to the **Extract** effect's controls:

- **Black Input Level: 0**

- **White Input Level: 40**

- **Softness: 0**

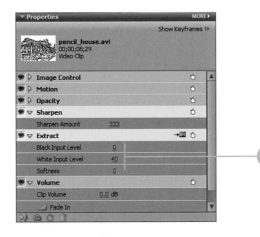

Did You Know?

You can customize your drawings with color.
After you've finished creating your "drawing," and have placed it on paper (which is the final step of this project), you can make the drawing appear to be on any color paper you want. Just apply the **Tint** video effect from the **Effects and Transitions** panel to the **pencil_house.avi** clip, and tint the picture to any color. Lighter colors work best. A tan color will make the drawing look like it was created on an artist's sketch pad.

Before Invert has been applied.

After Invert has been applied.

After the **Extract** effect has been adjusted.

Adding a "Paper" Background

To really "seal the deal" in terms of making the video clip look like it's a pencil sketch, we'll add an effect that gives the illusion of a slight texture of paper to the video clip. To achieve this effect, we'll first bring in a bitmap image of textured paper. Then, in the step that follows, we'll use a built-in Premiere Elements effect to apply that paper texture to our video clip.

Add Paper for the Pen

1 For this project, we need to be in **Timeline** view because we are working with clips on multiple video tracks. If the **My Project** panel is not already in **Timeline** view, click the **Timeline** button (shown below) to switch.

2 Click the **Get Media from** button on the **Media** panel to access the **Get Media from** view, if it's not already active.

3 Select **DVD, Digital Camera, Mobile Phone, Hard Drive Camcorder, Card Reader**.

4 When the **Media Downloader** displays, click the **Advanced Dialog** button to switch to Advanced mode.

5 Select the **drawingpaper.bmp** clip.

6 Click the **Get Media** button. Premiere Elements copies the **drawingpaper.bmp** clip from the DVD onto your hard drive and adds it to the Available Media list for this project.

7 From the **Media** panel, select **drawingpaper.bmp** and drag it to the Timeline onto the **Video 2** track so that the head (front) of the clip is at the very beginning of the track.

8 Grab the tail of the **drawingpaper.bmp** clip and stretch the clip so that it is the same length/duration as the **pencil_house.avi** clip on the **Video 2** track.

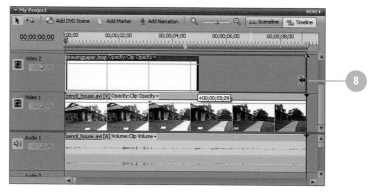

Applying the Paper Texture to the Drawing

Texturizing Puts the Picture on Paper

1 Click the **Effects and Transitions** button to switch to the **Effects and Transitions** view on the **Media** panel, if it's not already visible.

2 Type **texturize** in the **text box** on the **Effects and Transitions** view.

3 Select the **Texturize** effect from the **Stylize** subfolder of the **Video Effects** folder and drag and drop it onto the **pencil_house.avi** clip in the **Video 1** track.

4 On the **Properties** panel, click the **triangle** next to the **Texturize** effect. (Be sure that the **pencil_house.avi** clip is selected.)

5 From the **Texture Layer** drop down, select **Video 2**. Leave all of the other settings as is.

6 Back on the **Timeline**, right-click on the **drawingpaper.bmp** clip in the **Video 2** track and from the contextual menu, uncheck **Enable** to disable the clip.

> **IMPORTANT** *The Texturize effect won't take effect until the clip with the texture has been disabled.*

For this step, we'll use one of the Premiere Elements effects that don't work just on the clip/track that you apply it to, but which also require something—in this case an image—on another track working in tandem in order for the effect to work. We've already added our "paper." By applying the **Texturize** effect and pointing it to the track where the "paper" is, we'll be able to add the illusion that the "pencil sketch" has been "drawn" on paper.

7

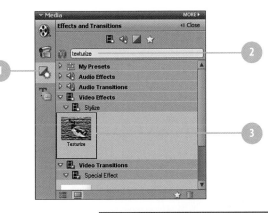

The clip before texturizing. Notice that the white areas appear smooth.

The clip after texturizing. Notice that the white areas, especially in the sky, now have a textured appearance.

The Pencil Sketch Effect **115**

Making Adjustments, Rendering, and Exporting

Finishing the Project

1 After you have played back your clip and made the necessary adjustments, press the **ENTER** key on your keyboard to render your project.

2 Press **CTRL-S** to save your project (or you can select **File, Save** from the menu).

3 Finally, export your work as an AVI file. To export the clip, select **File, Export, Movie**.

TIP *You can optionally bring this clip into a larger project, show it on your computer, upload it to an Internet video sharing site, or burn it to a DVD.*

When you have everything in place, press the **Spacebar** on your keyboard to run through the clip and check that everything looks right. You may notice that things look a bit rough right now. To get a better sense of how the final version will look, press the **ENTER** key to render your project . Keep in mind that the **Pencil Sketch** effect will naturally be a bit "wiggly," even in its finished state, but this adds to the pencil sketch illusion.

The clip, with the **Pencil Sketch** effect applied, playing in the Windows Media Player.

The Watercolor Painting Effect

MEDIA:
space_ship.avi
kickinback.wav

8

COMPLEXITY:	Simple	Moderate	Complex
SKILL LEVEL:	Novice	Intermediate	Advanced
MATERIALS:	None	Some Props	Greenscreen

Introduction

While Premiere Elements doesn't have a true "watercolor" or other painterly effects such as those found in Photoshop Elements, we can, by combining a number of Premiere Elements' built-in effects, create a close and convincing approximation.

To achieve the Watercolor Painting Effect, we'll actually work with two copies of the clip. One will be used to apply a watercolor-like effect. This effect simulates the blurry, watery look of a watercolor painting. However, it doesn't give us the natural pen or pencil sketch marks that typically show through in a watercolor painting. Again unlike Photoshop, Premiere Elements doesn't have a "pen and ink" effect, either. Nonetheless, we can approximate this effect, too, by applying an edge effect to the second clip. By making the top clip somewhat transparent, it will act as an overlay of the pen sketch, simulating how watercolor paints are laid on top of the original drawing.

The Watercolor Painting Effect can be used in wedding, honeymoon, anniversary, and other romance- or nostalgia-themed videos, or anytime you want to achieve a softer feel to a scene. This effect is best used for short sections of a clip. For example, when the bride and groom kiss, you could freeze the moment, dissolve to the watercolor look, and then superimpose their names and the date. In this chapter, we'll be applying the Watercolor Painting Effect to a still from a video clip, but you can apply it to an entire clip, should you want to.

What You'll Do

Load the Video Clip

Select and Create the Still Image

Add the Still Image to the Timeline Twice

Apply a Watercolor Effect to the Upper Snapshot

Adjust the Opacity of the "Faceted" Clip

Apply a Pen and Ink Effect to the Lower Snapshot

Add a Matte Border to the Still Image

Add a Music Track

Fade Out All Clips

Make Adjustments, Render, and Export

Loading the Video Clip

Although you can apply this effect to an entire video clip, this effect works best when it is applied to only a part of a clip, such as a few seconds or even a single frame. The first thing you'll need to do is load the clip into your project from which you want to create a still image. You then apply the effect to that image. By the way, you can "stop the action" multiple times in a clip and apply this effect with great results. For example, if you're editing a wedding video, you could stop and have a "watercolor moment" the first time the bride and groom kiss, the first time they dance, and just as they leave the hall for their honeymoon.

Load your clip to the Timeline

1. Start Premiere Elements and create a new project called **watercolor**.

2. Click the **Get Media from** button on the **Media** panel to access the **Get Media from** view, if it's not already active.

3. Select **DVD, Digital Camera, Mobile Phone, Hard Drive Camcorder, Card Reader**.

4. When the **Media Downloader** displays, click the **Advanced Dialog** button to switch to Advanced mode.

5. Select the **space_ship.avi** clip for this project.

6. Click the **Get Media** button. Premiere Elements copies the **space_ship.avi** clip from the DVD onto your hard drive and adds it to the Available Media list for this project.

7. From the **Media** panel, drag the **space_ship.avi** clip to the **Video 1** track on the Timeline.

   IMPORTANT *Be sure that the head (front end) of the **space_ship.avi** clip is at the front of the **Video 1** track.*

   TIP *If you are in **Sceneline** view, just drop the clip onto the first scene placeholder.*

8. For this project, we'll need to be in **Timeline** view because we are working with multiple clips on multiple video tracks. So, if the **My Project** panel is not already in **Timeline** view, click the **Timeline** button to switch.

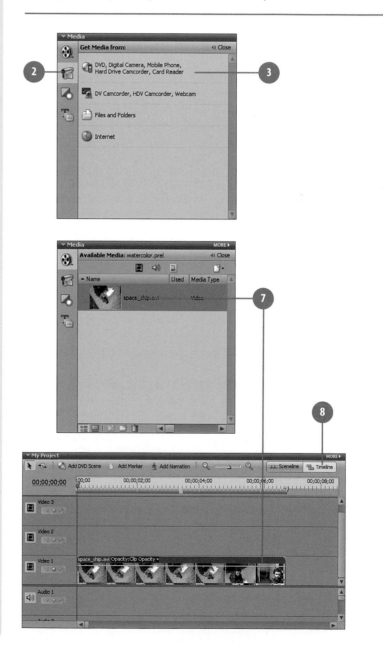

Selecting and Creating the Still Image

Still images work best for this effect. You can pause your clip multiple times, if necessary, and apply this same effect to multiple stills. For this example, we are going to use the very last frame of the sample clip, **spaceship.avi**. To this snapshot, or "freeze frame," we will apply numerous effects to give it a convincing watercolor painting look.

Find the Right Frame or "Still" and Save It as a Snapshot

1 Move the **CTI** to the last visible frame of the spaceship.avi clip on **Video 1**, 00;00;06;24.

> **TIMESAVER** *You can optionally jump right to the end of the clip by pressing the **Page Down (PgDn)** key on your keyboard, and then pressing the **right arrow** key.*

2 Click the **Freeze Frame** button on the **Monitor** panel.

3 From the **Freeze Frame** dialog box, click the **Insert in Movie** button.

> **NOTE** *A new clip, **watercolor_FF.bmp**, should now be in place on the Timeline, directly beside and to the right of the **spaceship.avi** clip on the **Video 1** track.*

Did You Know?

You may have to "clean up" after creating a Freeze Frame. Due to the way Premiere Elements captures the freeze frame image and inserts it into the Timeline, a single frame can end up being orphaned immediately to the right of the clip you took the freeze frame image from. This only occurs when the freeze frame image is from the very last usable frame in a clip. You most likely won't even notice that it's there, but you will probably notice it when you click the **Play** button on the **Monitor** panel to view the project. Therefore, you may want to zoom in (using the **Zoom In** button on the Timeline, or the **plus** "+" key on your keyboard), select this single-frame clip, and delete it.

Adding the Still Image to the Timeline Twice

As explained in the introduction, you need two copies of the clip you want to use (in this case, the snapshot you just took). One to apply the "watercolor" effect to, and one to apply a "pen and ink" effect to. If you were to apply both effects to the same clip, it won't work because the two effects will combine in a muddy way (try it and see). We need to control the opacity of the two effects independently, and having copies of the clip lets us do that. In this case, we actually need three copies. The first is the original freeze frame "snap shot" already on the Timeline that will stop the action, and then appear to slowly transform into a watercolor painting.

Drag the "Snapshot" You Just Took to the Timeline onto Video 1 and Video 2

1 From the **Media** panel, drag the **watercolor_FF.bmp** clip directly next to the tail end of the **watercolor_FF.bmp** already on the **Video 1** track on the Timeline.

2 Drag the tail end of this clip to extend its length to **15** seconds.

> **TIP** *Watch the yellow popup next to the cursor as you stretch the clip and stop when it reads* **00;00;10;00**. *This is because you are adding 10 seconds to the clip's original length of 5 seconds.*

> **TIP** *Alternatively, you can watch the clip's length as it displays on the lower right corner of the* **Monitor** *panel. Stop when it reaches* **00;00;15;00**.

3 Drag the **watercolor_FF.bmp** clip again from the **Media** panel to the Timeline, this time to the **Video 2** track, directly on top of the second copy in the **Video 1** track, which starts at **00;00;11;23**.

4 Drag the tail end of this clip to extend its length to **15** seconds, as well.

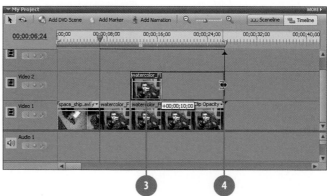

Applying a Watercolor Effect to the Upper Snapshot

In a real watercolor painting, the ink (or sometimes pencil) drawing occurs first, after which the watercolor is applied to the drawing. Sometimes the watercolor is painted first, and then the ink drawing is added on top. In this task, we'll add watercolor "paint" to the upper clip on the **Video 2** track with the **Facet** effect. In an upcoming task, we'll apply a "pen and ink" type of effect to the lower clip on the **Video 1** track.

Apply the Facet Effect to the Clip in Video Track 2

1 Click the **Effects and Transitions** button on the **Media** panel to switch to the **Effects and Transitions** view.

2 On the **Effects and Transitions** view, type **facet** in the text box.

3 Select the **Facet** effect and drag it onto the **watercolor_FF.bmp** clip in the **Video 2** track on the Timeline

> **NOTE** *The **Facet** effect in Premiere Elements has no controls, so there are no adjustments to make in the **Properties** panel. As with some other effects in Premiere Elements, such as the **Black & White** effect, this is simply a "drag, drop, you're done" function.*

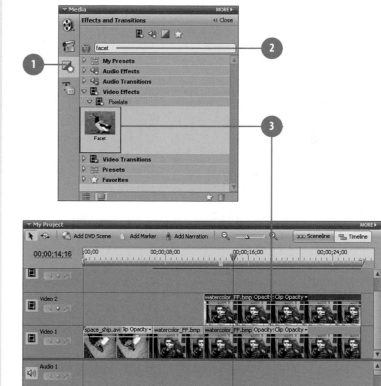

The **watercolor_FF.bmp** clip, before the Facet effect has been applied.

The **watercolor_FF.bmp** clip, after the Facet effect has been applied.

Adjusting the Opacity of the "Faceted" Clip

We'll be adding a "pen and ink" effect to the snapshot copy on **Video 1** next, but for that effect show through, we need to first adjust the opacity (transparency) of the **watercolor_FF.bmp** clip above it. All we need to do is set the opacity for the clip to at or around 70%. That should give us exactly what we need: enough of the watercolors, and just a bit of the pen and ink.

Adjust the Opacity to the Upper Clip

1. Select the **watercolor_FF.bmp** clip in the **Video 2** track on the Timeline.

2. In the **Properties** panel, click on the triangle next to **Opacity** to spin open the controls. Enter **70%** for **Clip Opacity**.

   TIP *If the label for the clip is **Opacity:Clip Opacity**, you can optionally grab the yellow rubberband directly on the clip in the Timeline and drag it down until it reads approximately 70%, and then release it.*

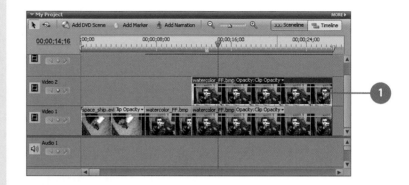

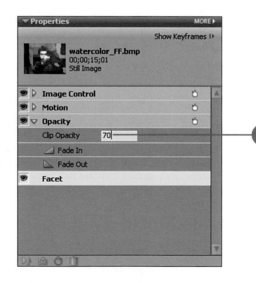

Applying a Pen and Ink Effect to the Lower Snapshot

Apply the Gaussian Sharpen Effect to the Snapshot in Video Track 1

1 Type **gaussian** in the **text box** in the **Effects and Transitions** view of the **Media** panel.

> **IMPORTANT** *Two Gaussian effects will appear: Gaussian Sharpen and Gaussian Blur. We are using the **Gaussian Sharpen** effect for this task.*

2 Drag and drop the **Gaussian Sharpen** effect onto the **watercolor_FF.bmp** clip on the **Video 1** track on the Timeline that is directly below the **watercolor_FF.bmp** clip on the **Video 2** track.

> **TIMESAVER** *The two tracks we're working with both start at **00;00;11;23** and end at **00;00;26;23**.*

> **NOTE** *Like the **Facet** effect, the **Gaussian Sharpen** effect has no controls, so there are no adjustments to make in the **Properties** panel.*

The **Facet** effect creates its "watercolor-ness" by defining geometric shapes, or facets, in the video or still image you apply it to. The effect also blurs the colors a bit, mimicking the effect of watercolor paints on paper. What you lose, however, is any sense of there being a drawing involved with the watercolor. To get that "pen and ink" look beneath the watercolor paints, we are going to add two different effects in a particular order (applied in the opposite order and the effect is considerably different, and harsher). We'll first apply the **Gaussian Sharpen** effect to bring out the edges that the **Facet** effect blurred. This will define the lines and begin to add the "ink." We'll then apply the **Find Edges** effect, which adds a faded, papery look.

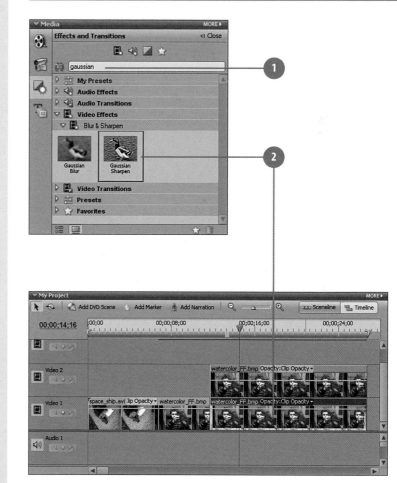

Apply the Find Edges Effect to the Snapshot in Video Track 1

 Type **find** in the **text box** in the **Effects and Transitions** view of the **Media** panel.

 Drag the **Find Edges** effect onto the **watercolor_FF.bmp** clip on the **Video 1** track on the Timeline.

3 On the **Properties** panel for the clip, click the triangle next to **Find Edges** to reveal the effect's controls.

4 Select the **Invert** check box.

5 Adjust the **Blend With Original** setting to **70%**.

NOTE *While 70% is the correct setting for the sample file for this project, you may find that to achieve the right effect with your own clips on future projects, you will need to adjust this somewhere between 50% - 75%.*

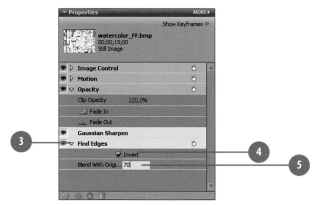

Before the Gaussian Sharpen and Find Edges effects have been applied.

After the Gaussian Sharpen and Find Edges effects have been applied.

Adding a Matte Border to the Still Image

In this stage, we'll use the Premiere Elements Titler to add the kind of border you often see in framed paintings, referred to as a *matte*. This will help increase the illusion that what your audience is looking at is a watercolor painting and no longer a video. To create this matte, we'll use the safe margins already supplied by the Titler as our guides to create even borders on all four sides. We'll also add a slight drop shadow to give the matte border some depth.

Create the Top Border

1 Click the **Add Text** button on the **Monitor** panel.

2 Click the **Selection Tool** (the arrow button).

3 **Right-click** the **Add Text** text box and select **Cut** from the contextual menu.

4 Click the **Rectangle Tool**.

5 To create the top border, draw a box at the top of the screen, so that the screen is covered from left to right, stopping just at the **Safe Title Margin** (the inner-most margin).

> **TIMESAVER** *To turn on margins, if they're off click the **MORE** button at the top right corner of the **Monitor** panel and select **Safe Title Margin** and **Safe Action Margin**.*

6 Click on the **Color Properties** button.

7 Set the following **RGB** values for the matte color on the **Color Properties** dialog box:

- ◆ **R: 249**
- ◆ **G: 255**
- ◆ **B: 207**

8 Click the **Drop Shadow** check box and then set the **Drop Shadow** options as follows:

- ◆ **Angle: 150.0 degrees**
- ◆ **Distance: 10.0**
- ◆ **Softness: 10.0**

9 Click **OK.**

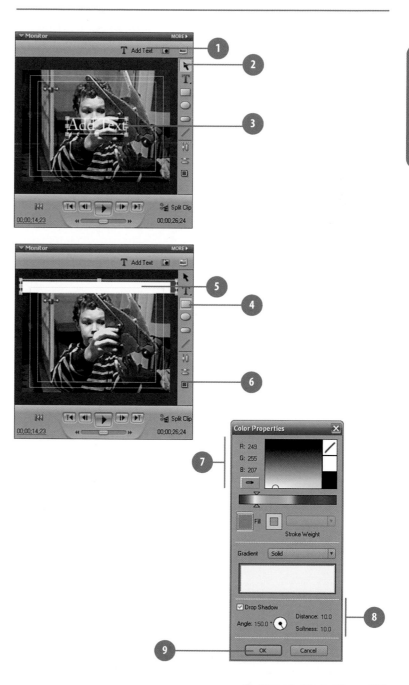

Create the Bottom Border

1. To create the bottom border, select the **Rectangle Tool** again (if necessary).

2. Draw a rectangle at the bottom of the screen so that the screen is covered from left to right. Again, stop just at the **Safe Title Margin**, as shown in the illustration.

3. Click on the **Color Properties** button.

4. Set the following **RGB** values for the matte color on the **Color Properties** dialog box:

   ◆ **R: 249**

   ◆ **G: 255**

   ◆ **B: 207**

5. Click the **Drop Shadow** check box.

6. Set the **Drop Shadow** for the bottom border slightly differently, as follows:

   ◆ Angle: **25.0 degrees**

   ◆ Distance: **10.0**

   ◆ Softness: **10.0**

7. Click **OK.**

Create the Side Borders

1. To create the left side border border, select the **Rectangle Tool** again (if necessary).

2. Draw a rectangle at the left of the screen, again so that the screen is covered from left to right, stopping just at the **Safe Title Margin**.

3. Click on the **Color Properties** button.

4 Set the same **RGB** values for the matte color on the **Color Properties** dialog box as for the top and bottom borders

- ◆ **R: 249**
- ◆ **G: 255**
- ◆ **B: 207**

IMPORTANT *The side borders do not use the* **Drop Shadow** *function.*

5 Click **OK.**

TIP *Make sure that when you create each side border, they overlap both the top and the bottom border*

6 Create the right side border in the same way.

7 To be sure that the two side borders are on top, **right-click** on the left border and the right border one at a time and select **Arrange, Bring to Front** from the contextual menu.

8 Finally, on the Timeline grab the tail end of the **Title 01** clip and stretch it out so that it matches the two snapshots in length.

IMPORTANT *If necessary, adjust this matte border clip so that the head of the clip also lines up with the head of the two* **watercolor_FF.bmp** *clips on the* **Video 1** *and* **Video 2** *tracks.*

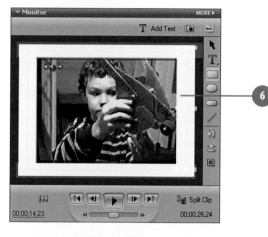

Adding a Music Track

On the DVD that accompanies this book, you'll find a music clip, **kickinback.wav**. This clip was created based on a SmartSound® QuickTracks™ software. SmartSound is a music generator program that will create music that works with your project of just the style and length you need. It comes complete with built-in tracks, and more tracks are available for purchase from the SmartSound Web site. You'll find more information about QuickTracks in *Chapter 4, "The Passing of Time Effect."*

Adding a Music Track to the Project

1 Click the **Get Media from** button on the **Media** panel to access the **Get Media from** view, if it's not already active.

2 Select **DVD, Digital Camera, Mobile Phone, Hard Drive Camcorder, Card Reader**.

3 When the **Media Downloader** displays, click the **Advanced Dialog** button to switch to Advanced mode.

4 Select the **kickinback.wav** clip for this project.

5 Click the **Get Media** button. Premiere Elements copies the **kickinback.wav** clip from the DVD onto your hard drive and adds it to the Available Media list for this project.

6 From the **Media** panel, drag the **kickinback.wav** clip to the **Audio 1** track on the Timeline.

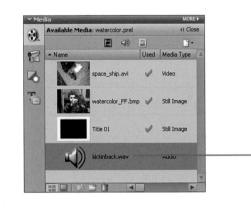

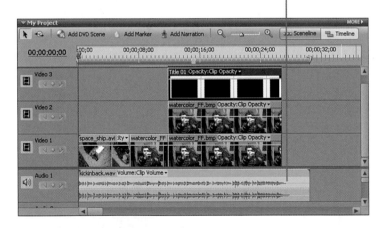

Fading Out All the Clips

To give this effect a nice emotional "punch," a nice fade out works perfectly. We'll use the new **Fade Out** button in Premiere Elements and select it for each of the clips that are still running at the end of this clip: the two "altered" images, the matte border clip, and the music clip.

Add a Fade Out to Each of the Video and Audio Clips

1. Select the **Title 01** clip on the **Video 3** track.

2. From the **Properties** panel, click the triangle next to **Opacity** and click on the **Fade Out** button.

3. Select the **watercolor_FF.bmp** clip on the **Video 2** track.

4. From the **Properties** panel, click the triangle next to **Opacity** and click on the **Fade Out** button.

5. Select the **watercolor_FF.bmp** clip on the **Video 1** track.

6. From the **Properties** panel, click the triangle next to **Opacity** and click on the **Fade Out** button.

7. Select the **kickinback.wav** clip down on the **Audio 1** track.

8. From the **Properties** panel, click the triangle next to **Volume** and click on the **Fade Out** button.

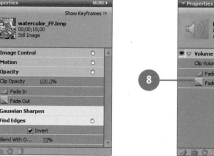

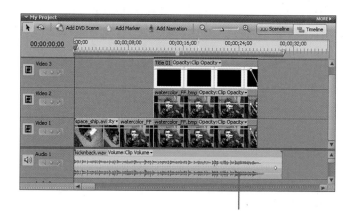

After the fade out has been applied to each of the tracks on the Timeline, each track will graphically show the fade out with white keyframes at the starting and ending points of the fade, and the descending yellow rubberband between them.

Making Adjustments, Rendering, and Exporting

Render your project by pressing **ENTER** to see if everything is working as expected. If not, now's the time to make adjustments and tweaks as needed. For example, you may want to add a **Cross Dissolve** between the original still image and the "painted" one so that the addition of the matte and the change to a watercolor painting happens gradually instead of all at once. Or, you may want to shorten the duration of the **watercolor_FF.bmp** clips to 10 seconds or even down to the original 5 seconds. (If you did so, you'd have to trim the **kickinback.wav** music clip to match.) Once you're ready, save, render, and share your movie.

Finishing the Project

1. After you have played back your movie and made the necessary adjustments, press the **ENTER** key on your keyboard to render your project.

2. Press **CTRL-S** to save your project (or you can select **File, Save** from the menu).

3. Finally, export your work as an AVI file. To export the clip, select **File, Export, Movie**.

   TIP *You can optionally bring this clip into a larger project, show it on your computer, upload it to an Internet video sharing site, or burn it to a DVD, and so on.*

The clip, with the **Watercolor Painting** Effect applied, playing in Windows Media Player.

The Faded Film Effect

Introduction

While Premiere Elements doesn't supply you with a push-button "old film" effect, it does give you almost limitless control over your clips to change brightness, contrast, and other properties over time. What it doesn't have is a "dust and scratches" filter. So as part of this project, we'll go and borrow those effects from Windows® Movie Maker, an entry-level video editing package included with Windows XP.

We will be applying a Movie Maker effect called, "Film Age, Old" to our clip. We will then save the clip and bring it into Premiere Elements 3 to complete the project. This lets us borrow the scratches, dust, and specks from Movie Maker. Then, by bringing the clip into Premiere Elements, we'll add bright spots over time to increase the illusion of faded film. By the way, if you prefer the more extreme fading, dust, and damage, there are two other Film Age effects in Movie Maker. By all means use them in your own projects.

What You'll Do

Start Movie Maker and Import the Clip

Apply the Old Film Effect to the Clip

Take a Look at Microsoft Movie Maker

Save the Clip as an AVI File

Bring the Clip into Premiere Elements and Colorize It

Add Some "Flash" to the Clip

Add Some Period Music to the Soundtrack

Make Adjustments, Render, and Export

Starting Movie Maker and Importing the Clip

You can use any video clip at all and transform it into an "aged film clip." However, what works especially well is footage taken at a country fair, an historical reenactment, or places such as Williamsburg, Plymouth Plantation, Monticello, or other historical settings—even at an antique car show. For this project, we've supplied you with a short clip from a reenactment of life in the mid-1800s, called **1850.avi**. In this task, we'll "creatively borrow" one of Movie Maker's video effects to add scratches and dust to our clip.

Start Movie Maker and Bring in the Video Clip

1 To start Movie Maker, click the Windows **Start** button and then click **All Programs.**

2 Choose **Accessories, Windows Movie Maker** (in come cases, Movie Maker may be found at **Accessories, Entertainment, Windows Movie Maker**).

> **IMPORTANT** *It's possible that your copy of Movie Maker may be located elsewhere on your All Programs list.*

3 From Movie Maker's **Capture Video** task list, select the **Import video** task.

> **TIMESAVER** *If the Movie Tasks menu isn't currently displayed, click the Tasks button on the toolbar to display it.*

4 Use the **Import File** dialog box and navigate to the DVD supplied with this book.

5 Navigate to the **Extras** folder, then to the **Media** folder, and finally to the **Video** folder.

6 Select the **1850.avi** clip and click **Import**.

7 Drag and drop the clip onto the storyboard.

> **TIP** *If the Storyboard view isn't displayed, click the Show Storyboard button.*

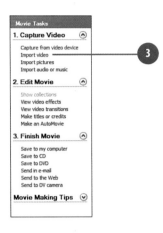

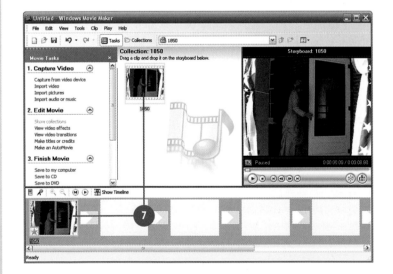

Applying the Old Film Effect to the Clip

There are three old film effects available with Movie Maker. They include "Film Age, Old," which applies some graininess, scratches, and dust. This is the one we'll be using. "Film Age, Older" fades the clip and removes frames to add jumpiness to the clip. It also increases the scratches and dust. "Film Age, Oldest," is the most extreme, and causes the clip to look as if it were from the Wild West, being viewed in a Nickelodeon device. It causes extreme "damage" to the clip, and the clip is very faded with many frames removed.

Apply the "Film Age, Old," Video Effect Filter to the Clip

1 Click **View video effects** in the **Edit Movie** task list in Movie Maker.

2 Scroll in the **Content** pane until you find the **Film Age, Old** effect.

3 Drag and drop the **Film Age, Old** effect onto the clip on the storyboard. The effect applies immediately.

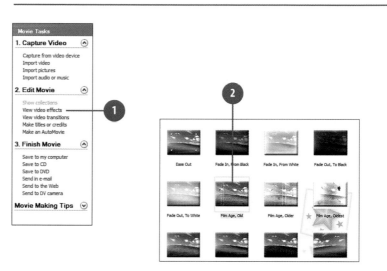

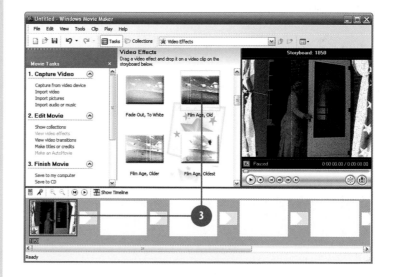

Did You Know?

You can read the stars to learn about effects. The "effects" star in the lower left corner of each clip is gray when no effects have been applied. Once you apply an effect, the star turns bright blue, as shown in the picture below. Multiple effects are indicated by two stars.

Did You Know?

Working among software packages is an accepted workflow in video editing. Moving a clip from program to program is a good skill to develop with video editing, and it is incorporated into many of the more advanced video editing workflows. For example, you might create a title in Adobe® Photoshop®, edit your video in Adobe® Premiere Pro®, add special effects in Adobe® After Effects®, and finally create a DVD menu using Adobe® Encore DVD®. Similar workflows can be followed with software suites from Apple®, Sony®, and Avid®.

Take a Look at Microsoft Windows Movie Maker

Windows Movie Maker, a great video editing program for beginners, has a surprisingly sophisticated set of video transitions and special effects. The software is setup so that you can follow a workflow of capturing or importing your clips; applying transitions and effects; adding titles, music, and narration; and "finishing" your movie by saving it to a number of different formats. While Movie Maker can't burn a DVD, it can save to a DVD-ready format.

You follow the workflow in Movie Maker along this left pane. Just click on the activity you want to complete, such as "Make titles or credits," and the screen changes to guide you through the process.

Video clips—stored as "collections"—appear here in this center pane, ready for you to select or to drag and drop onto the storyboard/timeline at the bottom of the Movie Maker screen. You can change the view from thumbnails to details, much like you can in the Media panel of Premiere Elements. Here you will also find Transitions (as shown) and effects.

You assemble clips in Movie Maker along the bottom of the screen, just as you do in Premiere Elements. Movie Maker has a single track for video, as well as a title overlay track and an audio track. You change the view back and forth from storyboard to timeline view, just as you can in Premiere Elements. The **Storyboard** view offers a convenient way to rearrange your clips by dragging and dropping them onto the squares of the storyboard. Switching back to the **Timeline** view lets you trim clips and view the timecode.

Movie Maker's monitor lets you preview your project and operates in a similar manner to the Monitor panel in Premiere Elements. There are the usual buttons for playing, stopping, and rewinding a video clip. The monitor also holds two additional buttons: one for splitting clips on the timeline and one for creating stills from a video clip, just like the **Monitor** panel in Premiere Elements. And just like Premiere Elements, Movie Maker's monitor lets you view your movie full screen.

Saving the Clip as an AVI File

Now that we have some quality "old film" scratches and dust applied to the video clip, we need to export it from Movie Maker so that we can bring it into Premiere Elements. The best format for saving the clip for our purposes is something Movie Maker calls "DV-AVI." Basically, this is a universal, high-quality AVI format. Because video formats are standard, the clip you export from Movie Maker can be opened in Premiere Elements.

Save the Clip from Movie Maker

1 Click **Save to my computer** in the **Finish Movie** task menu of Movie Maker.

2 The **Save Movie Wizard** starts. The first screen is the **Saved Movie File** screen. On this screen, change the name of the video file from the default name to **1850-old.avi**. Click **Next**.

> **NOTE** *You can optionally change the folder the clip is being saved to.*

3 The next screen in Save Movie Wizard is the **Movie Settings** screen. Select **Show more choices**. This will present three options, one of which is **Other settings**.

4 Click the **Other settings** radio button. From the **Other settings** drop down menu, select **DV-AVI**. Click **Next**.

> **NOTE** *Movie Maker shows you the progress it's making creating the movie file on the* **Saving Movie** *screen.*

5 When Movie Maker has finished, uncheck the **Play movie when I click Finish** check box.

6 Click **Finish** to close the Save Movie Wizard.

7 Close Movie Maker by selecting **File, Exit**.

8 You'll be prompted to save your changes. Click **No**.

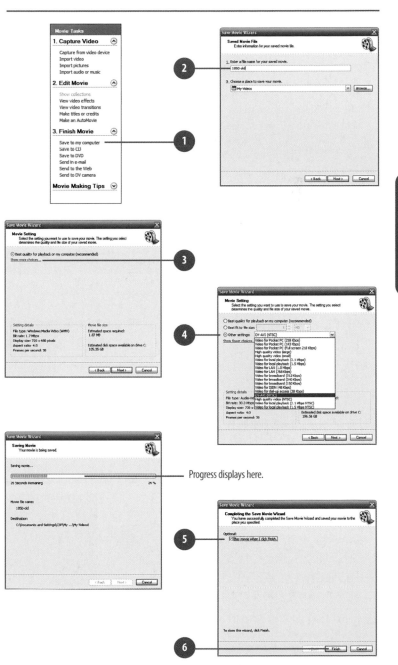

Progress displays here.

Bringing the Clip into Premiere Elements and Colorizing It

In Premiere Elements, we will import the "newly old" clip and add it to the Timeline. Once it's there, we'll need to add two simple color-related effects to the clip—the **Black and White** effect and the **Tint** effect—which will give it that "sepia tone" look of old film and photographs. This will add to the overall aged effect we're going for.

Add the "Old" AVI Clip to Your Project

1. Start Premiere Elements and create a new project called **fadedfilm**.

2. Click the **Get Media from** button on the **Media** panel.

3. Select **Files or Folders**.

4. Using the **Add Media** dialog box, find the **1850-old.avi** file you exported from Movie Maker and click **Open**.

    NOTE *By default, Movie Maker exports to your **My Video** folder, which is located under your **My Documents** folder.*

5. Drag and drop the **1850-old.avi** from the **Media** panel onto the **Video 1** track on the Timeline so that the head (front) of the clip is at the beginning of the track.

    TIP *If you are in **Sceneline** view, just drop the clip onto the first scene placeholder (as shown in the illustration).*

6. In the **Properties** panel for the clip, click the **Fade Out** button under **Opacity**.

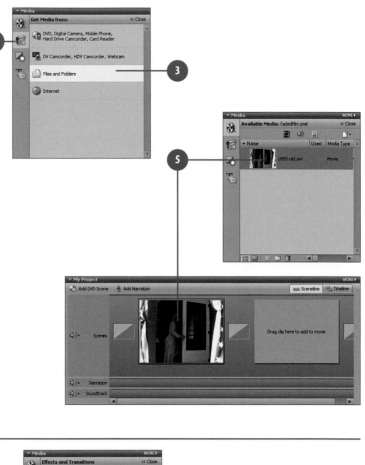

Change the Clip to Black & White

1. In the **Media** panel, click the **Effects and Transitions** button to switch to the **Effects and Transitions** view.

2. In the **Effects and Transitions** view of the Media, type **black** in the text box.

3. Drag and drop the **Black & White** effect on the **1850-old.avi** clip on the **Video 1** track on the Timeline.

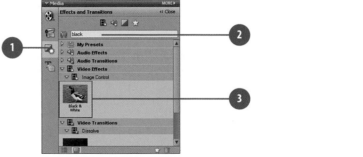

Tint the Clip

1. Return to the **Effects and Transitions** view of the **Media** panel and now type **tint** in the text box.

2. Drag and drop the **Tint** effect from **Effects and Transitions** view onto the **1850-old.avi** clip on the **Video 1** track on the **Timeline**.

3. In the **Properties** panel for the **1850-old.avi** clip, click the triangle next to **Tint** to open the effect's controls.

4. Click on the color picker for **Map Black To** and on the **Color Picker** dialog box set the following:

   ◆ H: **40%**

   ◆ S: **100%**

   ◆ B: **35%**

5. Click **OK** to close the **Color Picker** dialog box.

6. Click on the color picker for **Map White To** and on the **Color Picker** dialog box set the following:

   ◆ H: **45%**

   ◆ S: **70%**

   ◆ B: **100%**

7. Click **OK** to close the **Color Picker** dialog box.

8. Back on the **Properties** panel for the **1850-old.avi** clip, set the **Amount to Tint** to **50%**.

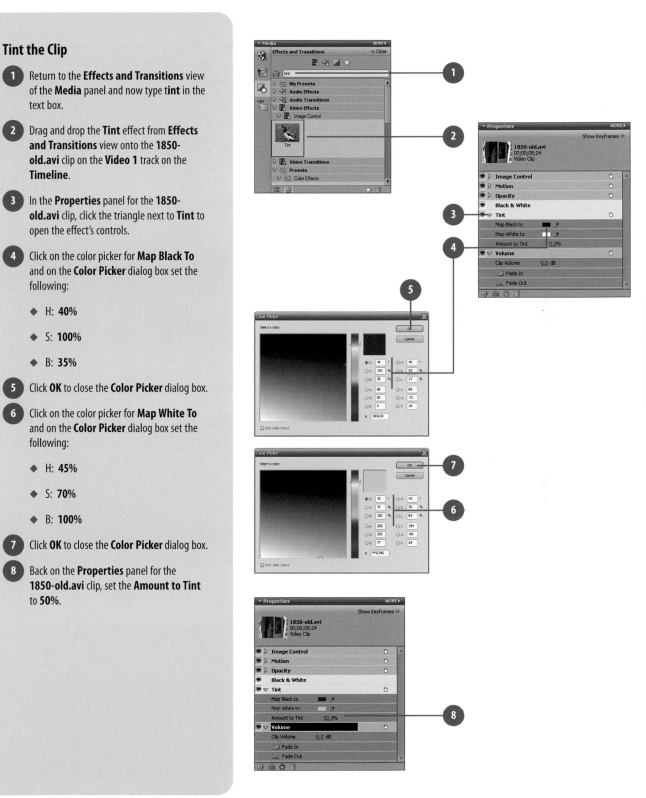

9

Adding Some "Flash" to the Clip

For the final effects task that we are applying to the video clip, we're going to add some real flash to our clip. Specifically, we are going to add that "flash" of light that you often see in old movies. As movies age, the celluloid wears and weathers differently, allowing for bright spots as the projector bulb shines through with varying intensity at different points in the film. We can simulate this by animating the Brightness control so that it changes dramatically and suddenly at different points over time. To do this, we'll use the keyframes in the **Properties** panel for the clip to set two bright flashes, one at three seconds, and one at five seconds.

Adjust the Brightness Over Time

1 Select the **1850-old.avi** clip on the **Video 1** track on the **Timeline**.

2 In the **Properties** panel, click the **Show Keyframes** button and expand the panel as needed to get a good view of the keyframes work area, as shown in the illustration.

*TIMESAVER We'll be starting at the beginning of the clip, so press the **Page Up** or the **Home** key on your keyboard to return the CTI to the start position of the track (the head of the clip), if it's not already there.*

3 With the **CTI** at the head of the clip, click the **Toggle animation** button.

4 Move the **CTI** three seconds into the clip (**00;00;03;00**).

5 In the **Properties** panel, under Image Control, set the **Brightness** level to **60.0**.

NOTE Premiere Elements automatically places a keyframe at this spot.

6 Move the **CTI** back 10 frames to **00;00;02;20** and reset the **Brightness** to **0.0**.

7 Move the **CTI** ahead to **00;00;03;10** and reset the **Brightness** here as well to **0.0**.

8 Repeat the process above and change the **Brightness** at these locations as follows:

◆ **00;00;05;00   60.0**

◆ **00;00;04;20   0.0**

◆ **00;00;05;10   0.0**

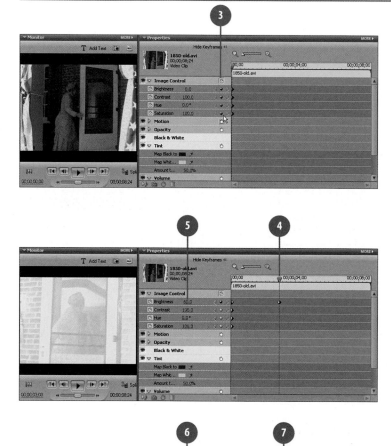

Adding Some Period Music to the Soundtrack

The final touch for this project is to add some period music to the soundtrack. On the DVD that accompanies this book is a song that has a "long ago" feel, **vintagesong.wav**. This is a song that is part of the SmartSound® Quicktracks™ software. We've renamed it for ease of use (its name as it appears in Quicktracks is *SmartSound - Piano Sonata - Gather [00;31;26].wav*). Add it to the soundtrack of your project, adjust the volume so that it sounds right, set it so that it fades out at the end, and we are done.

Add Some Vintage Music to the Project

1 Click the **Get Media from** button on the **Media** panel to access the **Get Media from** view, if it's not already active.

2 Select **DVD, Digital Camera, Mobile Phone, Hard Drive Camcorder, Card Reader**.

3 When the **Media Downloader** displays, click the **Advanced Dialog** button to switch to Advanced mode.

4 Select the **vintagesong.wav** clip.

5 Click the **Get Media** button. Premiere Elements copies the **vintagesong.wav** clip from the DVD onto your hard drive and adds it to the Available Media list for this project.

6 From the **Media** panel, select **vintagesong.wav** and drag it to the **Timeline** onto the **Audio 2** track so that the head (front) of the clip is at the very beginning of the track.

7 Drag the tail end of the clip and trim it back so that it extends about a few frames beyond the end of the **1850-old.avi** video clip. (You want it to end about **00;00;09;10** or so. It doesn't have to be exact.)

8 On the **Properties** pane, adjust the **Volume** of the clip so that it fades out at the end by clicking the **Fade Out** button.

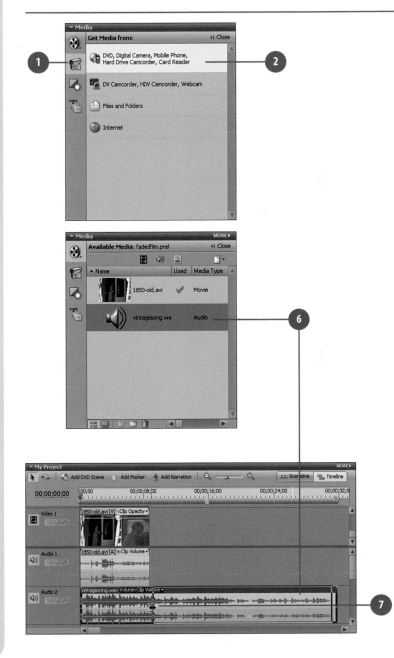

9

Making Adjustments, Rendering, and Exporting

Finishing the Project

1 After you have played back your clip and made any necessary adjustments, press the **ENTER** key on your keyboard to render your project.

2 Press **CTRL-S** to save your project (or you can select **File, Save** from the menu).

3 Finally, export your work as an AVI file. To export the clip, select **File, Export, Movie**.

> **TIP** *You can optionally bring this clip into a larger project, show it on your computer, upload it to an Internet video sharing site, or burn it to a DVD.*

When you have everything in place, press the **Spacebar** on your keyboard to run through the clip and check that everything looks right. You may notice that things look a bit rough right now. To get a better sense of how the final version will look, press the **ENTER** key to render your project.

Watch and enjoy your "old movie show."

Make Your Old Films Jump

Simulate the Jumpiness of Old Films by Splitting Clips

The reason people seem to jump about in old films—where a person could be standing in the middle of the room one second, and then suddenly a second later he or she is standing by the door—is because of the deterioration over time to which celluloid is prone. When film deteriorates, it eventually falls apart, and sections of it can no longer be run through the projector. When that happens, a film editor slices the film before and after the bad spot, and then tapes it back together in a process called "splicing." You can simulate this effect using the **Split Clip** button. Just move the **CTI** to any point in the clip and click the **Split Clip** button. Move the **CTI** again a few frames or even a few seconds into the future and click **Split Clip** again. Depending on the length of the clip you are "deteriorating," you can create one or many such "jump spots" to convincingly, and quickly, age any clip.

The Nightly News Effect

MEDIA:
144_Background1.mov
144_Lowerthird2.mov
anchor.avi
newstheme.wav
reporter.avi

10

COMPLEXITY:	Simple	Moderate	Complex
SKILL LEVEL:	Novice	Intermediate	Advanced
MATERIALS:	None	Some Props	Greenscreen

What You'll Do

Add Video and Graphics Clips to the Project

Create the TV News Background

Add the Anchorman

Remove the Green Background from Behind the Anchorman

Resize and Move the Anchorman

Understand Overlays, Backgrounds, and Lower Thirds

Add the Lower Third Graphic

Add Lower Third Text for the Anchorman

Add the "On Site" Reporter Clip to the Project

Add Lower Third Graphic and Text for the Reporter

Add "TV News" Theme Music

Save, Render, and Export the Movie

Introduction

For many of us, especially as kids, there is something inherently fun and interesting about being part of a news broadcast. Being the man or woman on the street is fun, too. But nothing beats being the "star," the anchorman or anchorwoman, as perfectly captured by Will Ferrell's documentary film, Anchorman.

The Nightly News Effect takes advantage of the incredible resources that are available today to give anyone's "basement tapes" the look and feel of a professional studio production. With the entire world, it seems, uploading their videos to One True Media, Mydeo, YouTube and even the Current cable network, we are all evolving into better videographers and video editors simply by exposure to others' videos. We are getting better, too, because we are all, to some degree, creating more small video clips than ever before. And why not? The world is watching! Now back to our main story…

Available from a variety of sources across the web are overlays, lower thirds, and what are variously referred to as "back drops," "motion loops," or "motion backgrounds." Not only do these look professional, they are professional. The exact same broadcast-quality backgrounds, overlays, and lower thirds that you can use in your productions are being used by Entertainment Tonight- and ESPN-type shows nationwide.

The Nightly News Effect is a great effect for having fun with kids who want to create a news broadcast—from developing the "stories," to creating a basic set (chair, table, paper and pen), to the "broadcasting" of the finished news program on your television. The techniques learned here can also be used by students for school television broadcasts or for incorporating into school projects.

Adding Video and Graphics Clips to the Project

In this step, we'll add the video clips for the project, **anchor.avi** and **reporter.avi**, as well as the background and foreground graphics clips, **144_Background1.mov** and **144_Lowerthird2.mov**. The **anchor.avi** clip is the anchorman for the project and the **reporter.avi** clip is the "girl on the street" reporting "live" from Hawaii.

Add the Video Clips to the Project

1 Start Premiere Elements and create a new project called **nightlynews**.

2 Click the **Get Media from** button on the **Media** panel to access the **Get Media from** view, if it's not already active.

3 Select **DVD, Digital Camera, Mobile Phone, Hard Drive Camcorder, Card Reader**.

4 When the **Media Downloader** displays, click the **Advanced Dialog** button to switch to Advanced mode.

5 Select the following clips for this project:

◆ **144_Background1.mov**

◆ **144_Lowerthird2.mov**

◆ **anchor.avi**

◆ **reporter.avi**

6 Click the **Get Media** button. Premiere Elements copies the clips from the DVD onto your hard drive and adds them to the Available Media list for this project.

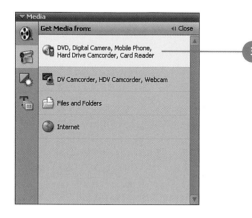

The video and graphics files loaded into the **Media** panel in Premiere Elements.

Creating the TV News Background

Add the Background Graphic

1 For this project, we'll need to be in the **Timeline** view because we are working with multiple clips on multiple video tracks. Therefore, if the **My Project** panel is not already in **Timeline** view, click the **Timeline** button to switch.

2 Select the back drop clip on the **Media** panel, **144_Background1.mov**, and drag it to **Video 1** track on the **My Project** panel. Be sure to line up the front of this clip with the start of the **Video 1** track.

3 Select the **144_Background1.mov** on the **Media** panel again, and drag it a *second* time to the **My Project** panel directly behind the first copy of the **144_Background1.mov** clip on the **Video 1** track.

> **IMPORTANT** *Why are we dragging the clip twice to the Timeline? This is because the duration of the clip is not sufficient to last as long as we need it to. Two copies of the clip are exactly right for this project. Had we needed the back drop to be longer, we would have added the clip again to the Timeline, as many times as we needed.*

We'll be using one of the "graphic loop" clips from Digital Juice, **144_Background1.mov**, along with text that we'll create in Premiere Elements later, to build a convincing background for our newscaster project. Once our background is in place, we'll move on to add our anchorman to the scene in the next task.

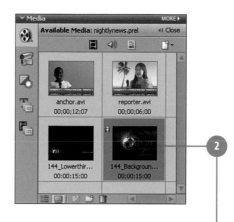

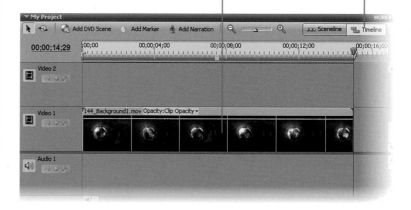

Create the Text

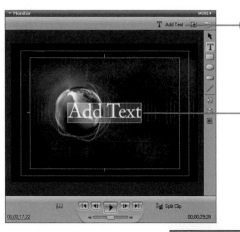

The default "Add Text" text box appears in a box centered on the **Monitor** panel as the Titler workspace loads.

1 Click the **Add Text** button at the top of the **Monitor** panel to begin to add a title for the news background.

> **TIP** *Safe margins should automatically appear. If they don't, you can turn them on yourself by clicking on the MORE button in the upper right corner of the **Monitor** panel. Then, click **Safe Title Margin**.*

2 Type **The Nightly News with Joe** in the text box. Press the **ENTER** key on your keyboard after the words **Nightly** and **News**. (Your text box should look like the one in the illustration.)

> **TIP** *Should the **Add Text** text box become unhighlighted before you start typing, click inside it and drag across the default text with your mouse to highlight it.*

3 Select **Times New Roman** from the fonts menu on the **Properties** panel.

4 Click the **Right Align Text** button to set the text to be right-justified

5 Click the **Selection Tool** (the "arrow" button) on the **Monitor** panel.

6 Click the text box and move it to the upper right corner of the panel, as shown in the illustration. Be sure to stay within the "safe text zone," which is represented by the inside white box.

7 Highlight **Nightly News** and change the size to **115**.

8 Highlight **The** and change the size to **55**.

9 Highlight **with Joe** and change the size to **55**, as well.

10 Grab the tail end of the **Title 01** clip on the **Video 2** track and drag it to the right until it is the same length as the background clips.

> **IMPORTANT** *If, for some reason, your Title 01 clip is not located on the Video 2 track and at the start location for the track (00;00;00;00), move it there now.*

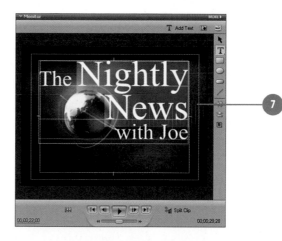

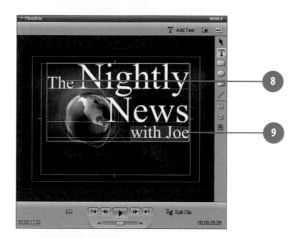

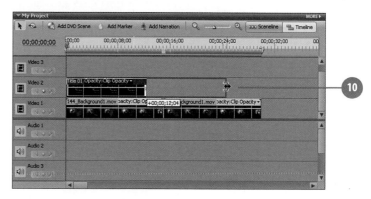

Adding the Anchorman

Now that we have our background in place—complete with spinning globe and other back drop elements in motion, as well as our title text—it's time to bring in the star of our show, Joe the Anchorman. Joe was filmed against a greenscreen, so when we first add him to the Timeline, we won't see the backdrop behind him. In order to see the backdrop, we'll have to first strip away the green background using the **Green Screen Key**, which we'll do in a later task.

Add the Anchor Clip to the Timeline

1 With your mouse, select the clip, **anchor.avi** on the **Media** panel from the **Available Media** view.

2 Drag and drop it onto the Timeline of the **My Project** panel onto the **Video 3** track. You want to position the clip precisely so that the head (start) of the clip is at the **8 second** mark (00;00;08;00).

> **TIP** *To make it easy to place the clip at the 8 second mark, first move the **Current Time Indicator** (**CTI**) to 00;00;08;00. Then, as you drag the clip from the **Media** panel, all you have to do is align it to the **CTI**.*

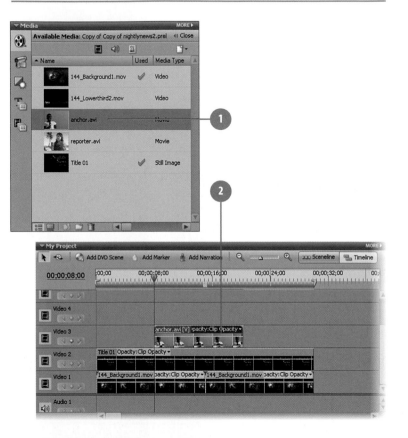

Did You Know?

Snap to it.
By using the Snap feature of Premiere Elements, it's even easier to get clips to align to the **CTI** and to align to other clips on the Timeline. To turn on the Snap feature, use the **MORE** button on the **My Project** panel and select **Snap**. If you don't see the **MORE** button, go to the Premiere Elements menus at the top of the screen and select **Windows**, **Show Docking Headers**.

If you look at the anchorman in the **Media** panel, you'll see that behind him is nothing but a vast stretch of green, which is the greenscreen material. We'll need to remove the green before the background we created can be seen.

Removing the Green Background from Behind the Anchorman

While Joe looks good in green, we still want to remove it so that we can reveal the back drop we created earlier. By presenting the anchorman in front of our professional backdrop, we can add a real newsroom look to our clip. In order to rid ourselves of the green, we'll need to apply the **Green Screen Key**. As you'll learn, the **Green Screen Key** gets out most, but not all, of the green. To get rid of the persistent green glow, we'll also apply our good friend, the **Non Red Key**, which you may have already become familiar with from other projects in this book.

Apply the Green Screen Key

1. On the **Media** panel, click the **Effects and Transitions** button to switch to the **Effects and Transitions** view.

2. Type **green** in the text box to bring up the **Green Screen Key**.

3. Select the **Green Screen Key** from the Keying category of **Video** Effects and drag and drop it onto the **anchor.avi** clip on the **Video 3** track.

4. In the **Properties** panel for the **anchor.avi** clip, click the **triangle** next to the **Green Screen Key** to twirl it down and reveal the effect's controls.

5. Set the following for the **Green Screen Key**:

   ◆ With your mouse, scrub across the **Threshold** setting to change it to **35%**.

   ◆ Scrub the **Cutoff** setting to **35%**.

   TIP *You can optionally click in the **Threshold** and **Cutoff** fields and type **35** directly.*

   ◆ Set the **Smoothing** level to **High**.

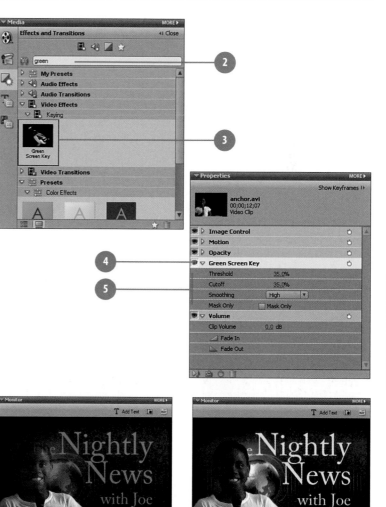

Did You Know?

You can view a white silhouette.
If you want to see how well a **Green Screen Key** is keying out the green, select the **Mask Only** check box. When you do, the **Monitor** panel will change to show a white cookie cutter shape of the actor. If the settings are correct, you should see no artifacts (holes) within the white silhouette. If you do, tweak the **Threshold** and **Cutoff** settings until all you see is a pure white silhouette.

Here, the **Green Screen Key** has been applied with default values. Notice the hazy way the foreground and background look merged.

Here, the **Threshold** and **Cutoff** settings have been tweaked. Notice how the anchorman stands out sharply from the bright background.

10

Apply the Non Red Key

1 Type **red** in the text box to bring up the **Non Red Key**.

   NOTE *If the **Media** panel is not displaying the **Effects and Transitions** view, click the **Effects and Transitions** button to switch to it.*

2 Select the **Non Red Key** from the Keying category of **Video** effects and drag and drop it onto the **anchor.avi** clip on the **Video 3** track.

3 In the **Properties** panel for the **anchor.avi** clip, click the **triangle** next to the **Non Red Key** to twirl it down and reveal the effect's controls.

4 Make the following changes for the settings for the **Non Red Key**:

   ◆ With your mouse, scrub across the **Threshold** setting to change it to **35%**.

   ◆ Scrub the **Cutoff** setting to **35%**.

   TIP *You can optionally click in the **Threshold** and **Cutoff** fields and type **35** directly.*

   ◆ Set the **Smoothing** level to **High**.

5 Click the **Defringing** drop-down menu and select **Green**.

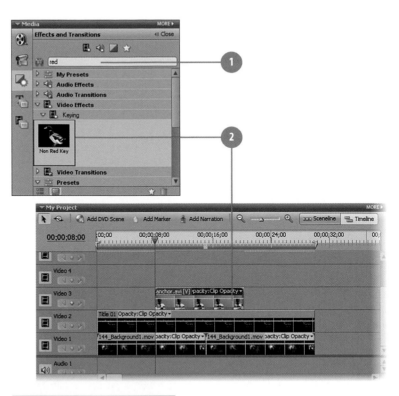

Did You Know?

You can Defringe green or blue.
Sometimes, as a result of lighting or other factors, you may end up with more of a bluish tinge to a clip (and, of course, if you are using a bluescreen instead of a greenscreen that's always the case). Whenever that happens, choose **Blue** from the Defringing menu.

The clip with only the **Green Screen Key** applied. Notice the green "fringe" and tone on the anchorman, and the desk.

The clip with the **Non Red Key** applied and adjusted. The green tinge is gone, and the overall color looks richer and more natural.

Adjust the Brightness

1 With the **anchor.avi** clip still selected, twirl down the triangle next to **Image Control** in the **Properties** panel for the **anchor.avi** clip to twirl it down and reveal the effect's controls.

TIP *The effect controls for **Image Control** may already be showing, in which case this step can be skipped.*

2 Make the following changes for the **Image Control** settings:

◆ **Brightness: 5.0**

◆ **Contrast: 105.0**

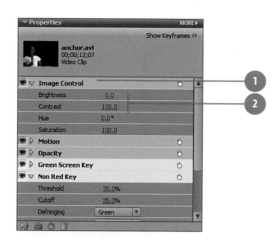

Did You Know?

There can be too much of a good thing.
As you work with the Image Control effect controls, including Brightness, Contrast, Hue, and Saturation, use a light touch. Where the keying effects allow you to make big adjustments up or down to get the effect you want (removing the green, for example), controls such as Brightness can have an immediate positive or negative effect on a clip with an adjustment of just one or two steps up or down. Be especially careful adjusting the Hue or Saturation settings on any clip that has had a keying effect applied, such as the **Green Screen Effect**. Again, even a minor adjustment here can alter the green that the **Green Screen Effect** was keying on.

The anchorman clip with the default **Brightness** and **Contrast** settings .

The anchorman clip with the **Brightness** and **Contrast** settings adjusted slightly to bring out the details in Joe's face a little better .

10

Resizing and Moving the Anchorman

Our anchorman is not quite in the right place, so we will adjust both his location and his size. We're adjusting his size so that we can see a bit more of the background. On news shows, the upper right corner of the screen is where graphics are displayed representing the next story, such as the graphic of clouds and sun to indicate that the weather report is up next.

Move and Shrink the Anchorman

1 If the **anchor.avi** clip is no longer the selected clip, reselect it now.

2 We need the safe margins on, so if they are not already displayed, click **MORE** on the Monitor panel and select **Safe Margins** to display them.

3 In the **Properties** panel for the **anchor.avi** clip, twirl down the triangle next to **Motion** to twirl it down and reveal the effect's controls.

4 Make the following changes for the **Motion** settings:

◆ **Position: 315.0   200.0**

◆ **Scale: 80.0**

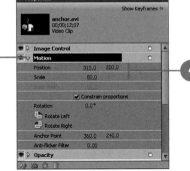

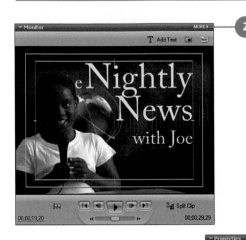

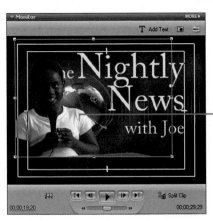

The **anchor.avi** clip, now resized and moved to its new location.

Did You Know?

You can make your initial adjustments right in the Monitor panel. After you click on the **Motion** effect in the **Properties** panel for the **anchor.avi** clip, a white box appears around the clip in the **Monitor** panel. You can optionally drag a corner of the box to resize the clip, and then click in the center of the box to move the clip to its new position. Use the **Position** and **Scale** controls to fine-tune those settings after you've made your manual adjustments on the **Monitor** panel.

Understanding Overlays, Backgrounds, and Lower Thirds

Animation Clips

What are animation clips, in terms of broadcast-ready clips used in video productions? These are simply pre-created, computer art variously referred to as overlays or back drops or motion backgrounds—Digital Juice calls them "jump backs"—which are used to enhance a production and give an ordinary-looking clip some "pizazz" or "punch."

Now that we are all in the business of producing small, fun, and informative clips, it doesn't hurt to add an overlay or lower third when needed to give our productions a little "somethin' somethin'" and add a real professional touch to our videos. In fact, these clips are very effective when added to a simple video of a soccer game, bike race, or other action-oriented "extreme" sports moment that you or your family are involved in.

Digital Juice

There are many companies on the Web that create unique and high-quality still and animated clips for the television industry, independent producers, wedding videographers, and home video producers. These are clips we all need, but don't have the time or expertise to create ourselves.

One of the best is Digital Juice (you can find them at **www.digitaljuice.com**). They also provide music software, sound effects, royalty-free video, and other packages useful to professional and amateur video producers alike. Digital Juice has provided the animation clips used in this chapter. If you like these, they have many more available that you can download immediately or have shipped to you on DVD.

Digital Juice Sample Clips

An example of a sports-themed back drop or "motion background." This one is 215_Jumpback from Jump Backs 5: Sports.

An example of a wedding- or romance-themed overlay. This is 150_Overlay3 from Editor's Toolkit 7: Wedding Tools II.

An example of a holiday-themed lower third. This one is 226_Lowerthird2.mov from Editor's Toolkit 9: Christmas Tools.

10

Adding the Lower Third Graphic

The lower third graphic is used in most news and sports programming as a back drop for displaying the reporter's name or location, the name of the person being interviewed, or any other pertinent information for the story. Our lower third clip is called **144_Lowerthird2.mov** and we'll simply drag it to the Timeline and make an adjustment or two.

Add the Lower Third

1 Select the clip, **144_Lowerthird2.mov,** from the Available Media view in the **Media** panel.

2 Drag and drop it onto the Timeline of the **My Project** panel onto the **Video 4** track. You want to position the clip so that the head (start) of the clip is at the **8 second** mark.

TIP *Don't worry if you currently have only three available video tracks. When you drag the* **144_Lowerthird2.mov** *clip to the blank area just above the* **Video 3** *track, Premiere Elements automatically creates a new video track to hold the clip.*

TIP *As mentioned earlier in this chapter, you can help place this clip at the 8 second mark by first moving the* **CTI** *to the 00;00;08;00 mark and then drag the clip from the Media panel to the* **Video 4** *track where the* **CTI** *is sitting.*

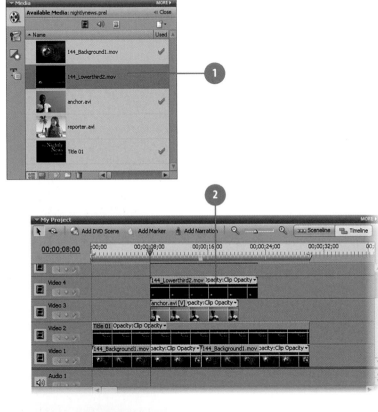

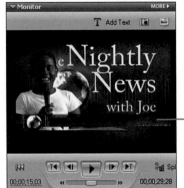

The lower third graphic, displaying in the Monitor panel at its default location and in its default orientation.

Adjust the Lower Third

1. On the **Media** panel, click the **Effects and Transitions** button to switch to the **Effects and Transitions** view.

2. Type **horiz** in the text box on the **Effects and Transitions** view to bring up the **Horizontal Flip** effect.

3. Select the **Horizontal Flip** effect from the **Video Effects Transform** category and drag and drop it onto the **144_Lowerthird2.avi** clip on the **Video 4** track.

   TIP *The Horizontal Flip effect will flip the 144_Lowerthird2.avi clip so that the globe is on the right side of the screen. This will be a better look for our "set," since we already have the big gold globe spinning away on the left, behind our anchorman. By the way, note that the the Horizontal Flip effect has no effect controls to adjust in the Properties panel. In the steps below we will, however, use the Properties panel to change the 144_Lowerthird2.avi clip's position.*

4. In the **Properties** panel for the **144_Lowerthird2.avi** clip, twirl down the triangle next to **Motion** to reveal the effect's controls.

5. Make this change for the **Motion** setting (leaving all other settings "as is"):

   ◆ **Position: 360.0   300.0**

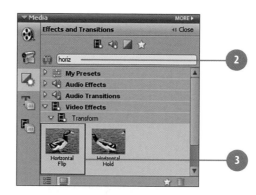

The lower third graphic, flipped horizontally.

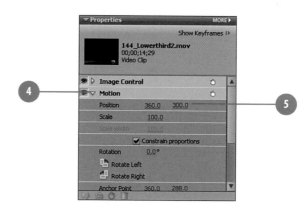

Adding Lower Third Text for the Anchorman

We'll now add some text to display over the lower third graphic at the bottom of the screen. In this case, we'll simply add the name of the anchorman and his title, which is "anchorman." As noted earlier, lower third text is usually used to identify the person on the screen, and their location. But it can also be used to convey highlights from other news stories, sports scores, and so on. This type of text typically crawls across the bottom of the screen, from right to left (so that we can read it from left to right). If you want to use this technique, it's easy with Premiere Elements. Just use click the **Roll/Crawl** options button and select Crawling text.

Type the Text and Choose a Style

1 Click the **Add Text** button to switch to the Titler workspace:

2 Replace the default text, "Add Text," with **Joe, Your Anchorman**.

3 Select the **New Times Roman** from the fonts menu on the **Properties** panel.

4 Resize the text to **32** points.

5 Style the text to be bold, italic by clicking the **Make Text Bold** and **Make Text Italic** buttons, respectively.

6 Reposition the text, by dragging it, so that it is positioned over the lower third graphic.

7 On the Timeline, do the following:

◆ Position the **Title 02** clip on the **Video 5** track so that the head of the clip lines up with the head (start) of the **anchor.avi** and the **144_Lowerthird2.avi** clips.

◆ Grab the tail of the **Title 02** clip and drag it across the **Video 5** track until it matches the length of the **anchor.avi** clip.

NOTE *We want the Title 02 clip to be the same length as the anchor.avi clip so that the text displays for as long as the anchorman is on the screen. If you want the text to appear later or end sooner, just adjust the start and end points accordingly.*

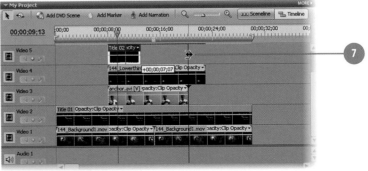

Adding the "On Site" Reporter Clip to the Project

As part of this project, the anchorman is introducing a report out in the field, in Hawaii. After his introduction, we "cut away" to the on-site reporter. Since this is a cut away, we'll add the clip to the Timeline by dropping the clip right next to the anchor clip on the same video track.

Add the Reporter

1 With your mouse, select the **reporter.avi** clip from the **Available Media** view on the **Media** panel.

2 Drag and drop the **reporter.avi** clip onto the **Video 3** track on the Timeline of the **My Project** panel, directly to the right (and touching) the **anchor.avi** clip, as shown in the illustration.

> **TIMESAVER** To easily make the two clips "fit together," be sure you have the Snap feature turned on. Remember, you can turn Snap on and off by selecting the **MORE** button at the top right of the **My Project** panel, and then selecting **Snap**. But perhaps the fastest way to activate and deactivate Snap is to just press the "**s**" key on your keyboard.

Did You Know?

You are using A and B Clips.
When you have two clips side-by-side like this on the Timeline, the arrangement creates one of the basic editing situations in film and video. The **anchor.avi** clip is referred to as the "A" clip. It is the current, but outgoing, clip. The **reporter.avi** clip is called the "B" clip. It is the incoming, and soon to be current clip. Finally, the cut between these two clips, then, is the classic A/B cut.

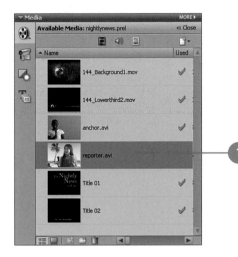

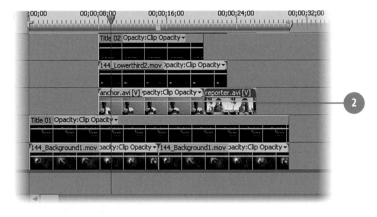

10

Adding Lower Third Graphic and Text for the Reporter

Just as for the anchorman, the on-scene reporter needs her own lower third graphics, as well as some identifying text. We'll use the same lower third graphics (a consistent look is a good thing). But this time, for the text, we'll identify the location, rather than the reporter. (The anchorman introduces the reporter by name right before the **reporter.avi** clips starts.) You can place multiple titles in sequence on the Timeline to display changing "headlines" in the lower third area, such as sports scores, birthdays, school grades, and other important dates and achievements.

Create the Reporter's Text

1 Since we've already created lower third text for the anchorman, why go through all those steps again? We'll just copy it and change it, a much simpler process. So, in the **Media** panel, **right-click** on the **Title 02** clip.

> **TIP** If the **Media** panel is not in the **Available Media** view, click the **Available Media** button (shown below) to switch.

2 In the contextual menu that displays, select **Duplicate**.

> **TIP** A new title clip appears now in the **Media** panel, called **Title 02 Copy**. You can optionally rename this clip by right-clicking on the new clip and selecting **Rename**.

> **TIMESAVER** You can also create a duplicate clip by selecting a clip, pressing the **CTRL** key on your keyboard, and dragging the clip to an empty spot on the **Media** panel. However, if you use this method, you'll have two clips with the exact same name so be sure to rename the copy.

3 Select **Title 02 Copy** and drag and drop it onto the Timeline onto the **Video 5** track, directly next to its brother, **Title 02**.

4 **Double-click** on the **Title 02 Copy** clip and in the **Titler** workspace, replace the text "Joe, Your Anchorman" in the text box with new text that reads, **On location in Hawaii**.

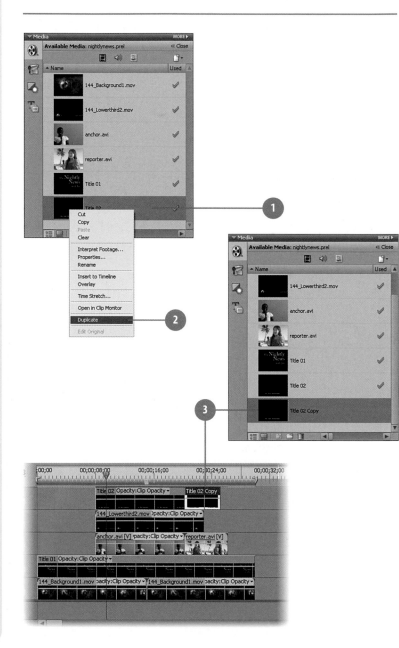

Add the Lower Third Graphic and Resize the Clips

1 Select the clip, **144_Lowerthird2.mov,** from **Available Media** view in the **Media** panel.

2 Drag and drop it onto the Timeline of the **My Project** panel onto the **Video 4** track, directly next to (and to the right) of the **144_Lowerthird2.mov** already there.

3 On the **Media** panel, click the **Effects and Transitions** button to switch to the **Effects and Transitions** view.

◆ Type **horiz** in the text box to bring up the **Horizontal Flip** effect.

◆ Drag and drop the **Horizontal Flip** effect onto the second **144_Lowerthird2.avi** clip on the **Video 4** track.

4 In the **Properties** panel for the second **144_Lowerthird2.avi** clip, adjust the **Motion** effect as follows:

◆ **Position: 360.0   300.0**

TIMESAVER *We could have chosen to simply copy the **144_Lowerthird2.avi** clip already on the Timeline and paste the copy again in line on the Timeline. It's a bit of a coin toss here as to which method would be quicker. Use whichever method you prefer.*

5 Grab the tail end of the second **144_Lowerthird2.avi** clip and pull it back so that it matches the length of the **reporter.avi** clip on the **Video 3** track.

6 Grab the tail end of the **Title 02 Copy** clip on the **Video 5** track and adjust it so that it, too, matches the length of the **reporter.avi** clip on the **Video 3** track.

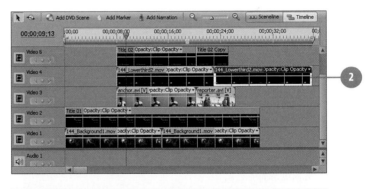

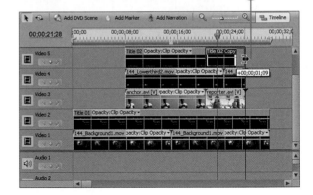

10

Here is the lower third for the on-site reporter. Note that it is in the right position and has the new text as well.

Adding "TV News" Theme Music

What makes the news the news? The news theme, of course! Well, that and the news. But we certainly can't call our newscaster project complete without having a news theme. Our news theme is brought to you once again by SmartSound and their Quicktracks software. We're using a tune from their catalog (SmartSound - Olympic - Soaring [00;30;00].wav), which we've renamed, **newstheme.wav**, for the purposes of this project.

Add the News Theme

1 Start Premiere Elements and create a new project called **nightlynews**.

2 Click the **Get Media from** button on the **Media** panel to access the **Get Media from** view, if it's not already active.

3 Select **DVD, Digital Camera, Mobile Phone, Hard Drive Camcorder, Card Reader**.

4 When the **Media Downloader** displays, click the **Advanced Dialog** button to switch to Advanced mode.

5 Select the **newstheme.wav** clip.

6 Click the **Get Media** button. Premiere Elements copies the **newstheme.wav** clip from the DVD onto your hard drive and adds it to the Available Media list for this project.

7 Drag the **newstheme.wav** clip from the **Available Media** view of the **Media** panel to the **Audio 1** track on the Timeline. Be sure to line up the head of the **newstheme.wav** clip with the start of the **Audio 1** track.

TIMESAVER *If you have the Quicktracks plug-in installed, you can optionally launch Quicktracks and load the same music track. First, select* **Orchestral Style** *from the SmartSound Maestro window. Then, select the* **Olympic** *track. Back on the Quicktracks window, select the* **Soaring** *variation. Then, click* **OK**.

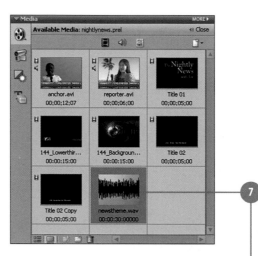

Adjust the Music's Volume Over Time

1 With the **newstheme.wav** clip selected, go to the **Properties** panel and click the **Show Keyframes** button:

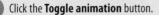

TIP *You may need to drag the **Properties** panel wider to show more of the timeline.*

TIP *If the effect controls for Volume aren't visible, twirl the triangle by Volume down to display them.*

2 Move the **CTI** to the seven second point (**00;00;07;00**).

3 Click the **Toggle animation** button.

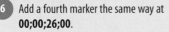

TIP *Premiere Elements automatically places a keyframe at 00;00;07;00 to mark the first point where we want to change the volume .*

4 Move the **CTI** to **00;00;08;00** when our anchorman first appears on the screen and it's here that we'll want to turn the volume of our news theme down. So, click the **Add/Remove Keyframe** button to add a keyframe.

  ◆ Set the **Clip Volume** here to **-9.0 dB**.

5 Add a third marker the same way at **00;00;25;00**.

  ◆ Set the **Clip Volume** here to **-15.0 dB**.

6 Add a fourth marker the same way at **00;00;26;00**.

  ◆ Set the **Clip Volume** for this final marker back to **00.0 dB**.

Once clicked, the **Show Keyframes** button becomes the **Hide Keyframes** button.

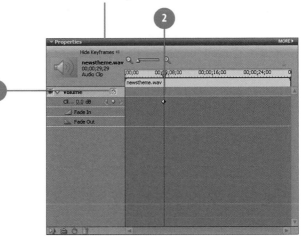

You will have four markers, each with an associated volume setting.

The yellow rubberband running the length of the **newstheme.avi** clip (representing Volume) should now look similar to the one shown here.

Making Adjustments, Rendering, and Exporting

We're done! It's goes without saying that you've been pressing **CTRL-S** on your keyboard (or selecting **File, Save** from the Premiere Elements menu) all along, but do it one last time here. Also, it doesn't hurt to render as you go either (by pressing the **ENTER** key on your keyboard, or by selecting **Timeline, Render Work Area** from the menu). Now that we're all set, it's time to share the fruit of our labor. To do so, we'll export our project to a finished file format.

Finishing the Project

1 After you have played back your clip and made the necessary adjustments, press the **ENTER** key on your keyboard to render your project.

2 Press **CTRL-S** to save your project (or you can select **File, Save** from the menu).

3 Finally, export your work as an AVI file. To export the clip, select **File, Export, Movie**.

> **TIP** You can optionally bring this clip into a larger project, show it on your computer, upload it to an Internet video sharing site, or burn it to a DVD.

The finished project "broadcasting" in Windows Media Player.

The "24" Effect

MEDIA:

24clock.wav
dublin.avi
MinorReleaseL2.mp3
newyork.avi
sanfran.avi
urban.avi

11

COMPLEXITY:	Simple	Moderate	Complex
SKILL LEVEL:	Novice	Intermediate	Advanced
MATERIALS:	None	Some Props	Greenscreen

What You'll Do

Bring in the Clips for the Project

Create the Opening Text

Animate the Opening Text

Create the Digital Countdown Clock

Animate the Clock Using Title Clips in Sequence

Synchronize the Title and Clock Clips and Add the "Beep"

Add the Four Video Clips on the Timeline

Apply a PiP Effect to Each of the Video Clips

Make Final Changes and Add the Soundtrack

Make Adjustments, Render, and Export

Introduction

If you've followed the television show *24* (or played the Xbox® game), about the exploits of a now ex-Counter Terrorist Unit (CTU) operative Jack Bauer, then you're familiar with its dramatic opening: one after another, four distinct videos appear on the screen, each in its own quadrant, each telling its own part of the bigger story. Finally, one of the four video boxes gradually fills the screen and it is that thread of the story that we follow first. These effects are achieved through the use of what is called a "PiP"—or a picture-in-picture.

PiPs are a time-honored movie and television convention that were popular in the 1960's and '70's (*The Thomas Crown Affair* with Steve McQueen used them extensively, and of course the *Brady Bunch* used them famously). In this chapter we'll recreate *24's* "The following takes place between the hours of..." opening text, to give The 24 Effect verisimilitude. The 24 Effect can be used for vacation videos, sports videos, and many other purposes. By the way, like the Star Wars® Opening Sequence Effect, you should feel free to rewrite the standard opening in your future projects to be anything you want ("The following birthday party takes place between...").

As usual, remember that the techniques you'll learn in this chapter for using PiPs can be used beyond the purpose of recreating *24's* opening sequence. Like the techniques learned throughout this book, the 24 Effect can be applied to other projects in other ways. As you create your next project, think creatively about how you might be able to use a PiP effect in your own movies to help tell the story.

Bringing in the Clips for the Project

Although this project is not particularly complicated, it does incorporate four video clips, one music clip, and one sound effect file (which is used multiple times). By adding these clips to the **Timeline** in just the right way, we can recreate our version of the opening of the well-known *24* show using just the tools available in Premiere Elements.

Import the Project's Video Clips

1. Start Premiere Elements and create a new project called **24effect**.

2. Click the **Get Media from** button on the **Media** panel to access the **Get Media from** view, if it's not already active.

3. Select **DVD, Digital Camera, Mobile Phone, Hard Drive Camcorder, Card Reader**.

4. When the **Media Downloader** displays, click the **Advanced Dialog** button to switch to Advanced mode.

5. Select the following six media clips:

   ◆ **24clock.wav**

   ◆ **dublin.avi**

   ◆ **MinorReleaseL2.mp3**

   ◆ **newyork.avi**

   ◆ **sanfran.avi**

   ◆ **urban.avi**

6. Click the **Get Media** button. Premiere Elements copies the clips from the DVD onto your hard drive and adds it to the Available Media list for this project.

> ### Did You Know?
>
> *Video clips for this project were prepared from existing clips.* The **dublin.avi** clip is a version of Artbeats' **TL302.mov** clip, and the **urban.avi** clip is a version of Artbeats' **TC107.mov** clip. The **newyork.avi** and **sanfran.avi** clips are from the Footage Firm's **brooklynbridge1.avi** and **sanfranpaintehouses.avi**, respectively.

The clips we need, added to the project.

Creating the Opening Text

At the beginning of every episode of *24*, Jack Bauer, the series' protagonist, sets the stage in a very simple way: he tells you the time of day. The premise of the series is that a story will be told in twenty-four consecutive 1-hour episodes, each in relative realtime. So, for each episode, Jack intones something along the lines of, "The following takes place between the hours of 8:00 AM and 9:00 AM." We'll use that text to create a simple title.

Create Your Opening Text

1. Click the **Add Text** button on the **Monitor** panel.

2. Select **Arial Narrow** as the font.

3. Set the font size to **22**.

4. Click the **Center Text** button to center the text.

5. Make the text bold by clicking the **Make Text Bold** button.

6. Type (in all caps): **THE FOLLOWING TAKES PLACE BETWEEN 8:00 AM AND 9:00 AM**.

   IMPORTANT *When you type, your new text should replace the default **Add Text** in the text box on the screen. If not, select **Add Text** with your mouse and then start typing.*

7. Click the **Color Properties button** on the toolbar.

8. Set the text to a deep golden yellow color:
   - **R: 240**
   - **G: 186**
   - **B: 24**

9. Click **OK** to apply these settings and close the **Color Properties** dialog box.

10. Center the text up and down by clicking the **Vertical Center** button.

11. Center the text left to right by clicking the **Horizontal Center** button.

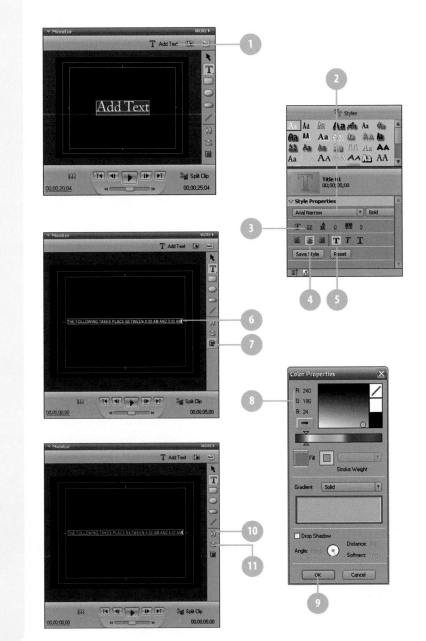

Animating the Opening Text

Now that we have our opening text created, it's time to animate it to look as if it's being typed, gradually appearing from left to right across the screen. At this point you could, if you wanted to, add a voiceover of yourself reading this text (using the Narration function in Premiere Elements), in imitation of the way Jack Bauer narrates these lines on the show. We won't be going to that length here because it's not absolutely necessary to do so for this effect to work.

Drag the Text to the Timeline and Apply a Transition

1 Click the **Effects and Transitions** button on the **Media** panel to switch to the **Effects and Transitions** view.

2 On the **Effects and Transitions** view, type **wipe** in the text box.

3 Select the **Wipe** transition and drag and drop it onto the front (head) of the **Title 01** clip on the **Video 1** track.

> **NOTE** You may need to scroll down a bit in the list of available wipes to find the Wipe transition.

4 Grab the tail end of the **Wipe.**

> **NOTE** Be sure you are selecting the **Wipe**, as shown in the illustration, and not the **Title 01** clip itself.

5 Drag the Wipe until it's the same length as the **Title 01** clip.

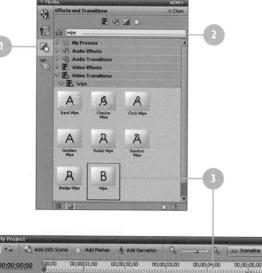

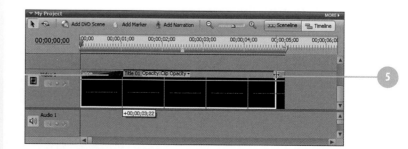

Did You Know?

You can add a narrator to the movie.
To get the full *24* effect, you could use the Narration feature in Premiere Elements to add a narration track. To do so, click the **Add Narration** button on the **My Project** panel. When the **Record Voice Narration** panel opens, click the **Record** button. With your microphone, read the text, "The following takes place between the hours of 8:00 AM and 9:00 AM." When you click **Stop**, the narration clip will be added to both the **Available Media** list on the **Media** panel and the Narration track on the **My Projects** panel.

Creating the Digital Countdown Clock

To create the illusion of a digital clock ticking on the screen, we'll place a set of "digital clock" titles on the **Timeline**, each displaying a time that is one second later than the title that proceeded it. We'll also add a "beep" sound in a later task. This "digital clock" sits in the center of the screen as the videos we'll add later will build around it in small windows called "PiPs."

Create the Prototype Clock Titles

1. Click the **Add Text** button on the Monitor panel.

2. Select **Arial Black** as the font.

3. Set the font size to **50**.

4. Click the **Center Text** button to center the text.

5. Type **07:59:55** to replace the default **Add Text** text.

6. Click the **Color Properties button** on the toolbar.

7. Set the text to to the same golden yellow as the opening text:

   ◆ **R: 240**

   ◆ **G: 186**

   ◆ **B: 24**

8. Click **OK** to apply these settings and close the **Color Properties** dialog box.

9. Center the text up and down by clicking the **Vertical Center** button.

10. Center the text left to right by clicking the **Horizontal Center** button.

11

Adjust the Duration for Title 02 on the Timeline and on the Media Panel

① Click anywhere on the **Timeline** to return to the **Edit** workspace.

② **Right-click** on the **Title 02** clip on the **Video 2** track and select **Time Stretch** from the contextual menu. This opens the **Time Stretch** dialog box.

③ Set the **Duration** to **00;00;00;20**.

④ Click **OK** to close the **Time Stretch** dialog box.

⑤ On the **Available Media** view of the **Media** panel, **right-click** on the **Title 02** clip and again select **Time Stretch** from the contextual menu.

⑥ Set the **Duration** to **00;00;00;20** here as well.

⑦ Click **OK** to close the **Time Stretch** dialog box.

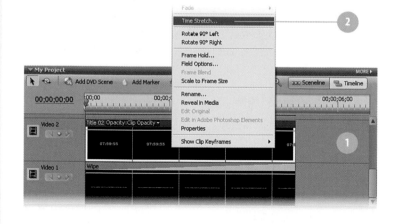

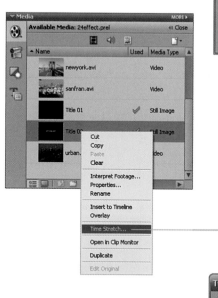

Did You Know?

You can download digital fonts from the Web.
Free fonts are available from many sources on the Internet and many variations on that "digital" look would work well for the clock we're building here. The digital numerals aren't essential, so we're building our clock for this project using a standard Windows font. However, if you want that digital look, use your favorite Internet search engine and search for free fonts. One of our favorite sources for free fonts is **www.pizzadude.dk**. Of their many free fonts (pizzadude also has fonts for sale), ***DigitaldreamFat.ttf*** is perfect for this project. If you'd rather purchase your font directly from a more well-known font company, Monotype's web-site, **www.fonts.com**, has a huge browsable and searchable font collection.

Animating the Clock Using Titles Clips in Sequence

Animating the clock involves nothing more than creating five duplicates of your original clock title clip, dragging and dropping the duplicates onto the **Timeline** in sequence, and "resetting" the time for each of the duplicate clips in sequence so that the clips, when played, will appear to be one "clock" ticking off the seconds leading up to eight o'clock: 07:59:55, 07:59:56, 07:59:57, 07:59:58, 07:59:59, 08:00:00...

Create Five Copies of the Title 02 Clip and Add Them to the Timeline

1. **Right-click** on the **Title 02** clip on the **Available Media** view of the **Media** panel and select **Duplicate** from the contextual menu.

2. **Right-click** on the **Title 02 Copy** clip you just created and select **Rename** from the contextual menu.

3. Rename the clip **56**.

4. Drag the **56** clip to the **Timeline**, directly next to the **Title 02** clip.

5. **Double-click** on the **56** clip to open the **Titler**.

6. Change the clock readout for this clip so that it reads **07:59:56**.

7. Create four additional titles in the same way by repeating **Steps 1 through 6** until you have title clips on the **Timeline** named **57**, **58**, **59**, and **8:00**. Edit the clips on the **Timeline** using the **Titler** so that the clips read as follows:

   ◆ **57** Clip : **07:59:57**

   ◆ **58** Clip : **07:59:58**

   ◆ **59** Clip : **07:59:59**

   ◆ **8:00** Clip: **08:00:00**

   TIP As you work, move the **CTI** over the latest "clock" clip on the Timeline so you can view your progress in the **Monitor** panel.

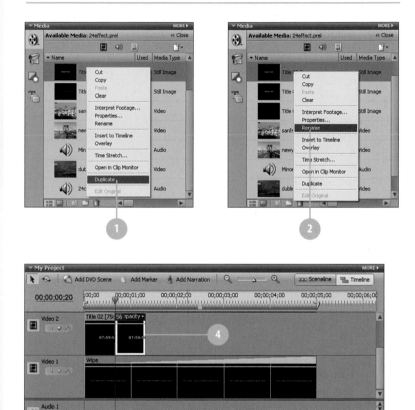

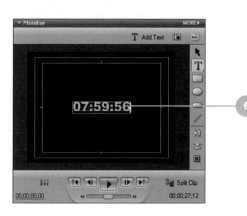

11

Synchronizing the Title and Clock Clips and Adding the "Beep"

To give the clock more credibility (and to more exactly match the clock on the TV show), we're going to add a sinister "beep, beep, beep" as the time changes on our clock. We'll be using a sound effect file called **24clock.wav**, placing a copy of it at the beginning of each of the "clock" title clips. But first, we need all of our title clips to be on the same video track.

Move the Clock Clips to the Video 1 Track

1. Press and hold the **Shift** key on your keyboard.

2. Click each of the "clock" clips on the **Video 2** track: **Title 02**, **56**, **57**, **58**. **59**, and **8:00**.

3. Drag the clips so that they sit in a row, right next to the opening text clip, **Title 01**, on the **Video 1** track. These tracks will now all play in sequence.

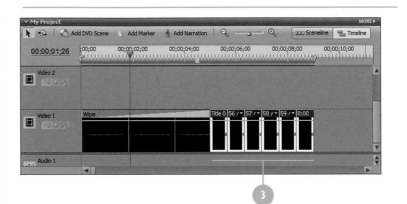

Add a Beep Each Time the Clock Changes

1. From the **Available Media** view of the **Media** panel, drag the **24clock.wav** clip onto the **Audio 1** track on the Timeline so that it lines up with the **Title 02** clip on the **Video 1** track.

   TIMESAVER *Scrub the CTI so that it lines up with the head of the video clip and drag the 24clock.wav file and line it up to the CTI.*

2. Drag the **24clock.wav** clip onto the **Audio 1** track again, so that it lines up with the **56** clip on the **Video 1** track.

3. Repeat this procedure until all of the "clock" clips have an associated **24clock.wav** clip on the **Audio 1** track, as shown in the illustration.

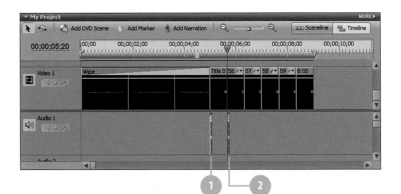

Adding the Four Video Clips to the Timeline

For this task, we will add to the **Timeline** the four video clips that will populate the four PiPs in each of the four corners of the screen. The lower-left and lower-right PiPs work perfectly as is, but in a later task we'll need to make a very small adjustment to the upper-left and upper-right PiPs so that they are positioned correctly in relation to the digital clock we created.

Import or Capture Your Video Clips

1. From the **Available Media** view of the **Media** panel, drag and drop the **newyork.avi** clip onto **Video 2**, aligned with the third "beep" on the **Audio 1** track at **00;00;06;10**.

2. Drag and drop the **sanfran.avi** clip onto **Video 3** track, aligned with the fourth "beep" on the **Audio 1** track at **00;00;07;00**.

   TIP *Press the **Page Down** (**PgDn**) key on your key board to jump the **CTI** to the start of the next clip on the Timeline. When the **CTI** is at the start of the next **24beep.wav** clip, drag the video clip to line up with the **CTI**.*

3. Drag and drop the **urban.avi** clip onto **Video 4** track, aligned with the with the fifth "beep" on the **Audio 1** track at **00;00;07;20**.

   TIMESAVER *If you currently only have three video tracks (the default number of tracks in Premiere Elements), you don't need to manually create the track first. Simply drag the **urban.avi** clip onto the dark gray area just above the **Video 3** track (as shown in the illustration) and Premiere Elements will automatically create the new track for you.*

4. Drag and drop the **dublin.avi** clip onto **Video 5** track, aligned with the sixth "beep" on the **Audio 1** track at **00;00;08;10**.

   NOTE *As noted above, if you don't have a **Video 5** track, one will be created for you. When you are done, the video clips will be arranged in a stair-step fashion (as shown in the illustration to the right) so that each clip starts a few beats after the preceding clip, synchronized with the "beep."*

Applying a PiP Effect to Each of the Video Clips

For this task, we'll apply a different PiP to each clip, transforming the clip so that it plays in only one quadrant of the screen (for example, the upper left corner). Doing so will create the effect of multiple smaller video screens popping open on the screen revealing action and the storyline details beat-by-beat. We'll split the **newyork.avi** clip into two clips, and apply a different PiP to the second **newyork.avi** clip so that it grows to fill the entire screen, just as in *24*.

Apply a Unique PiP to Each Clip

1. Click the **Effects and Transitions** button on the **Media** panel to switch to the the **Effects and Transitions** view.

2. On the **Effects and Transitions** panel, type **PiP 40% LL** (LL stands for lower left).

3. Drag and drop the **PiP 40% LL** PiP onto the **newyork.avi** clip in the **Video 2** track on the **Timeline**.

4. Add the following PiPs to the three remaining video clips:

   ◆ **sanfran.avi: PiP 40% UR** (upper right)

   ◆ **urban.avi: PiP 40% UL** (upper left)

   ◆ **dublin.avi: PiP 40% LR** (lower right)

   TIMESAVER *You only need to change the last two letters of the PiP in the text box, for example from **LL** to **UR**, to find the next PiP.*

   IMPORTANT *Be careful when you are selecting a PiP. PiPs have very similar names and it's easy to pick the wrong one. You may need to scroll down first to find the correct PiP.*

5. Scrub the **CTI** to **00;00;09;00**.

6. Click the **newyork.avi** clip in the **Video 2** track to select it.

7. With *only* the **newyork.avi** clip selected, click **Split Clip** in the **Monitor** panel.

8. On the **Effects and Transitions** panel, type **PiP 40% LL Scale Up to Full**.

9. Drag and drop the **PiP 40% LL Scale Up to Full** PiP onto the *new* **newyork.avi** clip you just created (the one that starts at **00;00;09;00**).

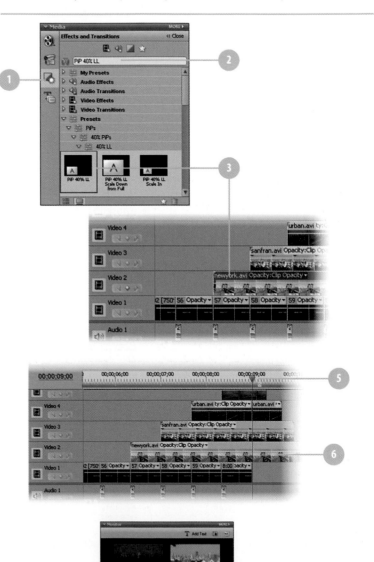

Making Final Changes and Adding the Soundtrack

What's an action-adventure style opening (or even a parody of it) without an exciting soundtrack? On the DVD supplied with this book we have just the thing, a tense track from the TwistedTracks folks called **MinorReleaseL2.mp3**. Before we add our music, we need to make a minor adjustment to a couple of clips. The default location for both the **PiP 40% UR** and the **PiP 40% UL** is just a bit too low, so that when the **sanfran.avi** and **urban.avi** clips first appear, they cover up our digital clock. Fortunately, this is easy to fix.

Adjust the Upper Left and Right PiPs

1. Click the **sanfran.avi** clip in the upper right corner of the **Monitor** panel.

2. In the **Properties** panel, click the triangle next to **Motion** to reveal the effect's controls.

3. Adjust the *vertical* **Position** of the PiP (the second number in the pair) to **115**.

4. Repeat **Steps 1 through 3** for the **urban.avi** clip in the upper left corner of the **Monitor** screen.

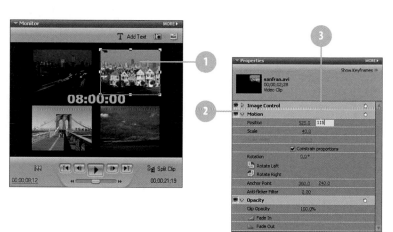

Add the Soundtrack

1. Click the **Available Media** button on the **Media** panel to switch to the **Available Media** view.

2. Drag the **MinorReleaseL2.mp3** clip from the **Media** panel onto the **Audio 2** track on the **Timeline**.

   IMPORTANT *Be sure that the start (head) of the MinorReleaseL2.mp3 clip is at the very beginning of the Audio 2 track.*

3. Drag the **MinorReleaseL2.mp3** clip a second time from the **Media** panel onto the **Audio 2** track on the Timeline. Position the clip so that it touches the end of the **MinorReleaseL2.mp3** clip already on the **Timeline**, as shown in the illustration.

4. On the **Properties** panel for the second **MinorReleaseL2.mp3** clip, click the **Fade Out** button under the **Volume** control.

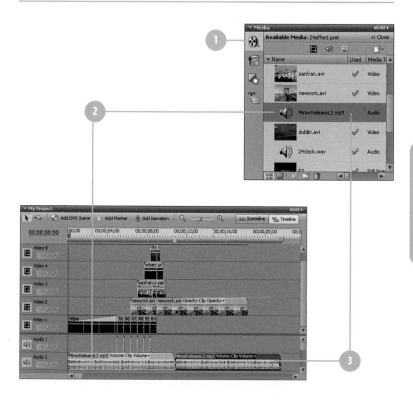

11

Making Adjustments, Rendering, and Exporting

Play your movie by pressing the **Spacebar** and make sure everything looks right. If not, make some adjustments until you like what you see. If everything looks good, you are ready to save your work one last time, and export your movie to the format of your choice. When you export, Premiere Elements will first render the project (applying effects and transitions to the clips on the Timeline) and then create the file.

Finishing the Project

1 After you have played back your clip and made the necessary adjustments, press the **ENTER** key on your keyboard to render your project.

2 Press **CTRL-S** to save your project (or you can select **File, Save** from the menu).

3 Finally, export your work as an AVI file. To export the clip, select **File, Export, Movie**.

> **TIP** *You can optionally bring this clip into a larger project, show it on your computer, upload it to an Internet video sharing site, or burn it to a DVD.*

> **NOTE** *Rendering can take a while, depending upon the speed of your computer and the number of frames that need to be rendered.*

Once the movie has been exported, sit back and enjoy your own version of *24*.

The Beam Me Up Effect

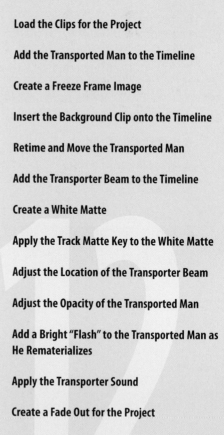

MEDIA:
transporterbackground.avi
transporterbeam.avi
transporterbeam.wav
transporterman.avi

12

COMPLEXITY:	Simple	**Moderate**	Complex
SKILL LEVEL:	Novice	**Intermediate**	Advanced
MATERIALS:	**None**	Some Props	Greenscreen

What You'll Do

Load the Clips for the Project

Add the Transported Man to the Timeline

Create a Freeze Frame Image

Insert the Background Clip onto the Timeline

Retime and Move the Transported Man

Add the Transporter Beam to the Timeline

Create a White Matte

Apply the Track Matte Key to the White Matte

Adjust the Location of the Transporter Beam

Adjust the Opacity of the Transported Man

Add a Bright "Flash" to the Transported Man as He Rematerializes

Apply the Transporter Sound

Create a Fade Out for the Project

Make Adjustments, Render, and Export

Introduction

"Beam me up, Scotty," has become a part of the American vernacular. We're all familiar with the expression, and we all know what it refers to: the transporter on the starship *Enterprise* from *Star Trek*® and its ability to deconstruct a person down to the subatomic level, transport them through space, and reconstruct them again in another location. We are all familiar with the transporter sound and the transporter sparkles. Recreating this effect, then, requires some faithfulness to the original effect used on the Star Trek television show for it to work.

There are actually two ways to create this effect. One is a complicated process using Adobe Photoshop or a similar program to manipulate a still image taken from Premiere Elements to create a matte of the person or persons being "beamed" up or down. This allows you to create a "beam me up" effect that's true to the television show in that the transporter particles are restricted to the outline of the person being transported. It's complicated, but effective.

However, there's a simpler way to do this that works just as well and creates a true "Sci-Fi" experience, with nowhere near the effort. What is surprising about this effect is that you don't need a greenscreen or any additional software beyond Premiere Elements 3. Basically, in this version, we place the transporter beam in front of the person we're transporting while we dissolve them into the scene (by adjusting the Opacity on the top clip of two nearly identical clips). An added "flash" of light adds a nice dramatic effect.

Loading the Clips for the Project

This effect uses four clips that are supplied, which you'll be loading into the project, and one clip—a still image—that you'll be creating. The **transporterbeam.avi** and **transporterbeam.wav** clips are two clips that you can use in your own projects to transport whomever you wish using the technique you'll learn in this chapter.

Add Your clips to the Project

1. Start Premiere Elements and create a new project called **BeamMeUp**.

2. Click the **Get Media from** button on the **Media** panel to access the **Get Media from** view.

3. Select **DVD, Digital Camera, Mobile Phone, Hard Drive Camcorder, Card Reader**.

4. When the **Media Downloader** displays, click the **Advanced Dialog** button to switch to Advanced mode.

5. Select the following clips to load:

   ◆ **transporterbackground.avi**

   ◆ **transporterbeam.avi**

   ◆ **transporterbeam.wav**

   ◆ **transporterman.avi**

6. Click the **Get Media** button. Premiere Elements copies the clips from the DVD onto your hard drive and adds them to the **Available Media** list for this project.

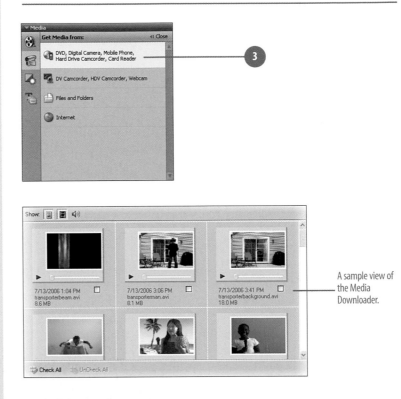

A sample view of the Media Downloader.

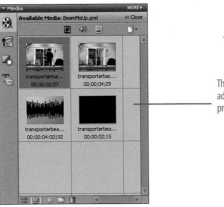

The project clips, added to the project.

Adding the Transported Man to the Timeline

The **transporterman.avi** clip is a clip, a few seconds long, of an actor standing in place for a brief moment before walking away. We'll be taking this very basic clip (which is exactly the kind of clip that you should shoot to use the Beam Me Up Effect with your own friends and family) and transforming it into a science fiction masterpiece. First, we'll add the actor to the Timeline, and then we'll take a snapshot of him standing in place.

Add the transporterman.avi Clip to the Timeline

 With your mouse, select the **transporterman.avi** in the **Media** panel.

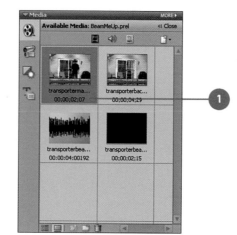

2 Drag and drop the **transporterman.avi** clip onto the **Video 1** track on the Timeline so that the head (front) of the clip is at the very beginning of the track.

> **TIP** If you are in **Sceneline** view, just drop the clip onto the first scene placeholder.

3 For this project, we'll need to be in **Timeline** view because we are working with multiple clips on multiple video tracks. So, if the **My Project** panel is not already in **Timeline** view, click the **Timeline** button (shown below) to switch.

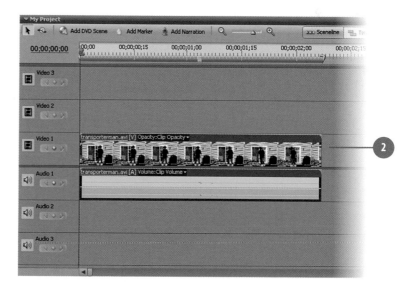

12

Creating a Freeze Frame Image

Most of the "effect" of the Beam Me Up Effect is applied to a still image which we will pull from the **transporterman.avi** clip on the Timeline using the **Freeze Frame** function in Premiere Elements. We'll place a background beneath the still image and the transporter beam above it to create the effect of someone "beaming in" from another dimension.

Adding a Still Image to the Project

1 With the **Current Time Indicator (CTI)** at the beginning of the **Video 1** track, click the **Freeze Frame** button on the **Monitor** panel.

> **TIP** *To send the CTI to the first frame of the Timeline, press the Home key on your keyboard.*

2 Click the **Insert in Movie** button on the **Freeze Frame** dialog box.

> **TIP** *The default for the freeze frame image is 5 seconds. If you have set this to be other than 5 seconds, reset it back to 5 seconds now.*

Did You Know?

You can edit an image in Photoshop Elements. Premiere Elements and Photoshop Elements are tightly woven together, which makes it easy to work with still images that are a part of a Premiere Elements project. One way that the two programs are connected is when you create a freeze frame image. At that time, you are given the option, through the Edit in Photoshop Elements after inserting check box, to open Photoshop Elements and edit the image you just created. Any changes you make to the image in Photoshop Elements are reflected immediately in Premiere Elements as soon as you save your work.

The freeze frame still image is inserted here, at the front of the **Video 1** track.

Inserting the Background Clip onto the Timeline

The actor who will be beamed into the scene needs a scene to be beamed into. We've shot the background of the same scene—using a tripod of course!—and we'll use that background. When we fade the actor in (using the **Opacity** settings over time), since the actor is the only thing different in this scene and the background scene, he'll appear to fade in, even though actually the entire clip is gradually fading in, not just the actor.

Add the transporterman.avi Clip to the Timeline

1 The background clip needs to be behind (or in video editing terms, "below") the still image. Select the **still image** on the **Video 1** track and drag it up to the **Video 2** track. Be sure that the front of the clip lines up with the start of the track.

2 Select the **transporterbackground.avi** clip in the **Media** panel.

3 Drag the **transporterbackground.avi** clip to the Timeline and drop it on the **Video 1** track so that the head (front) of the clip is at the beginning of the track.

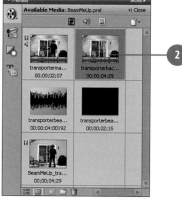

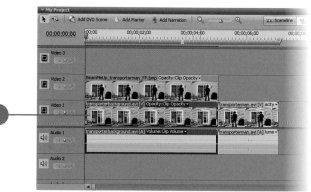

Retiming and Moving the Transported Man

We want, when the clip is playing, for the background (devoid of anyone appearing from out of nowhere) to appear on the screen for a few seconds to set the scene. Then, the transporter beam will appear, followed by the materialized man. To create this lag time, we'll simply shorten the timeframe for the still image clip, and then move it back so that it ends at the same time that the background clip ends.

Alter the transporterman.avi Clip

1. We want change the duration of the still image clip to 3 seconds, so move the **CTI** to the 3 second mark (**00;00;03;00**).

2. With your mouse, grab the tail end of the clip and drag it backwards until it lines up exactly with the **CTI**.

3. Next, click on the clip and drag it forwards until the tail of the clip lines up exactly with the tail of the **transporterbackground.avi** clip on the **Video 1** track.

Did You Know?

You can also an change the duration of any clip using Time Stretch. To access the **Time Stretch** dialog box, right-click on the clip and select **Time Stretch**. Then, on the **Time Stretch** dialog box, adjust the value for the **Duration**. When you're all set, click **OK**. Time Stretch functionality is also available right on the Timeline. Just click the **Time Stretch Tool** button (it's there between the **Selection Tool** button and the **Add DVD Scene** button in the upper left) and use the tool to increase or decrease a clip's speed and duration simultaneously.

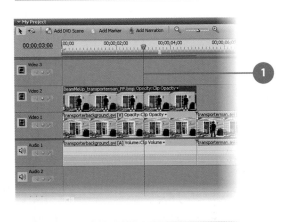

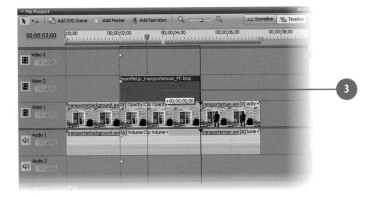

Adding the Transporter Beam to the Timeline

Now that the inter-dimensional traveller and the place he's traveling to are both on the Timeline, it's time to add the transporter beam to the Timeline to get him to his destination. The transporter beam is just a lighting effect animated so that it appears to move slightly down from above. It has no sound yet, but we'll be adding that critical component in a later task.

Transporter On!

1. We want the transporter beam to start appearing just slightly ahead of the **transporterman.avi** clip. so first let's set the **CTI** at the **00;00;01;15** mark.

2. Then, with your mouse, select the **transporterbeam.avi** in the **Media** panel.

3. Drag and drop the **transporterbeam.avi** clip on to the **Video 4** track on the Timeline so that the head (front) of the clip lines up with the **CTI**.

   NOTE *We're dropping this clip onto the Video 4 track because we'll be placing another clip on the Video 3 track in a later task.*

Did You Know?

Premiere Elements creates tracks as needed.
If you don't have a spare track, in this case a **Video 4** track, for the **transporterbeam.avi** clip to drop on to, no problem. As you drag the clip, just drop it in the blank space above the topmost clip. Premiere Elements will go ahead and create the new track. Premiere Elements does have an explicit function to add more tracks. (To use it, right-click in the track margin and select **Add Tracks**, as shown in the illustration below.) However, there's really no need to go out of your way to use it unless you know you need to add a number of tracks. Adding audio tracks works the same way.

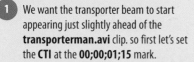

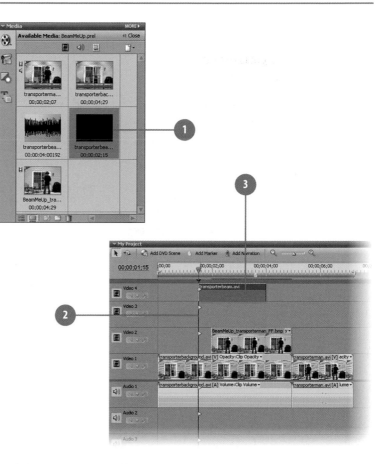

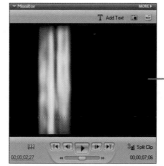

The **transporterbeam.avi** clip, as it appears in the **Monitor** panel.

12

Creating a White Matte

We'll create a color matte now that will serve two purposes. First, it will color our transporter beam a bright white, which will give it a bright light look. Second, it will, once we apply the matte effect in the next task, act as a color matte and allow the transport beam to show through on top of the still image by making all of the black in the **transporterbeam.avi** clip act as a transparent color.

Create a Matte and Color it White

1 Click on the **New Item** button in the **Media** panel.

> **TIP** *You should be on the **Available Media** view. If not, click the **Available Media** button on the **Media** panel to switch to that view.*

2 Select **Color Matte**.

3 On the **Color Picker** dialog box, drag the color picker circle all the way down to the lower left corner of the window.

> **TIP** *We want absolute white, so as an alternative you can type **FFFFFF** in the hexadecimal area (labeled "#") or **255, 255, 255** as the **RGB** values.*

4 Click **OK**.

5 The **Choose Name** dialog box displays. Type **White Matte** as the new name.

6 Click **OK**.

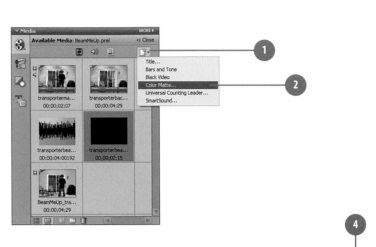

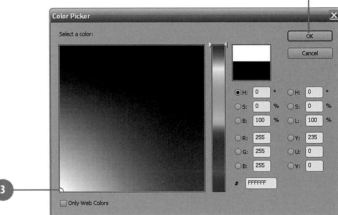

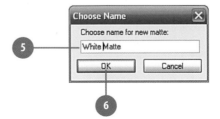

Add the White Matte to the Timeline and Adjust It

1 Select the **White Matte** from the **Media** panel.

2 Drag and drop the clip onto the Timeline onto the **Video 3** track so that the head of the **White Matte** clip lines up with the head of the **transporterbeam.avi** clip on the **Video 4** track.

> **NOTE** *Align the front of the* **White Matte** *clip with the front of the* **transporterbeam.avi** *clip.*

3 Grab the tail end of the **White Matte** clip and drag it back until it exactly lines up with the end of the **transporterbeam.avi** clip. This makes the duration of the two clips exactly the same.

Did You Know?

You can color a matte any color you want.
For this project, we've chosen to color the matte white because we think it works best for the effect we're going for (a beam of white containing a flash of white). However, you may think differently. Once you've learned and practiced this effect, you might decide that you'd prefer a green transporter beam. Or a magenta one. Or grape-colored. It makes no difference, technically speaking, what color you make the beam, so go ahead and design the transporter beam to be whatever color you choose. Perhaps you'll decide that humans and animals have different colored beams. Or, for your projects, perhaps men have yellow beams and women have purple beams. Or maybe beams that beam you up are a different color than the beams that beam you down.

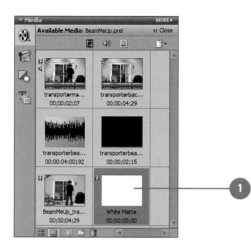

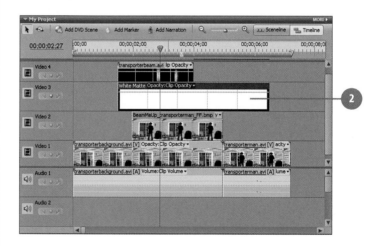

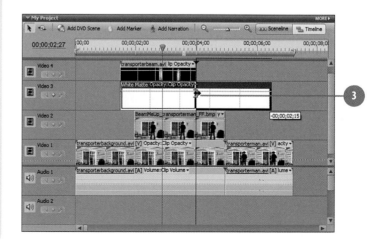

12

Applying the Track Matte Key to the White Matte

In order for the transporter beam to actually appear superimposed on the still image so that the actor actually appears to be transported, we need to apply the **Track Matte Key** from the Keying effects in Premiere Elements. We'll apply the key to the **White Matte** clip and point it at the track holding the **transporterbeam.avi** clip.

Apply the Track Matte Key

1. Click on the **Effects and Transitions** button on the **Media** panel to change to the **Effects and Transitions** view.

2. In the text box on the **Effects and Transitions** panel, type **matte**.

3. Drag and drop the **Track Matte Key** from the Keying section of the Video Effects on to the **White Matte** clip on the **Video 3** track on the Timeline.

4. In the **Properties** panel for the **White Matte** clip, click on the **triangle** next to the **Track Matte Key** to see the effect's controls.

5. From the **Matte** pull-down, select **Video 4**.

6. From the **Composite Using** pull-down, select **Matte Luma**.

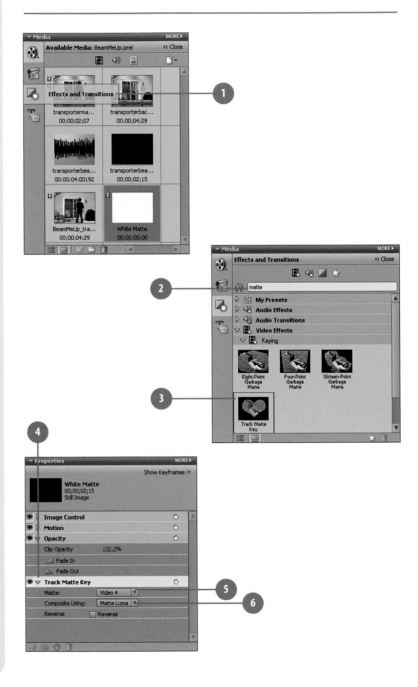

Adjusting the Location of the Transporter Beam

By default, the transporter beam runs down from top to bottom along the left side of the screen. Our transporter man is standing slightly off center, just to the right of center. In order for this illusion to work, we need the transporter beam to exactly overlay on top of the actor. To do so, we'll simply drag the **transporterbeam.avi** clip across the screen until it lines up correctly. When you use the transporter beam in future projects, use the same technique to relocate it as needed.

Relocate the beam

1 Scrub the **CTI** across the length of the **transporterbeam.avi** clip until you can see the beam fairly well in the **Monitor** panel, as shown in the illustration.

2 Click on the **transporterbeam.avi** clip in the Timeline to select it.

3 In the **Properties** panel for the **transporterbeam.avi** clip, click the **Motion** effect to select it.

> **TIP** *The name of the **Motion** effect should reverse (highlight in black) as shown in the illustration, if you've selected it correctly. In addition, handles should appear around the clip in the **Monitor** panel.*

4 Click on the **transporterbeam.avi** clip in the **Monitor** panel and drag the clip across the screen until the transporter beam overlays directly on top of the actor, as shown in the illustration.

Here's the default location for the transporter beam.

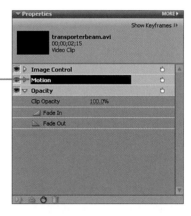

Here's the **transporterbeam.avi** clip, selected (notice the cross in the middle of the screen), ready to be moved.

Here's the same clip, having been moved across the screen and placed so that the transporter beam is now directly over the actor.

12

Adjusting the Opacity of the Transported Man

In order for our intergalactic traveller from another dimension to appear to dissolve into the scene, we need to adjust his opacity from 0% (invisible) to 100% (fully visible) over time. To do so, we'll make use of keyframes and animation and set the points at which we want the actor to be seen and at what percentage.

Set the Opacity to Increase Over Time

1 Select the freeze frame still image in the **Video 2** track on the Timeline.

2 In the **Properties** panel for the still image, click the **Show Keyframes** button to reveal the workspace for adding keyframe.

> **TIP** The **Show Keyframes** button, once clicked, becomes the **Hide Keyframes** button and its function changes to match.

> **TIMESAVER** Adjust the horizontal size of the **Properties** panel as needed so that you can work most effectively with keyframes. To expand the keyframe area of the **Properties** panel, drag the left side of the panel to the left. You want to see as much of the **Properties** panel timeline as possible.

3 Move the **CTI** to the beginning of the clip by pressing the **Page Up** key on your keyboard.

4 In the **Properties** panel, set the **Clip Opacity** to **0%** (zero).

5 Click the **Toggle animation** button to turn on the animation functionality of Premiere Elements.

> **TIP** Premiere Elements automatically inserts a keyframe at this point.

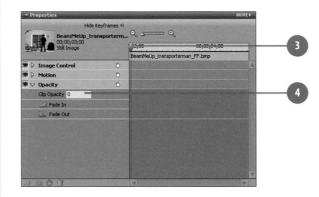

6 Move the **CTI** to the end of the clip by pressing the **Page Down** key twice.

TIP *We need to press the* ***Page Down*** *key two times because the first time you press the key, the* ***CTI*** *jumps to the end of the* ***White Matte*** *clip on the* ***Video 3*** *track.*

7 Set the **Clip Opacity** to **100%**.

TIP *Premiere Elements automatically inserts a keyframe at this point.*

8 We don't want our traveller to appear too quickly, so lets set one more keyframe. Scrub the **CTI** to **00;00;03;15**, which is roughly the half-way point for this clip.

9 Normally at this point, the clip would be around 50% opacity. But we want to slow things down a bit, so set the **Clip Opacity** to **25%**.

TIP *Again, Premiere Elements automatically inserts a keyframe at this point.*

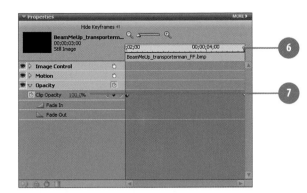

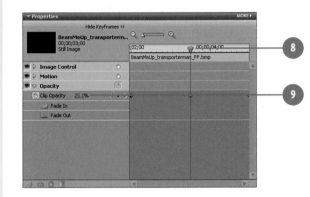

Did You Know?

Opacity is the opposite of transparency.
Opacity shares the same root word as opaque (to be non-transparent; a wall is opaque, but a window is transparent). It refers to the degree to which an image allows the images behind (below) it to show through; in other words, how "see through" the image is. An opacity setting of 100% means that the clip is completely *opaque*. An opacity setting of 0% means that the clip is completely *transparent*.

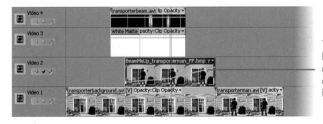

The rising yellow line indicates a gradual increase in opacity over the length of the clip.

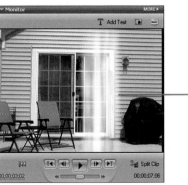

Here, you can just barely make out the actor starting to appear within the transporter beam as he rematerializes.

12

Adding a Bright "Flash" to the Transported Man as He Rematerializes

What will give our effect a convincing "punch"—or the cherry on top, if you prefer—is the addition of a bright flash just as the actor rematerializes. The flash of light seems to imply the power of the transportation and gives it the look of science fiction convention. By convention, we mean that the effect has a look to it that is understood and accepted by Sci-Fi fans.

Add a Lens Flare

1 Click the **Effects and Transitions** button on the **Media** panel to switch to the **Effects and Transitions** view.

2 In the **text box** on the **Effects and Transitions** panel, type **lens**.

3 Drag and drop the **Lens Flare** from the **Effects and Transitions** view onto the clip, **BeamMeUp_transporterman_FF.bmp**, in the **Video 2** track on the Timeline.

4 In the **Lens Flare Settings** dialog box, which pops up once you drop the **Lens Flare** effect on the clip, move the lens flare so that it sits in the middle of the actor, at about chest height, as shown in the illustration.

> **TIMESAVER** *You can also access the Lens Flare Settings dialog box from the Properties panel. Click the Setup button for Lens Flare (shown in the illustration) to do so.*

5 Click **OK**.

6 On the **Properties** panel for the **still image** clip, click the triangle for **Lens Flare** to reveal the effects controls.

7 Open the keyframe area if it's not already open by clicking the **Show Keyframes** button.

8 Scrub the **CTI** to **00;00;03;07**.

9 Set the **Brightness** for the lens flare to **250**.

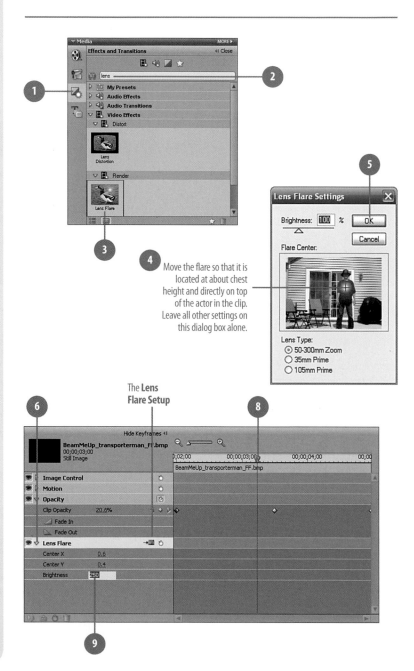

4 Move the flare so that it is located at about chest height and directly on top of the actor in the clip. Leave all other settings on this dialog box alone.

The **Lens Flare Setup**

Create the Appearance of the Lens Flare "Flashing"

1 Click the **Toggle animation** button to turn on the animation functionality of Premiere Elements.

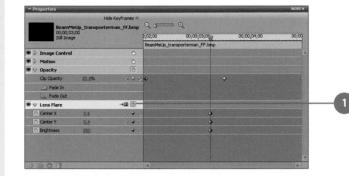

> **TIP** *Premiere Elements automatically places keyframes at this point for the Center X, Center Y, and Brightness controls.*

2 We only want to make a change to the **Brightness** control, so we'll quickly delete the other two keyframes. To do so, click the **Add/Remove Keyframes** button (shown below) for **Center X** and **Center Y**.

3 Scrub the **CTI** to the beginning of the clip.

> **TIP** *To jump right to the beginning of the clip, press the **Page Up** key on your keyboard.*

4 Set the **Brightness** to **10**.

> **TIP** *Premiere Elements automatically places a keyframe at this point.*

5 Scrub the **CTI** to the end of the clip.

> **TIP** *To jump to the end of this clip, press the **Page Down** key on your keyboard two times. (The first time you press it, the **CTI** jumps to the end of the **White Matte** clip, which is on the **Video 3** track.)*

6 Set the **Brightness** here at the end of the clip to **10** as well.

> **TIP** *Once again, Premiere Elements places a keyframe at this point.*

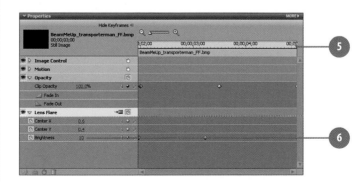

Use the **Add/Remove Keyframe** button to remove the keyframes for both Center X and Center Y.

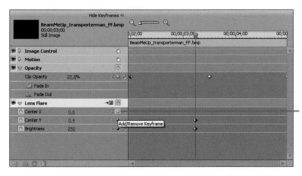

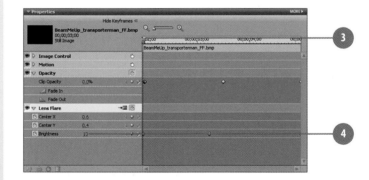

12

Applying the Transporter Sound

As visually interesting as we've made this effect, "it don't mean a thing if it ain't got that swing." That is, without the sound of the transporter the effect is somewhat lifeless. So, for this task we'll be adding the **transporterbeam.wav** sound file to the sound track, which will really bring this project to life.

Add the Transporter Noise to the Transporter Beam

1. Change to the **Available Media** view of the **Media** panel by clicking on the **Available Media** button.

2. Select the **transporterbeam.wav** sound file and drag and drop it onto the **Audio 2** track on the Timeline.

3. Position the clip so that its tail end exactly lines up with the tail end of the still image clip.

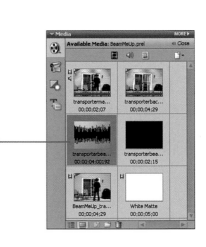

Did You Know?

You can use sounds creatively for effect. You may have noticed that the transporterbeam *sound* file is quite a bit longer in duration than the transporterbeam *video* file that it's supposed to be associated with. The reason this works is because we want to hear the transporter working before we actually see it. We also want to continue to hear the transporter fading away, even after the visual image of the transporter is no longer on screen. Working with sound is an art in itself and the more you use it, the more you'll see that sometimes you want sounds to fade in or fade out at different times other than when you might intuitively or logically expect. It's not unusual for a film editor to let viewers hear a sound first before showing the visual, such as the sound of a train whistle at the end of a scene of two people talking indoors. It's not until the next scene that we see the train.

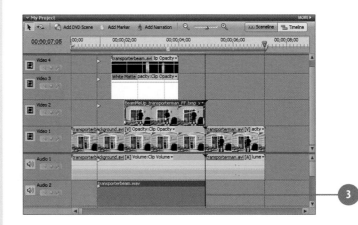

Creating a Fade Out for the Project

The final task for this project is to create a "fade to black" at the end. We'll use the Fade Out that's built in to every clip automatically with Premiere Elements. The default settings, however, aren't quite right (the fade out is too fast), so we'll make a small adjustment on the Timeline by dragging the keyframe on the clip.

Add a Final Fade Out to the transporterman.avi Clip

1. On the Timeline, click on the **transporterman.avi** clip on the **Video 1** track to select it.

2. In the **Properties** panel for the clip, click the **Fade Out** button (shown below) under Opacity:

3. Click on the white keyframe in the video portion of the **transporter.avi** clip on the **Video 1** track and drag it forward a bit, as shown in the illustration.

   TIP *By dragging the keyframe forward— that is, further in time—the fade out effect we just applied will therefore start later in the clip, which is what we want.*

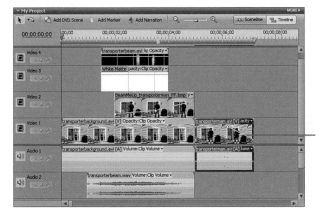

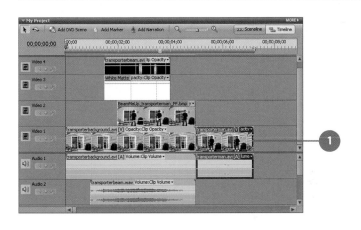

After you click the **Fade Out** button, the yellow opacity line gradual decreases here on the clip.

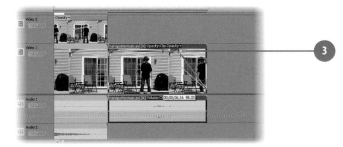

12

Making Adjustments, Rendering, and Exporting

Now that all of the tasks for this project have been completed, you're ready to "share" the movie, or incorporate it into a bigger project. You could burn a DVD or a VCD or share the clip on a video sharing web site. It's up to you. But always, make sure you save, save, save whenever you are working on a video editing project. You can, and should, render while you work. We will render one more time here, now that we have reached the end of our project.

Finishing the Project

1. After you have played your clip (using the **Spacebar** on your keyboard) and made the necessary adjustments, press the **ENTER** key on your keyboard to render your project.

2. Press **CTRL-S** to save your project (or you can select **File, Save** from the menu).

3. Finally, export your work as an AVI file. To export the clip, select **File, Export, Movie**.

   TIP *You can optionally bring this clip into a larger project, show it on your computer, upload it to an Internet video sharing site, or burn it to a DVD.*

The BeamMeUp clip, playing in the Windows Media player.

The Night Vision Effect

MEDIA:

bond.mp3
nightsuspects.avi

13

COMPLEXITY:	Simple	Moderate	**Complex**
SKILL LEVEL:	Novice	**Intermediate**	Advanced
MATERIALS:	**None**	Some Props	Greenscreen

Introduction

If you are a student creating a spy film or a sci-fi epic, you don't need to film your nighttime scenes at night. Use the Night Vision Effect instead. As a parent, if you want to give the film of your toddlers in a playpen a fake reality show's look at nighttime baby activities, use the Night Vision Effect. If you just want to have a little fun with an easy-to-use effect that can be applied to virtually *any* video clip, use the Night Vision Effect.

The techniques you'll learn in this chapter, like most of the techniques in this book, have broader applications than just simulating the night scope of a camera or other lens. In this chapter we'll create oval cutouts to simulate a night vision scope, but you can use this same technique in other projects to simulate the view through a telescope, a camera lens, or even a keyhole. The Night Vision Effect is a much-requested effect because of its many applications, especially in amateur filmmaking. It can be used to simulate the point of view of someone using night vision equipment, or to suggest a darkened room at night with low visibility.

The effect is great for spy flicks, as already mentioned, and can be used very effectively for thrillers and horror films as well. For example, if you're creating a spy film, videotape the view out your window and have your friends sit in a car across the street and act as if they are staking you out. Or for a horror film, do the same thing, but have your friends act like zombies moving slowly (but inexorably!) down the street. Next film your hero picking up special night vision-equipped scopes (also known as ordinary binoculars) to look out the window. In post production, cut in the zombie or stakeout footage, altered with the Night Vision Effect, and then cut to footage of your hero reacting. The entire scene will be instantly believable. So, let your imagination soar as you follow your vision—your *night* vision, that is.

What You'll Do

Add the Video Clip to the Project

Remove the Existing Colors from the Clip

Add the Green of Night Vision Using the Tint Effect

Add Noise to Simulate the Graininess of Night Vision

Add Darkness to the "Nightime" Clip

Add an Overlay to Simulate Night Vision Goggles

Add Motion to the Goggles to Simulate a Searching Movement

Add Blurriness to the "Goggles" for Additional Realism

Turn the Little White Circles into True Goggles

Add Mysterious Music "Under"

Make Adjustments, Render, and Export

Adding the Video Clip to the Project

We start this project just as we do all of the projects in this book: by starting Premiere Elements, creating a new project, and bringing in our initial clips. In this case, we are using a single video clip, **nightsuspects.avi**. Later, we'll modify this clip to look as if it's being viewed through nightvision goggles. We'll also create those "goggles" right in Premiere Elements.

Find a Clip and Add it to the Timeline

1 Start Premiere Elements and create a new project called **nightvision**.

2 Click the **Get Media from** button on the **Media** panel to access the **Get Media from** view, if it's not already active.

3 Select **DVD, Digital Camera, Mobile Phone, Hard Drive Camcorder, Card Reader**.

4 When the **Media Downloader** displays, click the **Advanced Dialog** button to switch to Advanced mode.

5 Select the **nightsuspects.avi** clip.

6 Click the **Get Media** button. Premiere Elements copies the **nightsuspects.avi** clip from the DVD onto your hard drive and adds it to the Available Media list for this project.

7 Drag on drop the **nightsuspects.avi** clip on the **Media** panel onto the **Timeline** in the **Video 1** track. Be sure to line up the head of the **nightsuspects.avi** clip with the start of the **Video 1** track.

> **TIP** *If you're in **Sceneline** view, drop the clip onto the first scene box. Premiere Elements automatically places it on the **Video 1** track.*

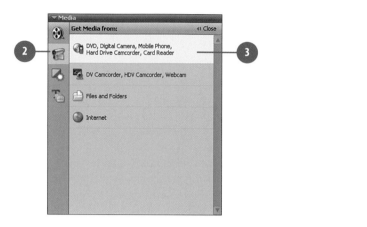

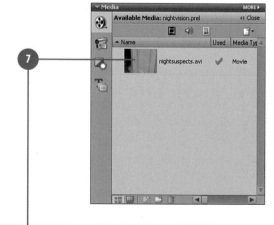

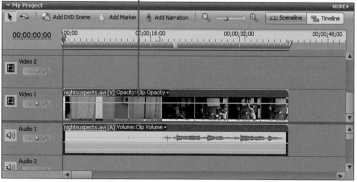

Removing the Existing Colors from the Clip

In order to effectively add the "night vision green" to our clip, we'll first need to remove the existing full-color palette from the clip. Otherwise, the tinting process will only "colorize" the clip, leaving a variety of shades of the original colors still showing through. To convert a color clip to a clip with no colors is simple with Premiere Elements: all you do is drag and drop the **Black and White** video effect onto the clip you want to change and the effect is instantaneous.

Start with a "Blank Palette"

1 Click on the **Effects and Transitions** button on the **Media** panel to switch to the **Effects and Transitions** view.

2 Type **black** in the text box in the **Effects and Transitions** view.

3 Select the **Black & White** video effect and drag and drop it onto the **nightsuspects.avi** clip on the **Video 1** track on the **Timeline**.

4 In the **Monitor** panel, view how your clip has changed from color to black and white.

TIP *In general, the more you type of the name of the effect you are looking for in the text box in the* ***Effects and Transitions*** *view of the* ***Media*** *panel, the more you'll narrow your search, and the less scrolling through the search results you'll need to do.*

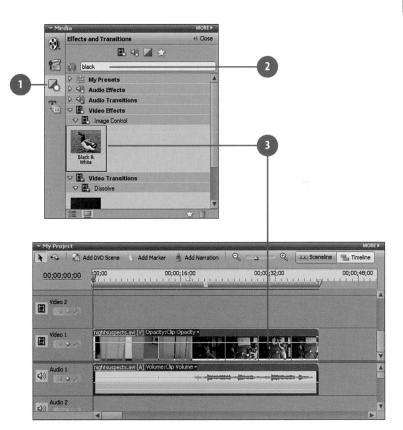

Adding the Green of the Night Vision Using the Tint Effect

Most people (correctly) associate the look of night vision with a dark green color. To capitalize on this association, we'll be tinting our clip a deep green as the next step in creating the illusion that our clip was filmed under "night vision" circumstances. To produce this "green-ness," we first apply the **Tint** video effect in Premiere Elements to the clip. We then tweak the color to achieve an acceptable night vision green.

Tint the Clip Green

1 In the text box on the **Effects and Transitions** view of the **Media** panel, type **tint**.

2 Select the **Tint** effect under the **Video Effects** in the **Image Control** category and drag and drop it onto the **nightsuspects.avi** clip on the **Video 1** track on the Timeline.

3 With the **nightsuspects.avi** clip selected on the Timeline, click the triangle next to the **Tint** effect on the **Properties** panel to reveal the effect's controls.

4 Adjust the **Black** color value by clicking the black color swatch next to **Map Black to** and entering the following values in the **Color Picker** dialog box.

   ◆ H: **150**

   ◆ S: **100**

   ◆ B: **30**

5 Click **OK** to close the **Color Picker** dialog box.

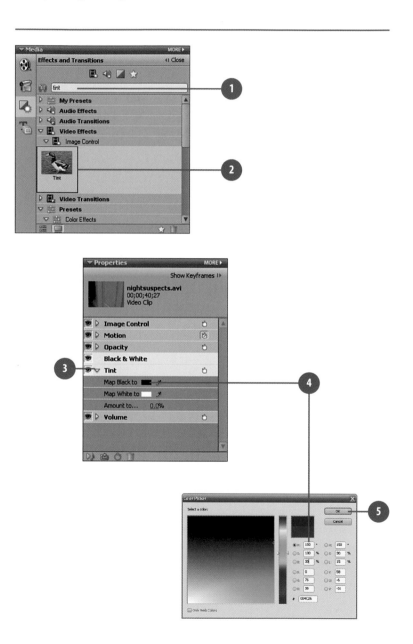

6 Adjust the **White** color value by clicking the white color swatch next to **Map White to** and entering the following values in the **Color Picker** dialog box and clicking **OK**.:

◆ H: **120**

◆ S: **80**

◆ B: **60**

7 Click **OK** to close the **Color Picker** dialog box.

8 Back on the **Properties** panel, set the **Amount to tint** to **100%**.

13

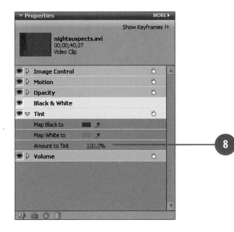

Adding Noise to Simulate the Graininess of Night Vision ▶

Because of the low-to-no light available at night (and the need for night vision technology), the images in the night vision "scope" are typically grainy. To simulate this graininess, we'll apply the **Noise** effect in Premiere Elements and adjust it slightly so that we have just the right amount of graininess in our clip.

A Noise in the Night

1 In the text box on the **Effects and Transitions** view on the **Media** panel, type **noise**.

> **NOTE** *The **Noise** effect appears in the **Stylize** folder in the **Video Effects** section of the **Effects and Transitions** panel. (You may need to scroll down to find it.)*

2 Drag and drop the **Noise** effect onto the **nightsuspects.avi** clip on the **Video 1** track on the Timeline.

3 With the **nightsuspects.avi** clip selected on the Timeline, click the triangle next to the **Noise** effect on the **Properties** panel to reveal the effect's controls.

4 Adjust the **Noise** level by entering **15%** as the **Amount of Noise**.

> **NOTE** *Leave the **Noise Type** and **Clipping** check boxes as is.*

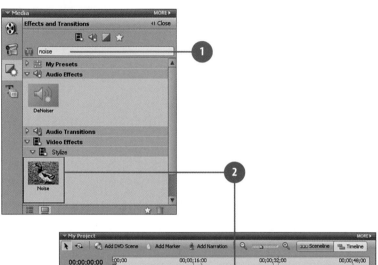

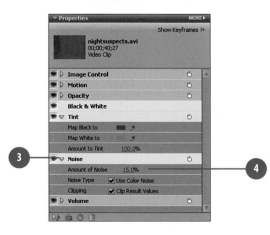

Adding Darkness to the "Nightime" Clip

To make the clip look truly like it is happening in the dark of night we need to darken it. With a simple adjustment to the **Opacity** setting for the clip, we can bring any clip, even one shot in the bright summer sunshine, into near total darkness— a darkness penetrated only by night vision goggles!

Adjust Opacity to Bring on the Night

1 Select the **nightsuspects.avi** clip on the **Video 1** track.

2 On the **Properties** panel for the clip, click the triangle next to **Opacity** to reveal the effect's controls.

3 Adjust the clip's **Opacity** to **80%**.

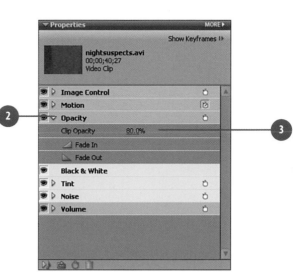

> ### Did You Know?
>
> **More "Noise" means less noise.**
> When you use this technique on your own clips, remember that things are just quieter at night. After you've darkened a clip to make it more like night, you may need to also dampen the noise level of the clip. To do so, simply select the clip, and in the **Properties** panel go to the **Volume** setting. Click the **triangle** to display the controls, then drag your mouse across the **Clip Volume** number to soften the volume. If you do this while the clip is playing, you'll get real-time feedback on the clip's volume while you adjust it.

If you look in the **Monitor** now and either click **Play** or use the **CTI** to scrub around, you'll see that the "ordinary" video image is now convincingly "night vision-ish." *Exactly what kind of craziness goes on under the cover of night...?*

Adding a Overlay to Simulate Night Vision Goggles

For this task, we'll use the Titler to create a simple binocular-like shape using two identical, overlapping circles. We'll add a couple of special effects to these circles a bit later in this chapter to bring out their "goggleness" and add to the realism of this effect. The purpose of this cutout shape is to create an opening as if your audience had the POV (movie-speak for "point of view,") of someone wearing night vision goggles usually worn by special forces personnel.

Add the First Cutout "Goggle" Shape

1. Click the **Timeline** button on the **My Project** panel to switch to **Timeline** view, if necessary. We need the **Timeline** view because we are working with two tracks.

2. Press the **HOME** key on your keyboard to return the **CTI** to the start of the tracks.

3. Click the **Add Text** button on the **Monitor** panel.

4. Click the **Selection Tool** (the arrow).

5. Click on the **Add Text** text box to select it and press the **DELETE** key on your keyboard to delete this text.

6. We won't be using the Titler to add text, but rather to add an object to the screen, so click on the **Ellipse Tool.**

7. Drag a circle on the **Monitor** panel so that it fills the upper left quadrant while staying within the **Safe Title Margin**, as shown in the illustration.

   TIMESAVER *Press the **SHIFT** key on your keyboard and you'll draw a perfect circle.*

8. Click the **Color Properties** button.

9. In the **Color Properties** dialog box, set the following **RGB** values:

   ◆ **R: 255**

   ◆ **G: 255**

   ◆ **B: 255**

10. Click **OK**.

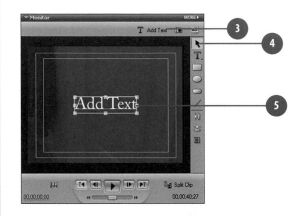

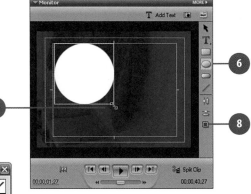

Add the Second Cutout "Goggle" Shape

1 With the circle you just created still selected, press **CTRL-C** to copy it, and then **CTRL-V** to paste the copy.

2 Drag the new copy of the circle to the right across the screen until the two circles are just overlapping, as shown.

3 Click the **Selection Tool**.

4 Hold down the **Shift** key on your keyboard and click both circles to select them.

5 We'll now center our goggles on the screen. First, click the **Vertical Center** button.

6 Now click the **Horizontal Center** button.

7 Finally, we want the goggles to appear for the full length of the movie, so back on the Timeline, grab the tail end of the **Title 01** clip (the goggles) on the **Video 2** track and drag it to the right until it lines up with the **nightvisitors.avi** clip in the **Video 1** track.

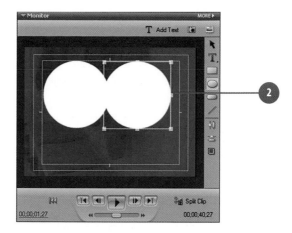

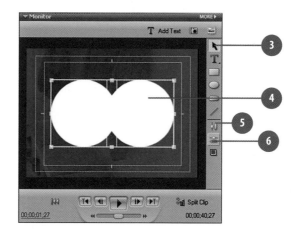

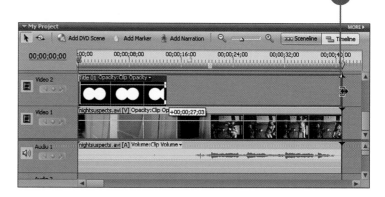

13

Adding Motion to the "Goggles" to Simulate a Searching Movement

By applying a motion effect to our "goggles," we can easily—and quite convincingly—create the further illusion of someone (or something) searching through the darkness of the night using night vision technology. We'll apply a simple tracking technique using the basic key frame functionality of Premiere Elements to move the goggles view around the clip, as if the "watcher" was concentrating on finding a particular person or studying the action.

Searching in the Night with a Motion Effect

1 Select the **Title 01** clip in the **Video 2** track on the Timeline so it is active in the **Monitor** panel.

2 In the **Properties** panel for the **Title 01** clip, click the **triangle** next to Opacity to reveal the effect's controls.

3 Set the **Opacity** to **35%**. This will allow us to see what's beneath the goggles as we move them about.

4 Click the **Show Keyframes** button to reveal the keyframes area, and adjust the **Properties** panel as needed for a better view of this area.

5 Turn on key frame animation for the **Title 01** clip by first clicking on the **triangle** next to **Motion** to reveal the effect's controls.

6 Then, click the **Toggle animation** button to enable motion effects.

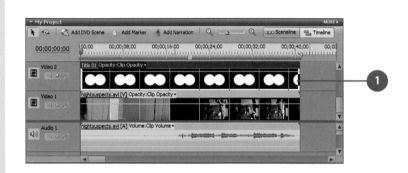

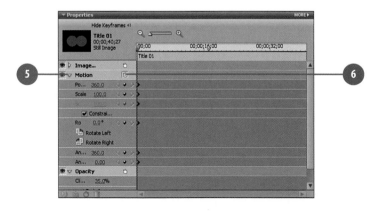

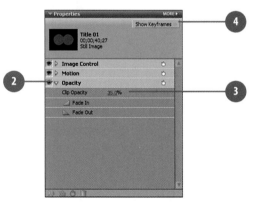

Creating the Motion

  If Safe Margins aren't visible, turn them on now by clicking the **MORE** button on the Monitor panel and selecting **Safe Margins**.

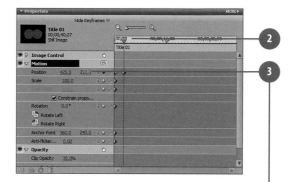

2 Using the **CTI** on the **Timeline**, advance the clip three seconds to **00;00;03;00**.

3 Reposition the goggles by clicking on them in the **Monitor** panel and moving them, or by typing these coordinates as the new **Position** under **Motion**:

   ◆ **Position: 425 210**

   TIMESAVER *Each time you move the goggles, Premiere Elements adds a new keyframe for you to mark the position that moment in time.*

4 Advance the clip to the eleven second mark: **00;00;11;00**.

5 Reposition the goggles again by clicking on them in the **Monitor** panel and moving them, or by entering these new coordinates under **Motion**:

   ◆ **Position: 330 175**

6 Advance the clip to the 25 second mark (**00;00;25;00**).

7 Reposition the goggles one last time to:

   ◆ **Position: 350 250**.

8 When you are done, reset the **Opacity** for the **Goggles** clip back to **100%**.

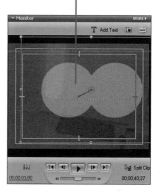

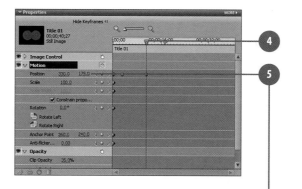

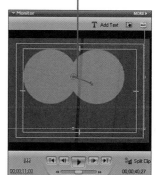

Adding Blurriness to the "Goggles" for Additional Realism

Well, you've created your night vision goggles, and you've got them successfully tracking your suspect. But there's still a problem. The "goggles" as we have them right now have very sharp, unrealistic looking edges. They look exactly like what they are: two overlapping circles. To help achieve a more realistic and subtle look, we only need to blur these sharp edges. This will make the goggles appear to be slightly out of focus, a convention your audience expects that will help "trick" them into believing this effect, and thereby enjoying your clip.

Add the Gaussian Blur Effect to Remove the Sharp Edges of the "Goggles"

1. Switch to the **Effects and Transitions** view in the **Media** panel by clicking the **Effects and Transitions** button.

2. In the text box in the **Effects and Transitions** view, type **gaussian**.

3. Drag and drop the **Gaussian Blur** effect from the **Blur & Sharpen** folder in the **Video Effects** section onto the **Title 01** clip on the **Video 2** track on the **Timeline**.

4. With the **Title 01** clip selected, go to the **Properties** panel and click on the **triangle** next to the **Gaussian Blur** effect to reveal the effect's controls.

5. Set the **Blurriness** to **50%**.

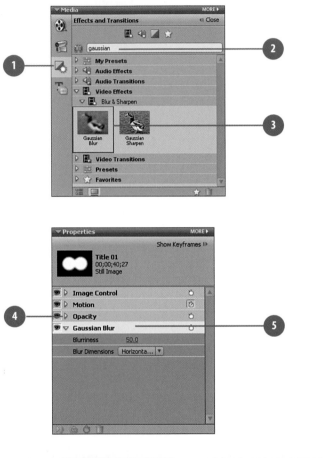

Before

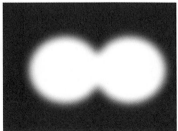

After

Turning the Little White Circles into True Goggles

Now that the "goggles" are in place, you're tracking your "subject" successfully, and the goggle lens are sufficiently blurred, it's time to turn your two, white, intersecting circles into actual goggles, while at the same time hiding everything but what the goggles "see." Fortunately, this is easily achieved by applying a **Track Matte Key** effect to the **nightsuspects.avi** video clip on the **Video 1** track and pointing the Track Matte at the **Title 01** clip in the **Video 2** track.

Apply the Track Matte Effect

1 In the text box on the **Effects and Transitions** panel, type **track**.

2 Drag and drop the **Track Matte Key** effect from the Keying category of Video Effects onto the **nightsuspects.avi** clip on the **Video 1** track on the **Timeline**.

3 With the **nightsuspects.avi** clip selected, access the **Properties** panel and click on the **triangle** next to the **Track Matte Key** effect to reveal the effect's controls.

Did You Know?

You can track a matte.
One of the purposes of the Track Matte is to create this "peephole" effect to show another track through it. Typically, it's used to superimpose one image over another, such as a bride and groom in a heart shape, superimposed on a clip of the chapel. It can be used to show the state champion (soccer or spelling) "super'ed" within a star shape. Here, we are using the technique a little differently. We don't want another clip showing through; we just want to use the **Track Matte Key** to hide most of our nighttime track and use the key as the point of view (POV) for our audience.

Point the Track Matte at the Video 2 Track to Activate the Night Vision Goggles

 From the **Matte** drop down, select **Video 2**.

> **IMPORTANT** *Leave the other* **Track Matte Key** *options as is.*

2 Note that in the **Monitor** panel, our night vision goggles are working! They've gone from opaque white discs to realistic night vision goggles with a click of the mouse.

Did You Know?

UniqueTracks is a great source for original, royalty-free music. The music for this project, **bond.mp3**, is provided by the folks at UniqueTracks. They have hundreds of music clips available in a variety of formats that you can download or order on CD. These are high-quality, multi-track clips in a styles that include Filmscapes, Spies, Cafe Metro, Cafe UK, The Martini Sessions, and more. The UniqueTracks website is a place to explore and learn about different musical styles. They have a newsletter about music, downloadable software, and links to other interesting sites. All of which make a visit to **www.uniquetracks.com** well worth the time.

UNIQUETRACKS

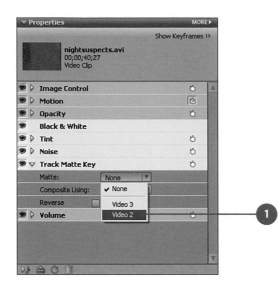

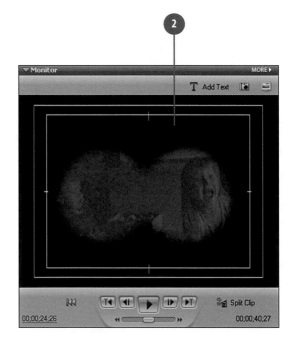

Adding Mysterious Music "Under"

By adding just the right music to your night vision scene, you can take a scene from technically interesting to tensely frightening, or at least "tensely interesting." When you add music to a scene so that it plays somewhat below the other elements in the soundtrack – the sound effects (footsteps, floor creaks, door hinge squeaks), dialog, and other incidental sounds (radio music, car horns from the street)—it is known in the film industry as placing the music "under" the other audio elements in the soundtrack. We'll be doing that here: placing the music "under" enough so as not to overpower the scene, but loud enough so that it's effect can be felt by the audience. On the DVD that accompanies this book, we've provided you with the perfect track, **bond.mp3**, courtesy of the folks at **uniquetracks.com**.

Add the Right Music for a Chilling Undercurrent

1. Click the **Get Media from** button on the **Media** panel to access the **Get Media from** view, if it's not already active.

2. Click **DVD, Digital Camera, Mobile Phone, Hard Drive Camcorder, Card Reader**.

3. When the **Media Downloader** displays, click the **Advanced Dialog** button and select the **bond.mp3** clip.

4. Click the **Get Media** button. Premiere Elements copies the **bond.mp3** clip from the DVD onto your hard drive and adds it to the Available Media list for this project.

5. Drag on drop the **bond.mp3** clip on the **Media** panel onto the Timeline in the **Audio 2** track.

6. Position the **bond.mp3** music clip on the audio track so it starts at the very beginning of the project, directly in line with the start of the **nightsuspects.avi** clip on the **Video 1** track.

7. The **bond.mp3** clip is one minute long. We only want to use the last 17 seconds. So, move the **CTI** to the 43 second point, or **00;00;43;00**. (60 seconds minus 17 seconds is 43 seconds.).

8. Grab the **front** (head) of the **bond.mp3** clip and drag it back until it exactly lines up with the **CTI** at **00;00;43;00**.

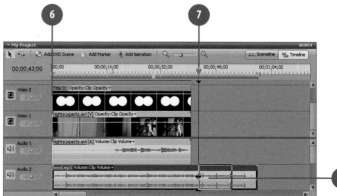

Making Adjustments, Rendering, and Exporting

Press the **Spacebar** on your keyboard or click the **Play** button on the **Monitor** panel to test your project and see that everything is working as expected. Remember, all of your clips are still in preview mode. If you want a better idea of how the whole thing will look when finished, press **ENTER** on your keyboard to render the project first. Make any final tweaks, as needed—for example, you might want to fade out both the goggles and the nightsuspects clips—and you'll be ready to export your project to a movie file.

Finishing the Project

1. After you have played back your clip and made the necessary adjustments, press the **ENTER** key on your keyboard to render your project.

2. Press **CTRL-S** to save your project (or you can select **File, Save** from the menu).

3. Finally, export your work as an AVI file. To export the clip, select **File, Export, Movie**.

   TIP *You can optionally bring this clip into a larger project, show it on your computer, upload it to an Internet video sharing site, or burn it to a DVD.*

As the project renders, Premiere Elements provides you with status information, including estimated time to complete and a status bar.

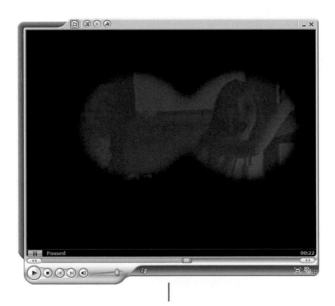

The finished movie, running in Windows Media Player.

The Hidden Identity Effect

MEDIA:
undercoverbaby.avi

14

COMPLEXITY:	Simple	Moderate	Complex
SKILL LEVEL:	Novice	Intermediate	**Advanced**
MATERIALS:	**None**	Some Props	Greenscreen

What You'll Do

Load the Video Clip

Add the Clip to the Timeline—Twice

Create a "Hider" Object to Hide the Face

Apply a Blur Effect to the Image

Synchronize the Hider Object to the Action

Apply the Mosaic Effect to the Second Clip

Apply the Track Matte Effect to the Second Clip

Make Adjustments, Render, and Export

Introduction

The Hidden Identity Effect is one of everyone's favorite effects simply because there are so many different ways that it can be used, and because it is one of those universally-recognizable effects. It's an effect that has been burned into our collective consciousness due to its use on such shows as *60 Minutes*, *Nightline*, and especially *COPS*. The effect has obvious comical applications, such as having parents and children comment on each other with their identities kept well "hidden" for use in birthday, graduation, or wedding videos; and for use with friends, relatives, and coworkers commenting "anonymously" at special occasions—such as promotions, award ceremonies, and retirement dinners.

While in this chapter we are applying the effect to a face—the most well-known use of this effect—you can use the effect to hide a poster on a wall, a license plate on a car, a hand gesture in crowd, a logo on a tee shirt, or a baby's diaperless bottom that, without this effect, might have left a great clip unusable. Now, you can simply "pixelize the problem" and save the clip!

When you are ready to use this effect on your own clip, the clip you use should follow the conventions of the "hidden identity" clip as much as possible for best effect: someone sitting in a chair, in their living room or dining room, talking directly to the camera or to an unseen person just off camera. Of course, any shot of any kind of action can also be used and have the hidden identity effect applied successfully to it.

Loading the Video Clip

This project uses just a single clip, **undercoverbaby.avi**, to create the effect. However, you will be using the clip twice, once as the base clip and once as the "pixelated" or blurred clip. For this task, we are bringing the video clip into Premiere Elements so that we can begin working on it.

Add the Video Clip to the Project

1 Start Premiere Elements and create a new project called **hiddenid**.

2 Click the **Get Media from** button on the **Media** panel to access the **Get Media from** view, if it's not already active.

3 Select **DVD, Digital Camera, Mobile Phone, Hard Drive Camcorder, Card Reader**.

4 When the **Media Downloader** displays, click the **Advanced Dialog** button to switch to Advanced mode.

5 Select the **undercoverbaby.avi** clip.

6 Click the **Get Media** button. Premiere Elements copies the **undercoverbaby.avi** clip from the DVD onto your hard drive and adds it to the Available Media for this project.

A sample view of the **Media Downloader** showing some of the clips on the DVD.

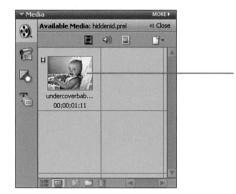

The **undercover.avi** clip, added to the

Adding the Clip to the Timeline—Twice

The clip for which you will be creating the "blurred features" in is actually used twice. This is because you are really blurring everything in the clip and essentially "poking a hole" through the good clip where you want the blur to occur, letting the underlying blurry clip show through. Therefore, you need to drop the clip on to the Timeline twice. If you are applying this effect to a clip already on the Timeline, you'll need to cut the clip where this effect is to take place, make a copy, and place the copy on the track directly above the original clip.

Add Your Clip

1 For this project, we'll need to be in **Timeline** view. So, if the **My Project** panel is in **Sceneline** view, click the **Timeline** button to switch.

2 Select the **undercoverbaby.avi** clip from the **Media** panel and drag and drop it onto the Timeline onto the **Video 1** track.

3 **Drag** a *second copy* of **undercoverbaby.avi** from the **Media** panel onto the **Video 2** track in the Timeline.

4 Since we have two clips that are identical, we'll change the display style for the **Video 2** track to help us keep track of which clip is which. To do so, click on the **Set Video Track Display Style** button for the **Video 2** track until there are no images displayed on the track, as shown in the illustration.

IMPORTANT *Be sure to line up each clip so that the head of the clip is at the front of the track, as shown in the illustration.*

Did You Know?

You have four video track display options.

 Use the **Set Video Track Display Style** button to change how video clips look on a given track. Clips can display on a track in one of four ways. First, a clip can display as a series of frames that run the full length of the clip to give you a good indication as to the contents of the clip. Second, a clip can display with just a single frame at the head and another at the tail of the clip. Third, a clip can display with just a single video frame at the start (head) of the clip. And finally, a clip can display with no frames at all.

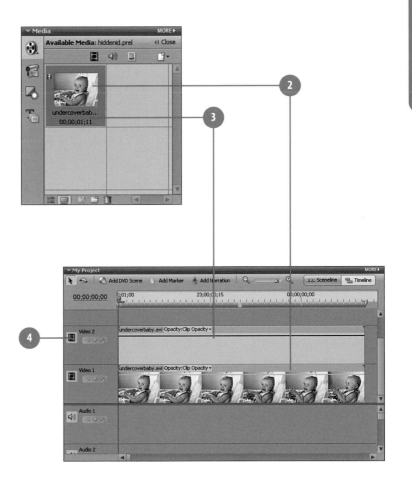

Creating a "Hider" Object to Hide the Face

Now that your two clips are set in place, we'll create the initial object that will be used to blur, or hide, the identity of the baby. Once you've mastered this technique, you can use it to hide anyone or any object. We'll be using the Titler to create this object, as the Titler enables you to create not just text, but geometric objects as well. Since a circle (actually, an ellipse) naturally matches the shape of a face, we'll be using that. In future projects, use a shape that matches the object you're looking to disguise. In other words, if the object more closely resembles a square or rectangle, then use one of those shapes instead.

Hide the Face

1 Click the **Add Text** button (shown below) at the top of the **Monitor** panel to begin to add a title for the news background.

TIP *Safe margins should automatically appear. If they don't, you can turn them on yourself by clicking on the **MORE** button in the upper right corner of the **Monitor** panel. Then, click **Safe Title Margin**.*

2 On the **Monitor** panel, click the **Selection Tool**.

3 Click on the **Add Text** text box to select it.

4 Press the **DELETE** key on your keyboard to delete this text. We won't be using the Titler to add text, but rather to add an object to the screen (next).

5 Select the **Ellipse Tool** from the toolbar.

6 Drag an ellipse in the general area of the baby's face, so we can keep her identity secret.

TIP *You want to err on the side of making this ellipse a little too big, rather than too small. We'll be applying a blur to the object a bit later. The blurred edges will cause the overall size of the object to shrink a bit.*

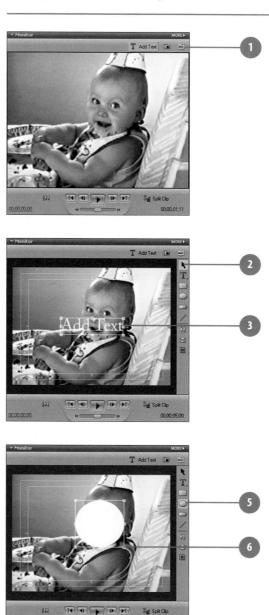

7 With the ellipse selected, click the **Color Properties** button.

8 Make sure that the ellipse is perfectly white. To ensure that it is, each of the **Red, Green, and Blue** (**RGB**) settings must be at 255. Adjust as necessary:

◆ R: **255**

◆ G: **255**

◆ B: **255**

9 Click **OK**.

10 Click anywhere on the Timeline to return to **Edit** mode and the **Edit** workspace.

11 If necessary, press the **BACKSLASH** (\) key on your keyboard to view the full project.

12 Resize the **Title 01** clip by grabbing the tail end of the clip and pulling it back so that it lines up with the two **undercoverbaby.avi** clips.

Did You Know?

Let the arrows be your guide.
If you have **Snap** turned on (**Timeline, Snap**), when you stretch the **Hider** clip to match the other two clips in the Timeline, Premiere Elements will show you that you've reached the right spot by using black arrows as indicators (as shown in the illustration). It's a useful visual clue to let you know that your clip is exactly the right length.

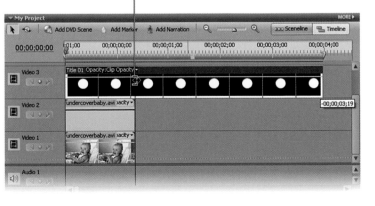

14

Applying a Blur Effect to the Image

By applying a subtle blurring effect to our clip, we can help achieve the overall blurred look that we're going for, and avoid hard edges in our final production. This step is very straight-forward and involves applying the **Gaussian Blur** video effect and tweaking the settings a bit.

Apply a Blur

1. Click the **Effects and Transitions** button on the **Media** panel to switch to the **Effects and Transitions** view, if it's not already displaying.

2. Type **blur** in the **text box** on the **Effects and Transitions** panel.

3. Select the **Gaussian Blur** and drag it onto the **Title 01** clip on **Video 2** track on the **Timeline**.

4. Go to the **Properties** panel for the Title 02 clip and click on the **triangle** next to **Gaussian Blur** to view the controls.

5. Adjust the **Gaussian Blur** this way:

   ◆ Increase the **Bluriness** amount to **40.0**.

   ◆ Leave the **Blur Dimensions** as is (Horizontal and Vertical).

Did You Know?

Track mattes work best in black and white.
This effect uses the **Track Matte** video effect as one of the elements that make it work. When you use track mattes for other projects, remember that you want to be sure that you are always using pure black (R: 0, G: 0, B: 0) and pure white (R: 255. G: 255, B: 255). Shades of gray will cause you shades of problems.

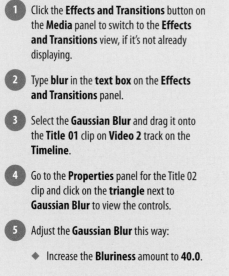

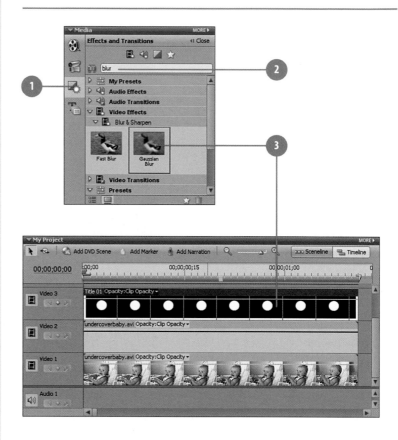

Synchronizing the Hider Object to the Action

Now we need to adjust the movement of the "hider" object so that it synchronizes with the movement of the baby's face. To do so, we use keyframes. To enable the ellipse to track correctly, we'll adjust its location over a series of keyframes to be sure that it moves on exactly the same track of motion as the object that it is supposed to be hiding. We only need to mark a small set of keyframes and Premiere Elements will do all of the work of "tweening," that is, filling in the points in between the keyframes that we set.

Enable Motion (Animation) for the Ellipse

1 Select the **Title 01** clip on the **Video 3** track on the **Timeline**, if it's not already selected.

2 Go to the **Properties** panel and click on the **triangle** next to **Motion** to view the controls.

3 Click **Show Keyframes** and expand this panel.

4 Click the **Toggle animation** button to enable motion effects.

Did You Know?

There are individual Toggle animation buttons for all of the Motion settings. Premiere Elements enables you to make large and small adjustments as needed to every possible motion-related setting. These include Position, Scale, Scale Width, Rotation, and Anchor Point. You can even control the **Anti-Flicker** setting frame-by-frame should you need to.

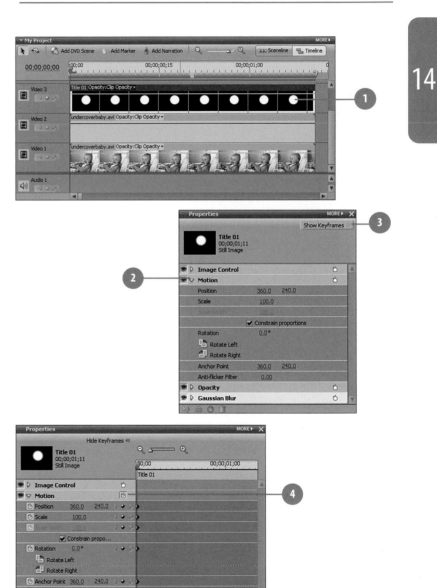

Setup the Motion Effect and Set the Initial Keyframes

1 Scrub the **CTI** to the end of the clip (**00;00;01;10**).

> **TIMESAVER** *Press the* ***Page Down*** *key on your keyboard to jump to the end of the clip. Then use the right-arrow and left-arrow keys on your keyboard to move back and forth through the clip, a frame at a time.*

2 Click directly on the clip in the **Monitor** panel. This will enable you to move the matte in the **Monitor** panel with your mouse, rather than have to enter numbers in the motion control area.

3 **Drag** the **Title 01** clip with your mouse as needed to better cover the baby's face:

◆ The new position should be at or near **345.0 215.0**.

> **TIMESAVER** *Premiere Elements automatically inserts a keyframe for Position at this point, because you made a change to the location of the object.*

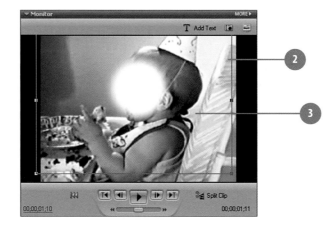

Insert Additional Keyframes

1 Move the **CTI** to the approximate center point of the clip.

2 Drag the **Title 01** clip again until it again covers the baby's face.

3 Move the **CTI** to a point halfway between the keyframe at the start of the clip and the keyframe at the middle of the clip.

4 Move the **Title 01** clip again, as needed.

5 Continue adding a few more keyframes in this way until most of the movement of the baby's head has been covered.

Did You Know?

You can use the Opacity control to keep an eye on things. You can set the **Opacity** for the hider clip (**Title 01**) down to around 70 or 80% or so while you're working. This can help you more precisely locate the **Hider** object for situations where there are, for example, multiple people walking down the street together or seated together on a couch and you need to see the action a little more clearly. Remember to reset **Opacity** back to 100% when you have finished setting all of your keyframes.

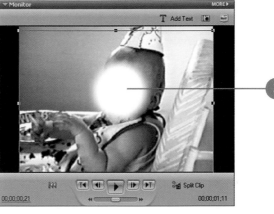

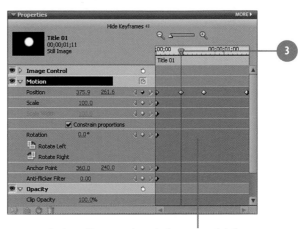

Continue adding more and more keyframes, as needed, always dividing the distance between two keyframes in half. Watch the location of the **Title 01** clip in the **Monitor** panel until you're confident that you have successfully tracked all of the baby's motion.

Applying the Mosaic Effect to the Second Clip

With the "hider" now tracking perfectly, we're ready to finish this effect. We next need to apply the **Mosaic** video effect to the copy of the clip to completely "pixelate" the image there, making unrecognizable anything on that clip. Since all we really need on that clip to be unrecognizable is the area where the ellipse is, we'll follow this up (in the next step) with the **Track Matte** effect to hide everything in the clip except where the ellipse is.

Apply the Mosaic Video Effect

1 Find the **Mosaic** effect in the list of effects by typing **mosaic** in the **text box** on the **Effects and Transitions** panel.

> **TIP** *If the Media panel is not in the Effects and Transitions view, click the Effects and Transitions button to switch to that view.*

2 Select the **Mosaic** video effect and drag it onto the clip in the **Video 2** track on the Timeline.

3 For the pixelization of the face to look right, we'll need fairly small (but not too small) blocks, or tiles. To adjust the size of the blocks, go to the **Properties** panel and make the following adjustments:

- ◆ **Horizontal Blocks: 25**

- ◆ **Vertical Blocks: 25**

- ◆ **Sharp Colors:** Leave unchecked

> **TIP** *The size of these blocks is a bit of a personal preference. Make these blocks a bit larger or a bit smaller as you prefer. Keep in mind that too large of a block will loose all facial definition, and too small of a block will end up revealing the identity that's supposed to be hidden.*

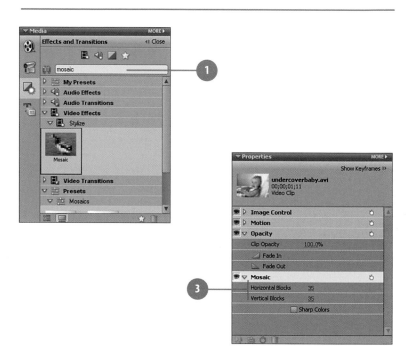

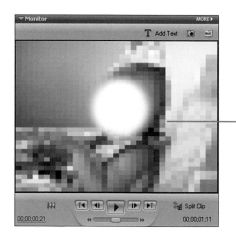

The **undercoverbaby.avi** clip (the copy) on the **Video 2** track is now fully pixelated. However, the identity of the baby in the video clip, while hidden by the circular shape, is not pixelated the way we want it. We need to do a quick switch so that the white in the circle is replaced with pixels.

Applying the Track Matte Effect to the Second Clip

We have our "hider" in place and tracking well with the baby's face. We've applied our **Mosaic** effect to the second **undercoverbaby.avi** clip in the **Video 2** track. Now we need to hide everything in the **Video 2** track *except* that small portion that we want to show through the ellipse which will thoroughly disguise the baby's face. To do that, we will apply the **Track Matte** effect to the clip in the **Video 2** track and select the **Video 3** track as the "target."

Apply the Track Matte Effect

1 Type **track** in the **text box** on the **Effect and Transition** panel to find the **Track Matte** effect in the list of effects.

2 Select the **Track Matte** effect and drag it onto the **undercoverbaby.avi** clip in the **Video 2** track on the **Timeline**.

3 In the **Properties** panel for the **undercoverbaby.avi** clip on the **Video 2** track, click the **triangle** next to **Track Matte Key** to reveal the effect's controls.

4 Set up the **Track Matte Key**:

◆ **Matte**: Video 3

◆ **Composite Using**: Matte Alpha

◆ **Reverse**: Leave unchecked

Did You Know?

You can browse through the list of effects to find the effect you're looking for. You could have navigated to this effect by selecting the **triangle** next to **Video** Effects in the **Effects and Transitions** panel to reveal the available effects. You would then click the **Keying triangle** to see the available keys, and then select the **Track Matte Key**. To make browsing easier, change the view (**MORE**, **List View** or **Icon View**) as suits your working style.

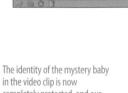

The identity of the mystery baby in the video clip is now completely protected, and our blurry effect moves perfectly with the baby as she moves.

Making Adjustments, Rendering, and Exporting

Press the **SPACEBAR** on your keyboard to run your clip and check out your effect. Now is the time to make a few small adjustments. If the hidden identity isn't hiding so well, go back and tweak the tracking path by adding a few more key frames or adjusting the location of the ellipse as needed. Are the blocks in the **Mosaic** effect too big or too small? That can be easily adjusted. And if it turns out you created your "hider" object a little too big or too small as well, just double-click on the **Title 01** clip in the Timeline to bring up the Titler workspace. Adjust the size of the object again in the Titler as needed.

Finishing the Project

1 After you have played back your clip and made the necessary adjustments, press the **ENTER** key on your keyboard to render your project.

2 Press **CTRL-S** to save your project (or you can select **File, Save** from the menu).

3 Finally, export your work as an AVI file. To export the clip, select **File, Export, Movie**.

> **TIP** You can optionally bring this clip into a larger project, show it on your computer, upload it to an Internet video sharing site, or burn it to a DVD.

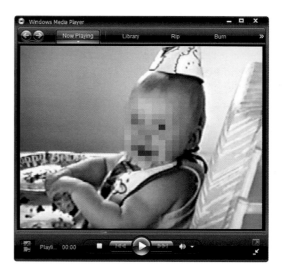

Even More Hidden Identity

Changing the Voice as Well as the Face

If the clip you're using lends itself to it, you can also try using Premiere Elements built-in voice modulator effects to alter the sound of the person's voice a bit. This will make it exceeding difficult to identify the person in the clip, if that's the goal. From the **Effects and Transitions** palette, go to the **Audio Effects** selections and drag the **PitchShifter** effect to the audio track for the clip. From the **Properties** panel, try using one of the preset effects, such as A quint up, A quint down, Cartoon Mouse, or Sore throat. Or use the **Pitch Shifter** knobs to make your own custom changes to the voice.

The Bleeping #$%&! Effect

MEDIA:

airhorn.wav
airwrench.wav
bleeping.avi
carhorn.wav
jalopyhorn.wav

15

COMPLEXITY:	Simple	Moderate	Complex
SKILL LEVEL:	Novice	Intermediate	Advanced
MATERIALS:	None	Some Props	Greenscreen

What You'll Do

Add the Video Clip to the Timeline

Find and Mark "Offensive Moments"

Remove the Audio at Each "Offensive Moment"

Import the Sound Effect Files

Acquire and Use Sounds

Add Sound Effects to the Audio 2 Track

Make Adjustments, Render, and Export

Introduction

We've all seen, or more accurately heard, that slip of the tongue, that inadvertent expletive spoken in a moment of embarrassment, anger, or even playfulness that suddenly and instantly makes a great family clip a bit "X-rated." Now what? You can delete the scene, which works if there's nothing else happening at that moment that was worth keeping. But what if there was? What if the funniest moment or the most "memory worthy" moment happened just as someone was reacting to pain or embarrassment (or, yes, joy) with a "bad" word? Well, this is very fixable, thanks to the sound capabilities of Premiere Pro and the fascinating world of sound effects.

Have you seen such shows as the Discovery® Channel's "Monster Garage" or "American Chopper?" Did you notice that whenever Senior at Orange County Choppers decides to vent at Junior, his string of curses always seems to coincide exactly with the sound of an pneumatic air wrench whirring or the sound of metal being cut, drilled, or welded? That's no coincidence, of course. The offending words have been dropped out of the soundtrack, and these other sounds from around the shop have been dropped in to cover up Senior's colorful language.

Now you can do this, too. This effect can be used to salvage clips that might otherwise be unusable (or at least in cases where the audio is unusable). It can also be used on any clip to add a comical effect to anyone's dialog, whether or not they are actually cursing a blue streak. It's an easy effect that's fun to do, and which produces an entertaining result.

Adding the Video Clip to the Timeline

The first step is to go and grab the video clip that you will be using for "bleeping out." We've provided you with a practice video clip, called **bleeping.avi.** It's on the DVD supplied with this book. To avoid harming sensitive ears, no actual expletives were uttered in the making of this clip. If you are familiar with the movie (and book) *A Christmas Story*, based on the early years of writer and raconteur Jean Shepherd, then you may be also familiar with the *frizzledazzlefriggle* style of "cursing" that you'll find on this clip.

Add the Supplied Video Clip to the Timeline

1. Start Premiere Elements and create a new project called **bleepeffect**.

2. Click the **Get Media from** button on the **Media** panel to access the **Get Media from** view, if it's not already active.

3. Select **DVD, Digital Camera, Mobile Phone, Hard Drive Camcorder, Card Reader**.

4. When the **Media Downloader** displays, click the **Advanced Dialog** button to switch to Advanced mode.

5. Select the **bleeping.avi** clip.

6. Click the **Get Media** button. Premiere Elements copies the clip from the DVD onto your hard drive and adds them to the Available Media list for this project.

7. Click the **bleeping.avi** clip on the **Media** panel and drag and drop it onto the **My Project Timeline** at the very beginning of the **Video 1** track (or onto the first scene box, if you're in **Sceneline** view).

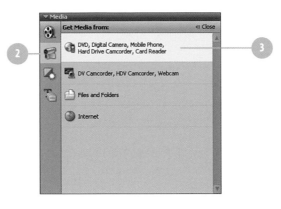

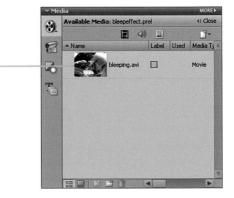

> ### Did You Know?
>
> ***You can drag and drop clips into Premiere Elements right from Windows Explorer.***
> You don't need to use the tools that Premiere Elements provides for bringing clips into a project from your computer. You can alternatively drag and drop any supported media (including entire folders of media) directly from Windows into Premiere Elements. Use whichever system best suits your working style.

Finding and Marking "Offensive Moments"

On this step, you'll first listen to the clip once through to find the sections of the video where "bad things happen." Next, you play it again with your finger poised over the **Spacebar** on your keyboard. As you reach each "bad place," you'll hit the **Spacebar**, place a marker, and hit the **Spacebar** again to move on. The marker will let you jump to each bad place to take remedial action in the next step.

Go on the Offense

1. We need the **My Project** panel to be in **Timeline** view, if it isn't already. To switch to **Timeline** view, click the **Timeline** button in the upper right of the **My Project** panel.

2. Press the **Spacebar** and listen carefully.

3. The first "bleepable" moment occurs at **00;00;08;25** (eight seconds, 25 frames in). Press the **Spacebar** to pause here.

4. Click the **Add Marker** button to place a marker at this spot.

5. Press the **Spacebar** again to continue.

6. The next "bleepable" moment occurs at **00;00;13;25** (thirteen seconds and 25 frames in). Press the **Spacebar** to pause here.

7. Click the **Add Marker** button again to place another marker at this spot.

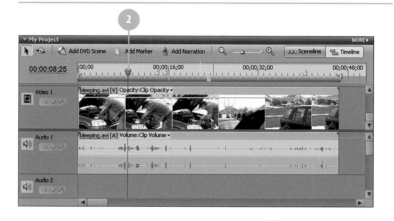

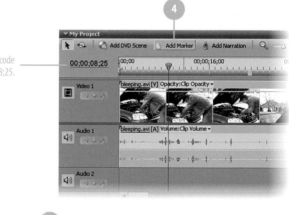

Notice the timecode at 00;00;08;25.

Did You Know?

You can use the arrow keys on your keyboard for frame-by-frame accuracy. You can "scrub" to the sound your looking for by dragging the **Current Time Indicator** (**CTI**) to the general vicinity. Then, for frame-level accuracy, use the right and left arrow keys on your keyboard to move along the Timeline, one frame at a time: 00;00;13;22, 00;00;13;23, 00;00;13;24...

15

8 Press the **Spacebar** again to continue.

9 The next "bleepable" moment occurs at **00;00;15;10** (fifteen seconds, ten fames in). Press the **Spacebar** again to pause here.

10 Click the **Add Marker** button again to place a third marker at this spot.

11 Press the **Spacebar** to continue.

12 The next "bleepable" moment occurs at **00;00;40;08** (forty seconds, 8 frames in). Press the **Spacebar** to pause here.

13 Click the **Add Marker** button again to place a fourth and final marker at this spot.

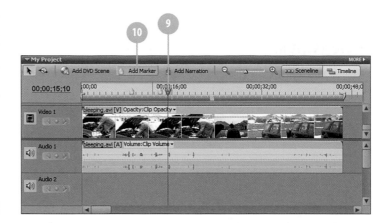

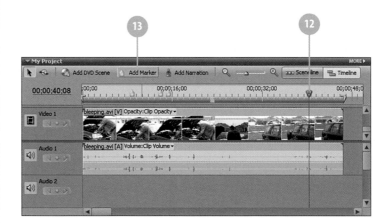

Did You Know?

You can access the marker contextual menu for additional options. The unnumbered markers you've been adding may be hard to see initially, due to the fact that they're light gray on a light gray background. Find a marker and right-click on it and you see a contextual menu that enables you to clear that individual marker or all markers; set a numbered marker, an unnumbered marker, or a DVD marker; jump to a marker: and so on. (Clicking anywhere on the **Timeline** ruler brings up the same menu, only with the **Clear Timeline Marker** option grayed out.)

You can add comments to markers. By double-clicking on a marker, you access the **Marker** dialog box. Here you can add comments, such as describing why you placed this marker. You can also add a URL link and frame information; create chapter links for use with Adobe Encore; change the duration of the marker; jump to the previous or next marker; or delete the marker.

Removing the Audio at Each "Offensive Moment"

In this task, we use keyframes and the yellow volume rubberband on the audio track in the Timeline to lower the volume where the "bad language" occurs. This is to ensure that, after we have applied the sound effects, none of the "offensive" words can accidentally be heard behind (or in video editing terms, *under*) the chosen sound effect. We have already placed markers at each of the four points in the clip where "bad words" can be found. We will now add a keyframe at the beginning and end of each word or phrase.

Lower the Sound for Each of the "Offensive Moments"

1 Each marker you placed already identifies the beginning of the audio we want to remove, so jump to the first marker by first pressing the **Home** key on your keyboard to return the **CTI** to the front (also known as the "head") of the clip.

2 Right-click in the timeruler and from the contextual menu, select **Go To Timeline Marker, Next**.

3 At the marker (at **00;00;08;25**), you can add a keyframe by clicking the **Add/Remove Keyframe** button.

> **TIP** *The clip must be selected or the **Add/Remove Keyframe** button won't work. This makes sense because without a clip selected, the keyframe won't know which clip on a track you want to mark.*

Did You Know?

Arrows are a quick way to jump to a marker.
The easiest way to move from marker to marker along the Timeline is to use the arrow keys again (remember how useful they were when originally placing the markers?). This time, however, you use them in conjunction with the **CTRL** ("control") key on your keyboard. To move to the next marker in the Timeline, press **CTRL-right** arrow. To move to the previous marker, press **CTRL-left arrow**.

You'll see the keyframe appear here at 00;00;08;25, marking the beginning of the first "bad spot."

4 Repeat the keyframe procedure again at the end of this "bleepable" phrase, by first moving the **CTI** to the end of the phrase (use your right-arrow key). The phrase ends at about **00;00;09;05**.

5 We don't want to remove the audio for the whole clip, just the single second between these two keyframes. To do this, we will need to add two more keyframes, one right next to the start keyframe and one right next to the end keyframe. Add these keyframes now.

◆ Click the **Add/Remove Keyframe** button at **00;00;09;04**.

◆ Click the **Add/Remove Keyframe** button at **00;00;08;26**.

TIMESAVER *Zoom in sufficiently to see what you're doing, otherwise you'll be looking at just a clump of keyframes on the screen.*

6 Drag the two keyframes you just added, one at a time, so that they are each down below the audio waveform at the bottom of the audio clip on the **Audio 1** track, as shown in the illustration. This will silence this portion of the clip.

7 Move to the next marker by pressing **CTRL-right arrow** on your keyboard.

TIMESAVER *You may want to zoom out while you navigate along the Timeline, then zoom back in while you add the keyframes.*

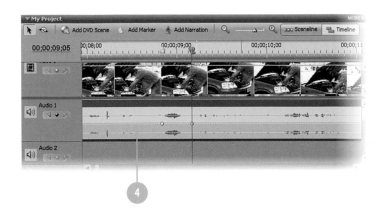

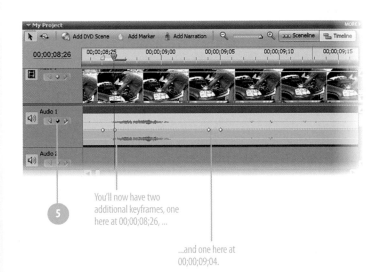

You'll now have two additional keyframes, one here at 00;00;08;26, ...

...and one here at 00;00;09;04.

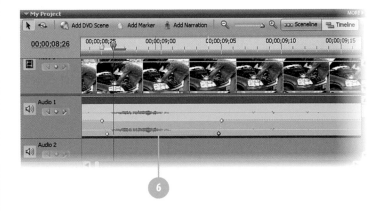

8 When you're at the marker (at **00;00;13;25**) add a keyframe by clicking the **Add/Remove Keyframe** button.

9 The next outbreak is close (00;00;15;10), so we'll encompass that one at the same time. Move to the third marker and then use the right arrow on your keyboard to move to the end of the "outrage" at **00;00;15;20**.

   ◆ Click the **Add/Remove Keyframe** button at **00;00;15;20**.

10 As before, so that we can mute these two outbursts as well, we need to add two more markers, one next to the start keyframe and one next to the end keyframe.

   ◆ Click the **Add/Remove Keyframe** button at **00;00;13;26**.

   ◆ Click the **Add/Remove Keyframe** button at **00;00;15;09**.

11 As you did for the first audio outrage, drag the two markers you just added, one at a time, to create that tell-tale dip in the yellow rubber band, as shown in the illustration. Doing so silences this part of the clip.

You now have a total of four keyframes for this outburst. Two here at 00;00;13;25 and 00;00;13;26, and...

...two here at 00;00;15;19 and 00;00;15;20.

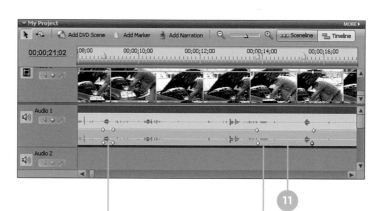

You now have two silent sections of audio in your clip, hiding the three verbal lapses. One more to go...

Did You Know?

You can Zoom in and out using your keyboard.
You no doubt already know how to zoom in and out on the Timeline using the zoom buttons and the slider (shown below). However, you might like to know that there's even an easier way to this. Simply press the "equal sign" key on your keyboard (=) to zoom in, or the "minus sign/dash" key (-) next to it to zoom back out. (The minus sign key on the numeric keypad won't work.)

15

12 Continue to the final keyframe (**CTRL-right arrow**) and add a keyframe there. Scrub to the end of this outrageous language at **00;00;40;08**).

◆ Click the **Add/Remove Keyframe** button at **00;00;40;08**.

TIMESAVER *Remember to zoom back out while you navigate along the Timeline.*

13 Move to the end of this final outbreak of swearing, at **00;00;43;09.**

◆ Click the **Add/Remove Keyframe** button at **00;00;43;09**.

14 Click the **Add/Remove Keyframe** button at **00;00;43;08** to add another keyframe.

15 Click the **Add/Remove Keyframe** button at **00;00;40;09** to add the final keyframe.

TIMESAVER *Again, zoom in as needed when working with keyframes.*

16 Finally, as you did for the previous two audio sections, drag the two keyframes you added, one at a time, to silence this part of the clip.

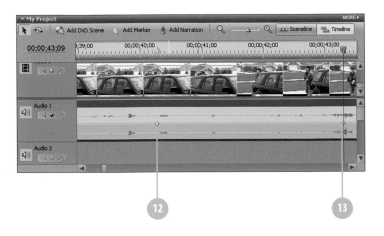

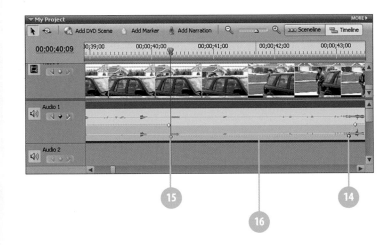

Importing the Sound Effect Files

We've supplied a number of sound effects files on the DVD that came with this book. You can use other sound effects, if you have them. There are also plenty of sound effects on the Internet, as well. You'll be "dropping and cropping" these sound files onto the Timeline where each of the expletives occur, matching the length of the sound effect (through cropping where needed) with the length of each of the "outbreaks."

Bring in the Sound FX Files

1 Click the **Get Media from** button on the **Media** panel to access the **Get Media from** view, if it's not already active.

2 Select **DVD, Digital Camera, Mobile Phone, Hard Drive Camcorder, Card Reader**.

3 When the **Media Downloader** displays, click the **Advanced Dialog** button to switch to Advanced mode.

4 Select the following clips:

- **airhorn.wav**
- **airwrench.wav**
- **carhorn.wav**
- **jalopyhorn.wav**

5 Click the **Get Media** button. Premiere Elements copies the clips from the DVD onto your hard drive and adds them to the Available Media list for this project.

The four sound effects files, now loaded in the **Media** panel. (Shown here in with the **Show Audio** button selected.)

Acquiring and Using Sounds

The addition of sounds to a project after the filming has been completed, in the phase known as "post production" (or simply "post"), is an important and often neglected part of assembling your final movie. Sound editing is a unique skill. Finding, creating, and adding sound effects is a unique skill *within* that skill that is known as "Foley" work, done by "Foley artists."

In this chapter we have used sound effects to mask sounds in the clip, but the more traditional use of sounds is to enhance a film. For example, if you filmed a conversation of two people walking along a beach, you might deliberately mic the scene to clearly capture just their conversation and as little as possible of the background sounds. Later, you would want to add in, in a controlled way, the sounds of waves and seagulls, and so on.

Skillful editors are known for the way they weave sound into a scene, especially sounds in the distance such as a church bell or a siren, of which you might not even be consciously aware.

Finding Sounds

There are a number of ways that you can gather the sounds you need for your production. The simplest way is to "film" the sounds with your camcorder at the scene. Just take a few minutes before and after you have finished taking the video footage you needed to capture additional footage for its "sound value." Premiere Elements 3 lets you bring in (capture) footage as "audio only."

As mentioned previously, if you are at the beach, capture some extra footage of the sound of the waves, children playing, dogs barking, and so on. You can use these audio clips to add in the background of your production later in your "studio" during post.

In addition to collecting these sounds, you can also create some of the sounds you need—such as a slamming door, glasses tinkling, car horns, and so on—by using your camcorder again and "filming" the sounds as they occur.

Sound Collections

Another source for sounds, besides creating them yourself, is "pre-packaged" sound effect CDs. You'll find these at most CD stores as well as online stores such as Tower Records, Amazon, and the like. They typically are inexpensive (around $10) and contain a wide variety of royalty-free clips.

You can find very good sound effects collections at your local library, as well. These tend to be theme-based, such as Halloween (horror), cartoon sounds, and the like. The sound effects in such collections might be copyrighted, so if you use them in any of your productions that are not just for personal use (other than for your own home movies, in other words), be sure to acknowledge the source.

Using Internet Sounds

Perhaps the best source for sound effects is the Internet. A quick search for "sound effects" brings up pages of sources. Among the more popular are FindSounds (**www.findsounds.com**), Partners in Rhyme (**www.partnersinrhyme.com**), and Sound Dogs (**www.sounddogs.com**). At each of these sites, you can search by category or keyword as well as listen to a sample of each sound.

If you like what you hear, download the file to your hard drive. Some of these sites offer sound effects collections on CD or DVD often with search software built in. If you like a company's product, consider buying a full set of their audio wares this way, and have it on hand without having to search the Internet. Sound Dogs represents a number of different companies who use Sound Dogs as their storefront. FindSounds is in the "public domain" game, finding sound files for you from across the Internet.

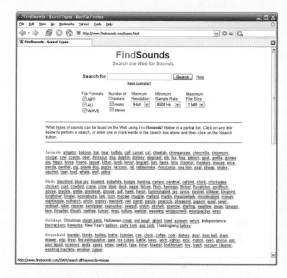

Copyrights and Permissions

Again, as with any files you use in your productions that you didn't create yourself, verify that the sounds you use are, in fact, in the public domain (which means they are not protected by copyright and essentially belong to all of us) or be sure to get permission to use from the owner/creator.

Adding Sound Effects to the Audio 2 Track

Add a Sound Effect at Each Marker

1 Return to the start of the tracks in the **My Project** panel by pressing the **Home** key on your keyboard.

2 Drag **airwrench.wav** from the **Media** panel to the **Audio 2** track and position it directly below the first "silent spot," that is, the first dip in the yellow rubberband, which starts at **00;00;08;25**.

3 Drag **jalopyhorn.wav** from the **Media** panel to the **Audio 2** track and position it directly below the second "silent spot." Notice that it doesn't quite fill the space, which would allow the "expletive deleted" to be heard (if the volume here wasn't already turned down, that is). There's a simple fix:

4 Drag **airhorn.wav** from the **Media** panel to the **Audio 2** track and position it to the right of **jalopyhorn.wav**. We now have sufficient sound effect coverage for the outburst.

It's now a matter of adding our "blooper" sounds at each of the "silent sections" that we created using the keyframes. Fortunately, these will be easy to spot and overlay with our sound effects, thanks to the obvious "dips" we created in an earlier task in the volume yellow rubberband in the audio track.

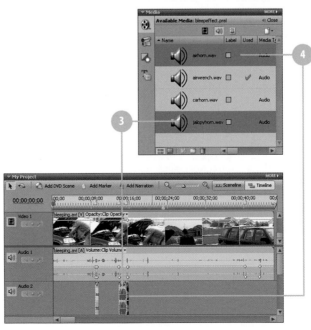

⑤ Drag **carhorn.wav** from the **Media** panel to the **Audio 2** track below the third "silent spot."

⑥ You may have noticed that this sound effect is a bit longer than the silence we created. To adjust this, select the "tail" end of the **carhorn.wav** clip on **Audio 2** track and trim the clip back by one second. (The length of the clip will show in the **Monitor** panel as **00;00;03;04**).

> **TIMESAVER** *Zoom in as needed for better control over the trim process. And, watch the pale yellow box that appears just to the right and below the clip as you begin to trim—you may need to pause slightly before trimming for this box to appear. It's showing you by how much you are trimming the clip. When you have reached one second and ten frames, or 00;00;01;10, you've trimmed enough. Release the mouse at this point.*

Did You Know?

You can use the CTI to control the focus of the zoom. When you zoom in on the Timeline, Premiere Elements will zoom in on the currently visible area only to a point. Once you loose your focus you'll find yourself having to scroll left and right to find where you were. An easy way to avoid this is to first move the **CTI** to where you want to work and then zoom in. In this case, press **CTRL-right arrow** until the **CTI** is at the final "silent space." Then, use either the shortcut key (the equals sign, =, on the keyboard) or the **Zoom In** button (the magnifying glass with the plus sign) to zoom in. Premiere Elements will continue to focus in on just that area by the **CTI**. A much better zooming experience when you're in control, isn't it? Note that you may need to tweak your view of the Timeline a bit using the left and right arrows to get it exactly the way you want it.

Making Adjustments, Rendering, and Exporting

Your audio surgery is complete! You are now ready to render. As always, save your work regularly. To preview your work, use the **Spacebar** on your keyboard or the **Play** button in the **Monitor** panel. For a truer "TV-like" experience, use the **Play Full Screen** button on the Monitor panel, or press **ALT-ENTER** on your keyboard.

Finishing the Project

1. After you have played back your clip and made the necessary adjustments, press the **ENTER** key on your keyboard to render your project.

2. Press **CTRL-S** to save your project (or you can select **File, Save** from the menu).

3. Finally, export your work as an AVI file. To export the clip, select **File, Export, Movie** and save as **bleepeffect.avi**.

    TIP *You can now bring this clip into a larger project, show it on your computer, upload it to an Internet video sharing site, or burn it to a DVD.*

The bleepeffect.avi movie clip,
playing in Windows Media player.

The Enchanted Elf Effect

MEDIA:

elf.avi
elfgarden.bmp
elfish_song.wav

16

COMPLEXITY:	Simple	Moderate	Complex
SKILL LEVEL:	Novice	Intermediate	Advanced
MATERIALS:	None	Some Props	Greenscreen

Introduction

It's a magical, mysterious world out there: Harry Potter flying on a turbo broomstick; Gandalf and Frodo going to extremes for a supernatural ring; and the children of the wardrobe sacrificing everything for Narnia. All around us there seem to be more dwarves, giants, faeries, and elves than we can shake a staff at. In this chapter, we're jumping on board the gilded bandwagon as it rolls magically past, by creating our own little magic. Here, we'll fashion out of thin air, or so it seems, an enchanting little elf ready to charm or annoy us (depending on how you feel about elves).

While we could use stage makeup, props, CGI animation, and special effects software to create this effect, who has that kind of time and money? More importantly, it's not necessary. Premiere Elements 3 gives us all of the tools we need to create this effect. The Enchanted Elf effect introduces two techniques in Premiere Elements that once you have them under your belt, you can use them for lots of different projects in different ways.

This chapter introduces you to the "shrinking" power of Premiere Elements. Using this technique, you'll be able to shrink anything—your dog, your house, your friends—and feature them as elves or fairies, or in miniature "Honey, I Shrunk the Kids" situations. Second, this chapter will introduce you to the color-changing abilities of Premiere Elements. We will change a child with normal coloring into a green elf. Again, using this technique, you can change anyone or anything—again, perhaps your dog or cat—to any color you want: orange, red, blue, purple.

This chapter also uses a technique introduced earlier in this book, the split screen. Here, we use the split screen to create a multi-dimensional background for the elf to interact with. We are only creating a single split in this project, but in your own projects you could create multiple splits to allow your character to appear to move in front of and behind objects in the background. This is a sophisticated technique that, with a little planning, is relatively easy to pull off.

What You'll Do

Add the Video Clips to the Timeline

Apply Color and Contrast Effects to the Elf Clip

Apply the Green Screen Key

Colorize the "Elf"

Troubleshoot a Greenscreen Project

Add the Foreground Clip

Crop the Foreground Clip to Create a Multi-Dimensional Environment

Shrink the "Elf"

Adjust the Elf's Starting Location

Make the Elf "Vanish"

Add Some Playful Elfish Music "Under"

Make Adjustments, Render, and Export

Adding the Video Clips to the Timeline

For this project, we have two video clips to add to the **My Project** panel. One, **elf.avi**, contains the footage of our actress that we will transform into an elf. The other, **elfgarden.bmp**, contains footage that we will use "as is" of a garden where the elf will appear. We'll arrange these two clips on the **My Project** panel's timeline one on top of the other, with the **elf.avi** clip on the **Video 2** track and the background garden clip on the **Video 1** track. Doing so will enable the background track, **elfgarden.bmp**, to show through **elf.avi** once we remove the green of the greenscreen.

Add the Background Clip to the Timeline

1. Start Premiere Elements and create a new project called **enchantedelf**.

2. Click the **Get Media from** button on the **Media** panel to access the **Get Media from** view, if it's not already active.

3. Select **DVD, Digital Camera, Mobile Phone, Hard Drive Camcorder, Card Reader**.

4. When the **Media Downloader** displays, click the **Advanced Dialog** button to switch to Advanced mode.

5. Select the following clips:

   ◆ **elfgarden.bmp**

   ◆ **elf.avi**

6. Click the **Get Media** button. Premiere Elements copies the clips from the DVD onto your hard drive and adds them to the Available Media list for this project.

7. Using your mouse, select the **elfgarden.bmp** clip on the **Media** panel and drag and drop it onto the **My Project** panel in the **Video 1** track.

   TIP *If you're in **Sceneline** view, drop it onto the first scene box. Premiere Elements will place it on the **Video 1** track.*

Add the Elf Clip to the Timeline

 If you are in **Sceneline** view in the **My Project** panel at this time, switch to **Timeline** view.

TIP *To switch to **Timeline** view, click the **Timeline** button in the right corner of the **My Project** panel:*

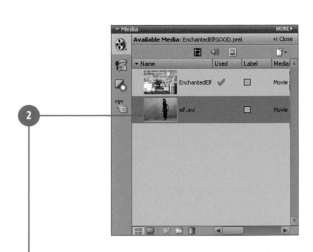

With your mouse, select the **elf.avi** clip on the **Media** panel and drag on drop it onto the **Video 2** track so that the head (front) of the clip is at the very beginning of the track, as shown in the illustration.

Did You Know?

There are scenes unseen.
We need to switch to **Timeline** view at this point in the project because we are working with multiple clips, and each clip needs to be on its own track. In **Sceneline** view, clips can only be added *in sequence* (one after another) on the **Video 1** track for visual media (still images and video clips), or the **Audio 1** track for sound media (narration, sound effects, and music).

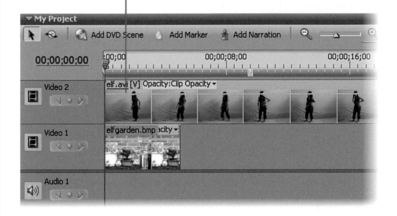

16

Applying Color and Contrast Effects to the Elf Clip

A best practice when working with green screen clips is to apply the **Auto Color** and **Auto Contrast** effects. This will help to successfully remove all of the green background from behind the clip. Premiere Elements' **Auto Color** and **Auto Contrast** effects make the colors in the clip richer and more vibrant, thus enhancing the green background as well. All this makes it easier to "key" out the green in a later task.

Apply the Auto Color Effect

1 Click on the **Effects and Transitions** button on the **Media** panel to switch to the **Effects and Transitions** view, if it's not already the current view.

2 In the **text box** on the **Effects and Transitions** view of the **Media** panel, type **auto**.

3 Select the **Auto Color** effect from the **Adjust** effects in the **Video Effects** list and drag and drop it onto the **elf.avi** clip on the **Video 2** track.

4 In the **Properties** panel, click the **triangle** next to the **Auto Color** effect to view the effect controls.

5 Set the **Auto Color** settings as follows:

- ◆ **Temporal Smoothing:** (leave at 0.00)

- ◆ **Scene Detect:** (unchecked)

- ◆ **Black Clip: 2.00%**

- ◆ **White Clip: 3.00%**

- ◆ **Snap Neutral Midtones:** (unchecked)

- ◆ **Blend With Original: 60%**

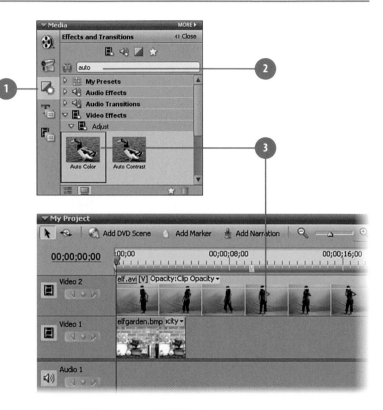

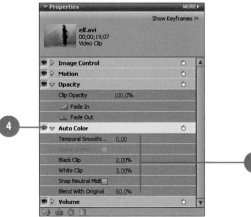

Apply the Auto Contrast Effect

1 Select the **Auto Contrast** effect from the **Adjust** effects in the **Video Effects** list and drag and drop it onto the **elf.avi** clip on the **Video 2** track.

2 In the **Properties** panel, click the **triangle** next to the **Auto Contrast** effect to view the effect controls.

3 Set the **Auto Contrast** settings as follows:

◆ **Temporal Smoothing:** (leave at 0.00)

◆ **Scene Detect:** (unchecked)

◆ **Black Clip:** 1.00%

◆ **White Clip:** 1.00%

◆ **Blend With Original:** 30%

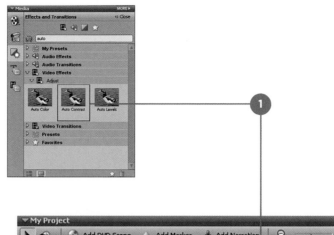

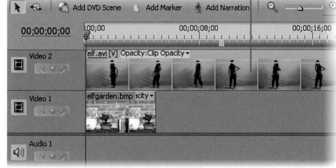

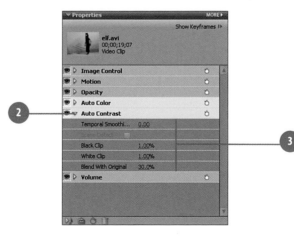

Did You Know?

It's a study in contrasts.
When using a green- or bluescreen effect in your future projects, apply the **Auto Color** and **Auto Contrast** effects, play with the effects' controls, and see what you come up with. Click the effect's toggle button (the eyeball, shown at left) to see what the clip looks like with the effect turned on and off. While brightening a clip and increasing the color saturation and contrast can improve how a clip responds to keying out the background, "results may vary," as they say on the infomercials. So, try the effect and if you like it keep it. If you don't or aren't sure, click the "eyeball" off and leave it turned off. Remember, video editing is both a science and an art, and it sometimes takes experimentation to get just the look you want.

16

Applying the Green Screen Key

The **elf.avi** clip is a special clip in that it is a clip of an actor who was filmed against a green-screen background. Now that the clip has been brought into Premiere Elements 3, we can apply one of Premiere Elements 3's standard Keying effects, the **Green Screen Effect**, to remove the green background.

Find and Apply the Key

1 Click on the **Effects and Transitions** button on the **Media** panel to switch to the **Effects and Transitions** view, if it's not already the current view.

2 Type **green** in the text field.

3 Select the **Green Screen Key** effect from the Keying effects in the **Video Effects** list and drag and drop it onto the **elf.avi** clip on the **Video 2** track.

4 In the **Properties** panel, click the **triangle** next to **Green Screen Key** to view the effect's controls.

5 Adjust the effect as follows:

- **Threshold: 38.0%**

- **Cutoff: 38.0%**

- **Smoothing: High**

TIP *To see a black and white version of your key (which can show you some details in the key that you might otherwise miss), with the subject as a cookie-cutter cutout in white, click the Mask Only check box. The clip in the Monitor panel will look something like this:*

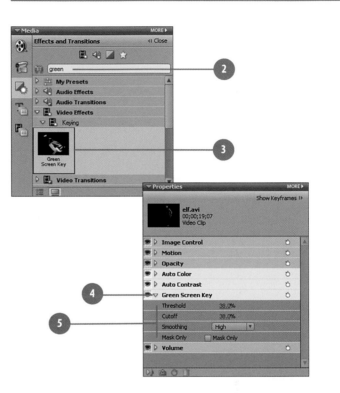

The clip before the **Green Screen Key** has been applied.

The clip after the **Green Screen Key** has been applied (but before the effect has been adjusted).

Colorizing the "Elf"

We now need to change the elf so that she is in her legitimate "elfen leaf green" color. Otherwise, she will not appear to be a real elf. Ironically, after all the trouble we took to remove every last pixel of green from the **elf.avi** clip, here we go making the whole thing green after all. After you've applied the **Tint** effect, you'll see two color swatches and eyedroppers in the **Properties** pane. We'll be leaving black mapped to black here, so we won't make any changes to the **Map Black to** color.

Apply the Tint Effect

1. If it is not already the current view, click on the **Effects and Transitions** button on the **Media** panel to switch to the **Effects and Transitions** view.

2. Type **tint** in the text field on the **Effects and Transitions** view.

3. Select the **Tint** effect from the **Image Control** effects in the **Video Effects** list and drag and drop it onto the **elf.avi** clip on the **Video 2** track.

4. In the **Properties** panel, click the **triangle** next to the **Tint** effect to view the controls.

5. Click on the **Map White to** color swatch (we're leaving the black "as is," that is, the black will stay mapped to black.)

6. The **Color Picker** window displays. Enter the following values and click **OK**:

   ◆ **H: 100**

   ◆ **S: 100**

   ◆ **B: 100**

7. Set the **Amount to Tint** to **50.0%**.

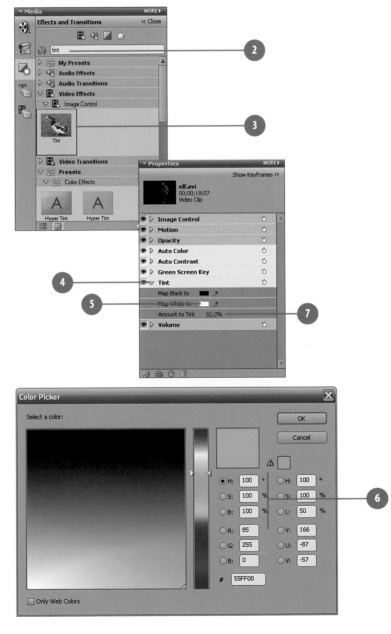

Troubleshooting a Greenscreen Project

Seeing Grey and Feeling Blue

Sometimes, no matter how well you thought you set up your green screen backdrop, or how well you thought you had the backdrop and your subject lit, when you get your clip into Premiere Elements and apply the **Green Screen Key**, what you see is mud. All you know is, the thing doesn't look like it's supposed to. Perhaps it's the color of your background. Maybe it's your lights (or lack of them). Maybe it's the fact that your greenscreen material has gotten a bit too wrinkled or you didn't quite stretch it (or iron it) enough this time. But no matter what the problem, there's a fix right in Premiere Elements.

Chroma Key to the Rescue

If you've applied the **Green Screen Key** as described in this chapter without satisfactory results, you can approach the problem from another angle. Try the **Chroma Key** instead. With the **Chroma Key**, you can choose the color by either selecting it from the background using an eyedropper tool or by picking it from a color swatch.

The **Chroma Key** can be found among the other keys in the **Video Effects** list on the **Effects and Transitions** view on the **Media** panel. After you've applied the key, go to the **Properties** panel, click the triangle next to the **Chroma Key**, and then, select the eyedropper tool. With the eyedropper, click on a color in the background of the clip in the **Monitor** panel. The color swatch next to the eyedropper tool will now be the same color as the color you selected.

Clicking on the color swatch next to the eyedropper brings up the **Color Picker** window. This is an alternative way to select your starting color for the **Chroma Key**. From the **Color Picker** window, you can either select a color by clicking on it or you can enter a numeric value.

Adjust the Chroma Key to Eliminate the Green

As you may notice the first time you use this effect, the **Chroma Key** at first does a rough cut, a kind of a wide sweep and removes a certain amount of the background. In order to remove the rest, you'll need to tweak the **Chroma Key**'s controls. On the **Properties** panel, you can adjust the Similarity setting for the **Chroma Key** by dragging your mouse across the setting (or by typing in a value) until as much as possible of the background disappears.

You can also tweak the controls to adjust the key until, hopefully, all of the background has been eliminated. Controls for the **Chroma Key** include Blend (how and to what degree it merges with the background), Threshold (the amount of shadows included in the selected color), and Cutoff (how dark or light the shadows are). (The green will disappear and reappear as you make adjustments.) Keep in mind that you can apply the **Chroma Key** as many times as necessary to completely eliminate all of the background color or colors in the clip.

Non Red is the Right "Non" Color

Premiere Elements has an another key that you can use to eliminate any final vestiges of green, especially the nefarious green "fringe" that sometimes remains around an actor after the green background has been removed. When you need to rid yourself of this pesky fringe, try the **Non Red Effect**. In the **Properties** panel, click the Defringing dropdown and choose Green. This should, in most cases, remove the green fringe. By the way, if your actor has a blue fringe from a blue background, select Blue instead.

As you make adjustments using the Chroma Key effect controls on the Properties panel, you'll see the green of the greenscreen begin to peal away and the background begins to show through.

Fringe around the actor's hair is clearly visible before the **Non Red Key** is applied, here. Notice the greenish "tinge" on her face.

After the **Non Red Key** is applied, the green fringe and tinge are gone.

16

Adding the Foreground Clip

We are going to create a trick of the eye by adding the background to another track in the Timeline. By cropping this track, we will create the illusion that our elf is really in that world by making it appear as if she is moving among the objects there, when in reality she is ten times bigger than the objects and the objects are actually part of a still picture.

Drop the Background Clip Again, Now as the Foreground

1 Once again, select the **elfgarden.bmp** clip on the **Media** panel and drag on drop it onto the Timeline, this time onto the **Video 3** track. Be sure that you drop it, or move it after you drop it, so that the head (front) of the clip is at the very beginning of the track.

> **TIMESAVER** *If you don't have a Video 3 track, by dragging and dropping the clip in the blank area of the Timeline above the Video 2 track, Premiere Elements automatically creates a new track for the clip. You need at least a little space above the last track for this to work, so if there's no space at all, expand the My Project panel a bit first.*

2 Adjust the length of the **elfgarden.bmp** clip on the **Video 3** track so that it matches the duration of the **elf.avi** clip.

3 Adjust the length of the **elfgarden.bmp** clip on the **Video 1** track, as well, so that it, too, matches the duration of the **elf.avi** clip.

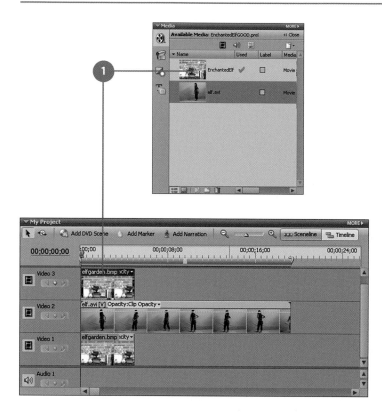

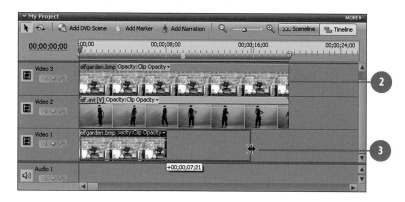

Cropping the Foreground Clip to Create a Multi-Dimensional Environment

Because Premiere Elements has multiple video tracks (up to 99 tracks, should you need them), you can create layer upon layer of backgrounds or images. Here, we are using another copy of the background image and cropping it to make the watering can appear to be in the foreground. If you wanted, you could add another track above (in **Video 4**) and crop that so that the bonsai plant could be effectively another object in the scene.

Use the Crop Effect to Create an Illusion of a Foreground

1 In the **Media** panel, select the **Effects and Transitions** button to switch to the **Effects and Transitions** view.

2 In the text box on the **Effects and Transitions view**, type **crop**.

3 Select the **Crop** effect from the **Transform** category of **Video Effects** and drag and drop it onto the **elfgarden.bmp** clip on the **Video 3** track on the Timeline.

4 In the **Properties** panel for the **elfgarden.bmp** clip on the **Video 3** track, click on the **Crop** effect so that it highlights. A box will appear around the **elfgarden.bmp** clip in the **Monitor** panel.

5 Select the top left handle of the box in the **Monitor** panel and drag it down towards the chrome watering can at the bottom right of the screen until you have framed the watering can (see illustration).

Did You Know?

You can create as many "layers" as you want. Here's how creative you can get with this: Film *your* elf standing on a chair peaking about. Then have him or her jump off, run around a bit, and exit. In "post," you can hide the chair behind the plant. The elf will appear to be jumping down from the plant. When the elf exits, he or she will appear to be running between the bonsai plant and the watering can.

5 Drag the crop box so that it frames the watering can.

Shrinking the "Elf"

In this task, we'll "shrink" the elf down to little, tiny elf size. This is a simple procedure in Premiere Elements 3. Later, when we have the elf down to true elf dimensions, we'll move her over to a slightly different starting location that will increase the illusion of having an elf in the garden even more. You will not believe how effective you will be with this illusion, even when created on your own home computer!

Shrink the Elf Down to Elf Proportions

1 Click on the **elf.avi** clip on the **Video 2** track to select it.

2 In the **Properties** panel, select the **Motion** effect.

3 The elf clip in the **Monitor** panel will now appear with sizing handles, as shown.

4 Grab one of the handles and drag to resize the elf.

> **TIP** In the next task, we will be hiding the elf behind the watering can, so eyeball the relative size of the elf as you shrink her. You want the elf to be slightly smaller than the base of the watering can.

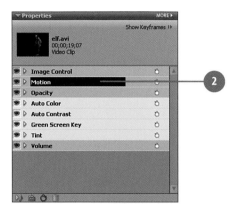

Adjusting the Elf's Starting Location

Move the Elf to Add Believability to Her Hiding Place

1 With the **elf.avi** clip still selected, in the **Properties** panel for the clip, select **Motion**.

> **TIP** *A box will appear around the **elf.avi** clip in the **Monitor** panel, enabling you to drag it across the screen.*

2 With your mouse, **click** anywhere inside the box and **drag** the **elf.avi** clip until the elf appears to be hidden behind the watering can.

Did You Know?

It's a piece of cake to add more layers.
Because you can have up to 99 video tracks in a Premiere Elements project, you could use the techniques learned in this chapter to create additional layers. For example, you could add a flower pot in front so that the elf could appear to hide behind, running from her hiding place behind the watering can to a new hiding place behind the pot. You could also create objects in the elf's "environment" that the elf could either pick up or push aside using this same technique or by filming the object first against a greenscreen. Have the actor act out lifting the object or pushing it. Then, in "post," place the object in the right position and use keyframes to make it appear as if the actor is affecting the object. As with most of the concepts introduced in this book, how far you take them is limited only by your own imagination.

Now that we've cropped the second instance of the **elfgarden.bmp** clip so that the chrome watering can can act somewhat as an object in the scene, we will move our actor "behind" the watering can (or in other words, behind the section of the **elfgarden.bmp** clip on the **Video 3** track that has not been cropped). This will create a very convincing illusion of the elf "peeping out" from behind the watering can. It's an illusion, of course, since the actor is really not that small (nor that green!) and isn't actually in the garden. But the illusion works like, well, magic!

1

Drag the elf.avi clip back behind the watering can, where she will start the show by appearing to peak out from behind it.

16

Making the Elf "Vanish"

In our clip, **elf.avi**, the actor playing the elf is surprised by the sound of approaching humans and so she decides to "vanish." To do so, because she has elfin powers, all she needs to do is snap her fingers and she's gone. The clip, **elf.avi**, ends when the elf snaps her fingers. To make it appear as if she's suddenly disappeared, all we need to do is keep the background on screen for a few seconds longer, and then fade to black.

Adjust the Background Clip's Ending Point Relative to the Elf Clip

1 With your mouse, grab the tail end of the **elfgarden.bmp** clip in the **Video 1** track and drag it out a few seconds more, so that it's longer than the **elf.avi** clip in the **Video 2** track.

> **IMPORTANT** The *elfgarden.bmp* clip on the **Video 1** track should now be 20 seconds and 20 frames long. As you resize the clip, watch the timecode in the **Monitor** panel and stop resizing when it reaches **00;00;20;20**.

2 In the **Properties** panel for the **elfgarden.bmp** clip in the **Video 1** track, click the **triangle** next to **Opacity** to reveal the effect's controls.

3 Click the **Fade Out** button for **Opacity**.

> **TIP** The Fade Out function in Premiere Elements is an easy way to create a professional ending for the clip, by having it slowly fade to black.

4 Back on the Timeline, grab the tail end of the **elf.avi** clip and trim it back a second or two. This will create the illusion of the elf vanishing immediately after she snaps her fingers.

> **IMPORTANT** The *elf.avi* clip on the **Video 2** track should now be 16 seconds and 10 frames long. As you resize the clip, watch the timecode in the **Monitor** panel and stop resizing when it reaches **00;00;18;10**.

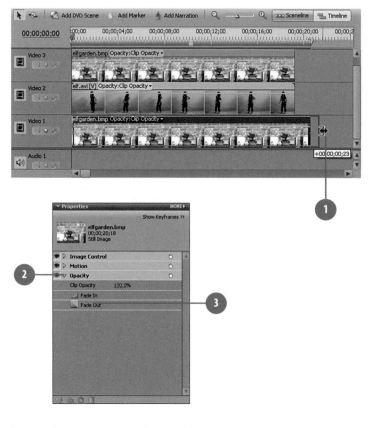

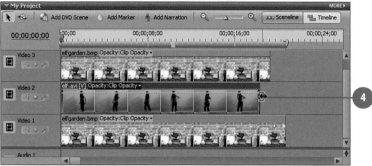

Adding Some Playful Elfish Music "Under"

This goes without saying, but we can't create a video clip that features an elf without having a bit of elfish music playing in the background. In this line of work, video editing, music in the background playing softly is known as playing "under." On the DVD that was supplied with this book, we've given you a bit of elf music, **elfish_song.wav**. (Actually, the real title as generated by SmartSound Quicktracks is "SmartSound - Synergy - Emergent [00;29;26].wav," but let's face it, that's not very catchy. So we renamed it.) Let's add that to the project now and we're just about ready to call it a "wrap."

Add the Music to the Project and Adjust the Audio on the Elf Clip

1. Click the **Get Media from** button on the **Media** panel to access the **Get Media from** view, if it's not already active.

2. Select **DVD, Digital Camera, Mobile Phone, Hard Drive Camcorder, Card Reader**.

3. When the **Media Downloader** displays, click the **Advanced Dialog** button to switch to Advanced mode.

4. Select the **elfish_song.wav** clip and then click the **Get Media** button. Premiere Elements copies the **elfish_song.wav** clip from the DVD onto your hard drive.

5. Drag and drop the **elfish_song.wav** clip onto the **Audio 1** track, so that the front of the clip is at the front of the track.

6. Grab the tail end of the **elfish_song.wav** clip and trim it back so that, at **00;00;21;14**, it's just slightly longer in duration than the **elfgarden.bmp** on the **Video 1** track.

7. With the **elfish_song.wav** clip still selected, go to the **Properties** panel and set the **Clip Volume** to **-12.0 dB**.

8. Click the **Fade Out** button.

9. **Right-click on the elf.avi** clip on the **Video 2** track. From the contextual menu, select **Audio Gain**.

10. From the **Clip Gain** dialog box, click the **Normalize** button and click **OK**.

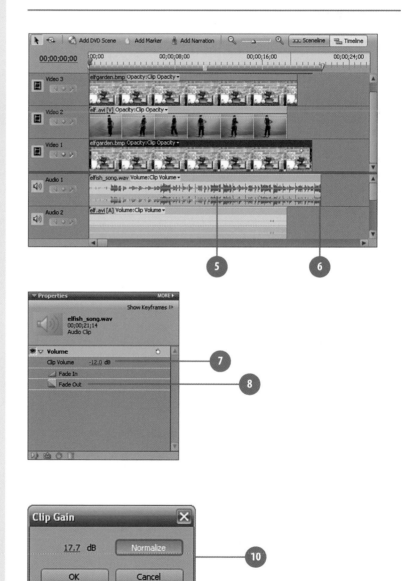

Making Adjustments, Rendering, and Exporting

We're now ready to render all of our effects, save our project one more time, and create our output file. Before we do so, you might want to play the clip (press the **Spacebar** on your keyboard or click the **Play** button on the **Monitor** panel) to see how it looks. If you need to, make any final tweaks. For example, the point at which the elf "vanishes" might require a slight adjustment. Then, you are ready to save, render, and make your movie.

Finishing the Project

1. After you have played back your clip and made the necessary adjustments, press the **ENTER** key on your keyboard to render your project.

2. Press **CTRL-S** to save your project (or you can select **File, Save** from the menu).

3. Finally, export your work as an AVI file. To export the clip, select **File, Export, Movie**.

   TIP *You can now optionally bring this clip into a larger project, show it on your computer, upload it to an Internet video sharing site, or burn it to a DVD disc.*

The finished project running in Windows Media Player. Notice the elf's size, color, and the illusion that she's hiding behind the watering can.

The Friendly Ghost Effect

MEDIA:

ghost.avi
no-ghost.avi
DarkCity30.mp3

17

COMPLEXITY:	Simple	Moderate	Complex
SKILL LEVEL:	Novice	Intermediate	Advanced
MATERIALS:	None	Some Props	Greenscreen

Introduction

The Friendly Ghost Effect, despite the specificity of its name, is more of an all-purpose supernatural effect than it is simply a "ghost maker." It's a technique that can be used (with minor variations) to produce the "incredible vanishing boy" (or girl)—you've probably seen this effect in old science fiction or horror films as the main character holds his hand up to his face and stares in disbelief at his own disintegrating flesh…

The effect can also be used to create a "visitor from another dimension" by reducing and increasing opacity over time using keyframes to show the visitor gradually becoming more solid looking as they enter our dimension. (Keyframes are explained in detail in *Chapter 1: The Retro Title Effect*.) Once you have mastered this technique, you'll no doubt invent some of your own applications for this supernatural effect.

In addition to the opacity controls used to produce the Friendly Ghost Effect, believe it or not Premiere Elements provides an additional effect called, literally, "Ghosting." This effect creates a residual copy of the actor's movements in the clip and adds an eerie look to an already other-worldly scene. While the addition of the "Ghosting" effect works perfectly in the context of the Friendly Ghost Effect, it wouldn't apply to the "vanishing boy," or the "visitor from another dimension" scenarios.

Have fun with this one: It's an easy-to-do effect that's a huge hit with the kids. It's an effect that can be used over and over again in your own horror movies or horror comedies and spoofs ("*horror*-dies?").

What You'll Do

Add the Video Media to the Timeline

Create a "Split Screen" Using the Crop Effect

Understand Opacity

Adjust the Opacity of the "Ghost" Clip

Adjust the Brightness or Contrast of Either Clip as Needed

Apply a Ghostly Effect

Add Transitions for the Ghost's Entrance and Exit

Add a Haunting Melody

Make Adjustments, Render, and Export

Adding the Video Media to the Timeline

Your first step in working on any project, even if that project is simply creating a short video segment, is to create a new Premiere Elements project and give it a descriptive name. Remember, project file names in Premiere Elements can be up to 100 characters long (including any spaces between words) and can therefore be very descriptive. Your next step, typically, is to bring in the media files you'll be using for the project. In this step, we'll first bring in the two video clips we'll be working with on this project.

Load the Two Video Clips into Premiere Elements

1 Start Premiere Elements and create a new project called **friendlyghost**.

2 Click the **Get Media from** button on the **Media** panel to access the **Get Media from** view, if it's not already active.

3 Select **DVD, Digital Camera, Mobile Phone, Hard Drive Camcorder, Card Reader**.

4 When the **Media Downloader** displays, click the **Advanced Dialog** button to switch to Advanced mode.

5 Select the following clips for this project:

  ◆ **ghost.avi**

  ◆ **no-ghost.avi**

6 Click the **Get Media** button. Premiere Elements copies the clips from the DVD onto your hard drive and adds them to the Available Media list for this project.

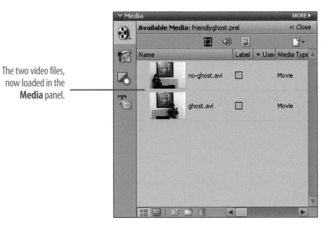

The two video files, now loaded in the **Media** panel.

Add the Two Video Clips the Timeline

1 Switch to **Timeline** view at this time by clicking the **Timeline** button on the upper right corner of the **My Project** panel.

2 Click the **no-ghost.avi** clip on the **Media** panel to select it and drag and drop it onto the **Timeline** in the **Video 1** track so that the head (front) of the clip is at the very beginning of the track.

TIP *Because you just added the file to the* ***Media*** *panel, the* ***no-ghost.avi*** *clip may already be selected. It's possible that when you clicked on it just now, you actually deselected it. If this happens to you, just click on the* ***no-ghost.avi*** *clip once more to select it.*

3 Drag the **CTI** six seconds and 25 frames into the video; in other words to **00;00;06;25**.

4 Click the second clip, **ghost.avi**, on the **Media** panel to select it, then drag and drop it onto the Timeline in the **Video 2** track. Position the clip directly against the **CTI** so that it starts at **00;00;06;25**.

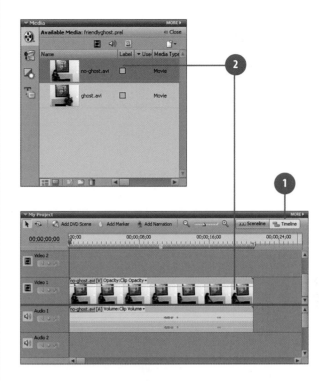

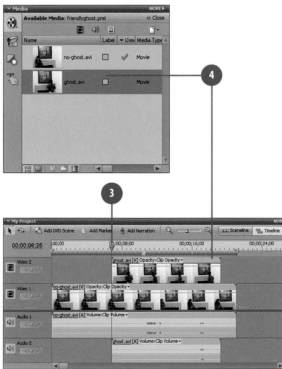

17

Creating a "Split Screen" Using the Crop Effect

Now that you have both clips loaded into the Timeline—one on the **Video 1** track and one on the **Video 2** track—you'll use the **Crop** effect on the "ghost" clip to make the two clips appear to be a single clip. This is a classic, time-honored technique used to make it appear that two actors are standing in the same scene when they actually are not. In fact, it's often used with a single actor to make it appear that there are twins in the scene. It's been used famously in films such as "The Parent Trap" (both the Haley Mills and Lindsay Lohan versions).

Apply the Crop Effect to the "Ghost" Clip

1. Click the **Effects and Transitions** button on the Media panel to switch to the **Effects and Transitions** view.

2. In the text box on the **Effects and Transitions** view, type **crop**.

3. Drag the **Crop** effect from the Transform section of the Video Effects and drop it on the **ghost.avi** clip in the **Video 2** track on the Timeline.

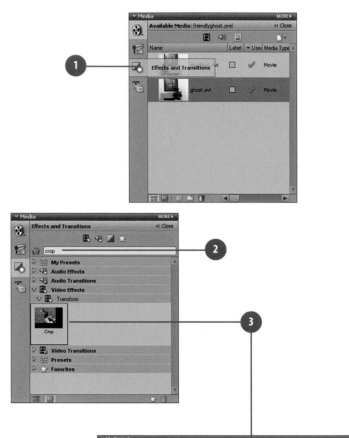

Did You Know?

You can choose among your favorites.
You don't always have to go through the process of searching for an effect among all of the effects and transitions that Premiere Elements has available. You can save any effect that you use regularly as a favorite. Premiere Elements makes this real simple. If you look at the bottom of the **Media** panel when the **Effects and Transitions** view is active, you'll notice a bright yellow star icon, right next to the Delete icon (the trash can). Just select any effect, preset, or transition that you like or use regularly. Then, click this star button (which is actually called the Add to Favorites button). The first time you use the button, it will create a new category in the **Effects and Transitions** panel, called Favorites, and it will use the yellow star as its icon. Notice, too, that at the top of the **Effects and Transitions** view is a row of buttons. Each one lets you filter the list by video effects, audio effects, transitions, and—you guessed it—your favorites.

Create the Split

1 Select the **Crop** effect on the **Properties** panel (so that it's highlighted). This will reveal the control handles for the effect in the **Monitor** panel.

TIP *Drag the **CTI** so that it is over the **ghost.avi** clip in the **Video 2** track so you can see it in the **Monitor** panel.*

2 Twirl the triangle next to **Crop** to view the effect's controls.

3 Grab the handle in the upper **left** corner of the **Monitor** panel and drag it across the Monitor until you have reached **40%** of the way across.

TIP *At 40%, the edge of the **ghost.avi** clip should now be just after the edge of the book that the actor in **no-ghost.avi** is reading (see illustration).*

Did You Know?

You can handle it differently .
Using handles is the easiest and most intuitive way to control a crop. However, if you're one of those folks who'd rather control the position of the "crop box" numerically, use the **Properties** panel. Just click the arrow next to Crop and adjust the percentages for the following parameters as needed:

- ◆ **Left**

- ◆ **Top**

- ◆ **Right**

- ◆ **Bottom**

Drag the handle until roughly a third of the underlying clip, **no-ghost.avi**, shows through.

17

Understanding Opacity

How Opacity Works

Premiere Elements supports the Friendly Ghost Effect through the use of a function called "opacity," which you may more readily understand as "transparency." That is, it's the quality (or lack of) "see-throughness," if you will, of a video clip.

When used by itself (that is, over an empty track or "nothingness"), decreasing opacity on a clip will appear to make the clip darker, as shown in the image at left (which is set at 50% opacity). When used over another clip, the second clip acts as a background clip (as shown in the sequence of pictures at the bottom of these two pages).

When two clips are for the most part identical, with only one element changing (specifically, it's becoming transparent, or in other words, losing opacity) it appears that only that element is changing, when, in fact, *everything* in that clip is actually changing.

An Apple Appears to Appear

Along the bottom of these two pages are illustrations from two clips, superimposed over each other. One is of a table without an apple; the other clip of the same table, with an apple placed on top.

The opacity of the "apple" clip is set to gradually increase over time, from 0% to 100%. This makes it seem as if the apple is appearing out of thin air. (This particular effect can also be accomplished by cross-dissolving from one clip to the other.)

This works because *all other elements*—the table, the placemats, the plants—are exactly the same in each shot. The only difference is the apple. This is simply an illusion, a kind of a magic trick created with a camcorder and video editing software.

Requirements for Success

Even in the clips below, which were filmed literally within seconds of each other, you can begin to see the shadows shifting as the sun moves slowly in the sky. This is rule number one whenever you plan to use the Opacity control in this way: the sun is your enemy. As light and shadows change, the effect will become less and less convincing. Film as quickly as you can whenever you are creating scenes like these.

The second requirement for success is the tripod. Without one, you will fail. It's that simple. Even the slightest variation in angle or position from one clip

to the other and the whole thing is ruined. It simply won't be believable. If you don't have a tripod or a monopod, find a way to rest the camcorder on a table, chair, shelf, or other rock-solid surface.

One Last Thing

One last trick of the trade. Once you switch on your camcorder to film your clips for this type of project, *don't turn it off*. This no doubt seems counter-intuitive because people (or their hands, in the case of props being moved in and out of the scene) will be filmed. This may appear to give the "trick" away, but it really won't. Remember, back in your "studio," you can edit all that out.

What you don't want when filming is even the slightest change in the camcorder's position, which even the gentlest pressing of the **Record** button to stop and start filming can do.

17

Adjusting the Opacity of the "Ghost" Clip

Right now, both of our clips have the same opacity; that is, both are "normal." For the **Friendly Ghost Effect** to work, however, our "ghost" clip needs to be faded out so that the actor playing the part of the spirit will appear to be see-through. To achieve this effect, we'll simply adjust the **Opacity** setting for the clip to less than 50%. A good setting for our purposes is 25%, but you can adjust this to your preferences. In addition, you can choose to adjust the opacity directly on the Timeline using the Opacity rubberband, or on the **Properties** panel. The instructions here cover using the **Properties** panel.

Make the Ghost Clip "See Through"

1 Click on the **ghost-avi** clip in the **Video 2** track, if not already selected.

2 In the **Properties** panel, click the arrow next to **Opacity** to display the effect's controls, if they aren't already visible.

3 Drag the number next to **Clip Opacity** and set the opacity to **50.0%**.

> **TIP** You can type 50 directly into this field.

Did You Know?

You can use the yellow rubberband to control opacity. You can use the yellow rubberband that runs the length of every video clip to set opacity. Be sure that the rubberband is controlling opacity (see the second *Did You Know?* below). Then click on the rubberband. With the mouse button held down the cursor changes to include small up and down arrows. Drag the rubberband down to decrease opacity, up to increase it. As you move the rubberband, Premiere Elements displays a small yellow box to show you the opacity amount.

You can choose what the rubberband controls. By default, the rubberband controls opacity, but you can set it to control other effects. To do so, click on the settings menu control in name bar at the top of the clip. It only appears at the head, or front, of the clip, so if you don't see it, scrub to the beginning of the clip. From the menu, select **Opacity, Clip Opacity**, as shown below.

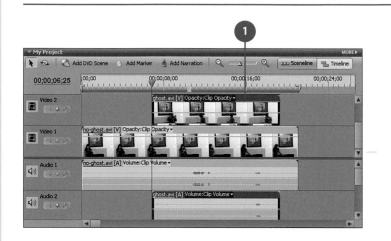

Notice how the actor playing the "ghost" now has faded convincingly and appears to be emerging right out of the wall to begin his dreadful haunting.

Adjusting the Brightness or Contrast of Either Clip as Needed

Match the Appearance of the Two Clips

1 Select the **no-ghost.avi** clip on the **Video 1** track.

2 In the **Properties** panel, click the arrow next to **Image Control** to display its controls, if they aren't already visible.

3 Drag the number next to **Contrast** and set the amount to **94.0**.

Did You Know?

Sometimes, the light is just right.
Adjusting the brightness, contrast, hue, or other settings on one or both video clips should only be necessary when filming outdoors during the day or indoors using natural light. You shouldn't need to make adjustments when filming using artificial light exclusively. In such cases, all of the lights and shadows should be consistent enough that the two clips are virtually identical in terms of their image values.

Now that we have our two clips happily co-existing side-by-side, and have cast a ghostly pallor upon our "ghost" using the **Opacity** control, we need to adjust some settings on the ghost clip so that the two clips more exactly match. This is because by overlaying the two clips and adjusting the opacity, the ghost clip is actually darkening the clip beneath it somewhat. In addition, even though the two clips were filmed within minutes of each other, changes in light and shadow have occurred, enough so that the two clips aren't exactly identical.

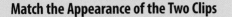

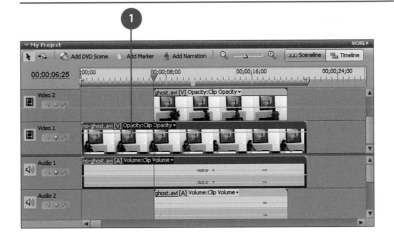

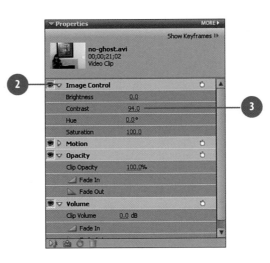

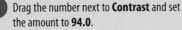

17

Applying a Ghostly Effect ▶

For this task, we'll be applying the aptly-named "Ghosting" effect from the set of available video effects in Premiere Elements. This effect creates a shadowy echo of the ghost as he moves about the room. It's a subtle effect, with no controllable parameters, but it gives our project, in an instant, just the right additional creepy touch.

Use the "Ghosting" Video Effect

1 Select the **Effects and Transitions** button on the **Media** panel to switch to the **Effects and Transitions** view.

2 In the text box on the **Effects and Transitions** view, type **ghost**.

3 Drag the **Ghosting** effect from the **Blur & Sharpen** section of **Video Effects** and drop it on the **ghost.avi** clip in the **Video 2** track.

Did You Know?

There's really nothing to it.
The **Ghosting** effect is one of the few video effects in Premiere Elements with absolutely no controls whatsoever. If you look at the effect on the **Properties** panel (a section of which is shown below), there's not even the triangle available for showing/hiding effect controls.

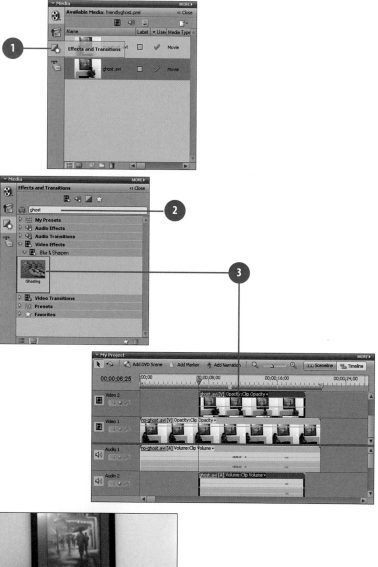

You can see the effect of the Ghosting here. As the actor playing the ghost moves through the room, an eerie, echo of a shadow follows him.

Adding Transitions for the Ghost's Entrance and Exit

When the ghost arrives and when he leaves, he abruptly pops in and out of the scene. Not a very convincing way for a ghost to materialize nor to vanish. It would be much better if he could somehow materialize by forming from tiny pieces and dematerialize in a similar way. Well, that is exactly what the **Cross Dissolve** transition does. This transition, when applied to an overlay such as this, appears to affect only the ghost character. Because the two clips are identical, there appears to be nothing "dissolving" between them except for the ghost. By applying the **Cross Dissolve** transition to the beginning and end of the **ghost.avi** clip, we create the illusion of a ghost materializing as he enters the room and dematerializing as he vanishes.

Add the Transition for the Ghost's Entrance

1 Select the **Effects and Transitions** button to access the **Effects and Transitions** panel, if it's not the active view.

2 In the text box on the **Effects and Transitions** panel, type **cross**.

3 Select the **Cross Dissolve** effect from the set of **Dissolve** effects and drag and drop it on to the front, or head, of the **ghost.avi** clip in the **Video 2** track.

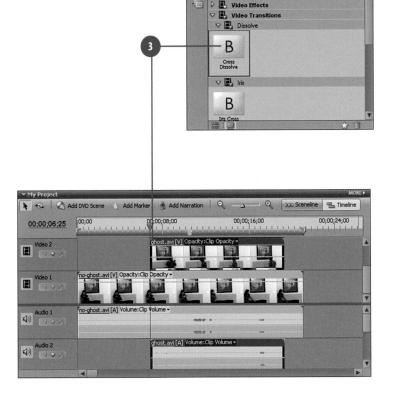

17

Adding a Transition for the Ghost's Exit

 Select the **Cross Dissolve** effect again from the the **Effects and Transitions** panel.

2 Drag and drop it on to the back, or tail, of the **ghost.avi** clip in the Video 2 track.

NOTE *When you're done, a purple and white band will appear at both ends of the clip's name bar, as shown in the illustration. The purple and white band will be labeled with the name of the effect, which in this case is **Cross Dissolve**. Depending on your zoom level, you may see only a small part of this band and the effect's name.*

The ghost materializes—out of nowhere!

Adding a Haunting Melody

What's a spooky clip without spooky music? We want to keep the focus on the short play we're creating, so we do not want the music to be overpowering. Once we bring the music in and drag it to the Timeline, we'll adjust the Volume for the clip so that it plays "under" the action in a subtle, but effective way. The music we're using is provided courtesy of the folks at Twisted Tracks. This particular twisted track is called, **DarkCity30.mp3**.

Add a Touch of Spooky Music

1 Click the **Get Media from** button on the **Media** panel to access the **Get Media from** view, if it's not already active.

2 Select **DVD, Digital Camera, Mobile Phone, Hard Drive Camcorder, Card Reader**.

3 When the **Media Downloader** displays, click the **Advanced Dialog** button to switch to Advanced mode.

4 Select the **DarkCity30.mp3** clip for this project.

5 Click the **Get Media** button.

6 Drag and drop **DarkCity30.mp3** onto the **Audio 3** track. Be sure that the head of this clip starts at the beginning of the track.

7 In the **Properties** panel for the clip **DarkCity30.mp3**, set the **Volume** to **-9.0 dB**. This will keep the music so that it's not to loud, and yet we'll still be able to hear it "under" the action.

8 Click the **Fade Out** button for **Volume** in the **Properties** panel so that the music fades out gracefully at the end of the movie.

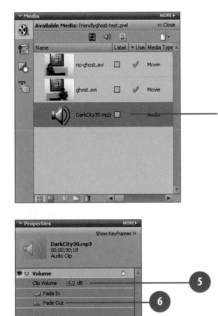

The **DarkCity30.mp3** music file loaded into the **Media** panel.

17

Making Adjustments, Rendering, and Exporting

Now that all the pieces of your production puzzle have been put in place, you're ready to go. Of course, throughout this project you should always save as you go (**CTRL-S**). Now, press the **ENTER** key on your keyboard to render the project. It will play automatically once it's done rendering. Watch the playback. If you see anything you don't like, go in and tweak things and press the **Spacebar** to play the clip again, or press **ENTER** to render again. After everything looks good to you, you're ready to export your project to a viewable movie file.

Finishing the Project

1 After you have played back your clip and made the necessary adjustments, press the **Enter** key on your keyboard to render your project.

2 Press **CTRL-S** to save your project (or you can select **File, Save** from the menu).

3 Finally, export your work as an AVI file. To export the clip, select **File, Export, Movie**.

4 You can optionally bring this clip into a larger project, show it on your computer, upload it to an Internet video sharing site, or burn it to a DVD.

The finished movie, playing in Windows Media Player.

The Multiple You Effect

MEDIA:

triplets.avi

18

COMPLEXITY:	Simple	Moderate	Complex
SKILL LEVEL:	Novice	Intermediate	Advanced
MATERIALS:	None	Some Props	Greenscreen

What You'll Do

Add the Video Clip to the Timeline

Identify, Mark, and Split Each Clip by "Triplet"

Separate and Move the Triplet Clips

Understand the Split Screen Function

Apply the Crop Effect to All Clips

Adjust the Crop Effect for Each Clip

Fine-Tune the Timing of the Conversation

Make Adjustments, Render, and Export

Introduction

From almost the very start of television, the need to have "twins" on the screen who talk alike, walk alike, and sometimes even think alike (what a crazy pair!) has been irresistible. With Premiere Elements 3, splitting the screen into two parts (or, if you are very, *very* careful, even more than two) is easy to do. The actor and his or her twin (which, of course, is the same actor again, in a second location) can appear to hold a conversation and walk in and out of the scene in a truly convincing way.

One of the nice things about the Multiple You Effect is, while it can be done using a blue- or greenscreen, such equipment is not necessary. If you want to create the illusion of a clone (or a twin), the classic split screen works just fine. With care, you might even be able to finesse triplets (as demonstrated in this chapter). Anything beyond that, such as an army of clones, does require that the actor be filmed in a number of locations against a greenscreen, so that the background can be stripped away (keyed out") and the various "clones" layered one over the other in the scene using the multiple tracks available in Premiere Elements.

In this chapter, however, we are concentrating on the much easier technique of splitting the screen using the Crop effect and creating the illusion of look-alikes engaged in casual conversation. The secret here is to script out the conversation ahead of time so that the "actors" know where to look and what to say. Then, when the scene is pieced together in Premiere Elements, it looks normal and natural as "they" point, talk, and look at each other in the course of conversation.

By the way, for the purposes of instruction, in this chapter we are intentionally violating some basic split screen rules. We are setting our actor against a horizontal plane (he is sitting in various locations on or around a couch) and he is casting a shadow which is cut off sharply at the crop. For your projects (as you'll learn in the section in this chapter, *"Understanding the Split Screen Function"*), these are definite no-no's. But here, they help demonstrate where each of the cropped clips begin and end. Even with such blatant violations, this effect is so convincing that the "trick," for the most part, still works.

Adding the Video Clip to the Timeline ▶

To ensure that the background stayed exactly the same from shot to shot, the **triplets.avi** clip was shot with the camcorder on a tripod (that goes without saying!). But even more to the point, the whole scene was done as one take. The clip that is on the DVD that came with this book has the intervening footage (wherein the actor walked from point A to point B) removed, but in the original clip, because the camcorder was left on, that footage was included. This is a recommended "best practice" for you, as well, when you create your "twin" or "triplet" footage: keep the camcorder running. There's no harm done by having that extra footage as you can delete it easily once you've brought the clip into Premiere Elements.

Add the "Triplets" Clip to the Timeline

1. Start Premiere Elements and create a new project called **multiyou**.

2. Click the **Get Media from** button on the **Media** panel to access the **Get Media from** view, if it's not already active.

3. Select **DVD, Digital Camera, Mobile Phone, Hard Drive Camcorder, Card Reader**.

4. When the **Media Downloader** displays, click the **Advanced Dialog** button to switch to Advanced mode.

5. Select the **triplets.avi** clip.

6. Click the **Get Media** button. Premiere Elements copies the **triplets.avi** clip from the DVD onto your hard drive and adds it to the **Available Media** list for this project.

7. With your mouse, select the **triplets.avi** clip on the **Media** panel and drag on drop it onto the Timeline in the **Video 1** track. You want to line up the head of the **triplets.avi** clip with the start of the **Video 1** track.

   TIP *If you're in **Sceneline** view, drop the clip onto the first scene box. Premiere Elements automatically places it on the **Video 1** track.*

Once you've brought the **triplets.avi** clip into your project (at right), just drag and drop it onto the Timeline in the **My Project** panel (below).

Identifying, Marking, and Splitting Each Clip by "Triplet"

In this task, we mark the start and end of each of the "triplet" characters so that we can create clips that contain only one triplet per clip. So, because we are talking triplets here, we'll go from one big triplet-packed clip, to three clips, each with its own unique triplet. We'll label each clip by triplet: TRIPLET1, TRIPLET2, and TRIPLET3.

Mark the Start Point for Each "Triplet"

1 Switch to **Timeline** view on the **My Project** panel, if necessary (that is, if you're in **Sceneline** view).

> **NOTE** *To switch to **Timeline** view, click the **Timeline** button in the upper right of the My Project panel.*

2 Using your mouse, grab the **Current Time Indicator,** or **CTI**, and glide it along the Timeline until you find the break between "Triplet" #1 and "Triplet" #2.

> **HINT** *The second triplet enters at 23 seconds into the clip, at **00;00;23;00**.*

3 Click the **Add Marker** button (shown below) to drop a marker here.

4 Move the **CTI** again until you find "Triplet" #3's entrance.

> **HINT** *The third triplet appears just about one minute into the clip, at **00;00;57;00**.*

5 Click the **Add Marker** button again to drop a marker here.

6 Press the **Home** key on your keyboard to return the **CTI** to the front, or head, of the **triplets** clip.

> **TIP** *If the full clip is not visible, press the backslash key, \, to view the full clip.*

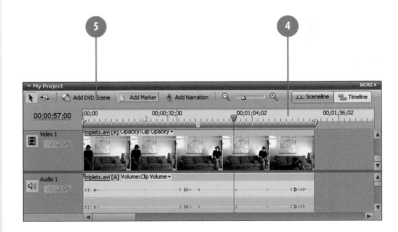

18

Split and Rename Each Triplet's Clip

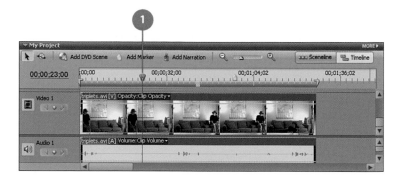

1 While holding down the **CTRL** key on your keyboard, press the **right arrow** key to jump to the first marker.

2 Click the **Split Clip** button on the **Monitor** panel to split the clip at this point (at **00;00;23;00**).

3 Press **CTRL-right arrow** again to jump to the next marker.

4 Click the **Split Clip** button on the **Monitor** panel again to split the clip here (at **00;00;57;00**).

5 **Rename** the clips:

◆ With your mouse, **right-click** on the first clip, at the front, and from the contextual menu that displays, select **Rename**.

◆ In the **Rename Clip** dialog box, rename the clip by typing **TRIPLET1** in the **Clip Name** field.

◆ Click **OK**.

◆ Repeat this process on the remaining two clips and rename them **TRIPLET2** and **TRIPLET3**, respectively.

Notice the split here.

Separating and Moving the Triplet Clips

Now that we have our clips split apart and named so that we can easily identify each one, in this step we'll move each of the "triplets" to their own video track. Actually, **TRIPLET1** remains right where it is on the **Video 1** track. We will just be moving the **TRIPLET2** clip to the **Video 2** track and the **TRIPLET3** clip to the **Video 3** track.

Move the Clips To Their Own Track

1 With your mouse, grab the **audio** track for the **TRIPLET2** clip and drag it straight down onto the **Audio 2** track.

2 Next, grab the clip **TRIPLET2** and drag and drop it onto the **Video 2** track directly above the clip in **Video 1**, **TRIPLET1**.

IMPORTANT *Be sure to line up the head of the TRIPLET2 clip with the start of the Video 2 track.*

3 Similarly, grab the **audio** track for the **TRIPLET3** clip and drag it down onto the **Audio 3** track.

4 Finally, grab the clip **TRIPLET3** and drag and drop it onto the **Video 3** track directly above the other two clips.

IMPORTANT *Again, be sure to line up the head of the TRIPLET3 clip with the start of the Video 3 track.*

Did You Know?

Sometimes manual intervention is required. If we were simply adding the **TRIPLET2** clip from the Media panel to the **Video 2** track, Premiere Elements would automatically place the audio for **TRIPLET2** on the **Audio 2** track. Because we are dragging and dropping and don't want to overlay or insert (we want to create a stack), we need to manually place the audio on the **Audio 2** track ourselves. The same concept applies to the **TRIPLET3** clip.

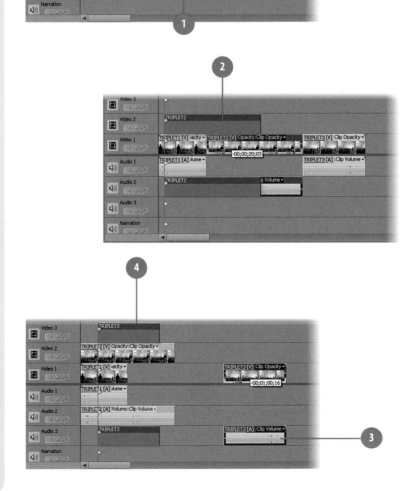

Understanding the Split Screen Function

The Split Screen

Creating a convincing scene using the tried-and-true split screen is simple to do, yet surprisingly effective. There are three key factors that make this technique work: the actor, the setting, and the timing.

The Actor

The first key factor is the actor's talent. The actor's ability to remember lines so that he or she can time their pauses to allow the "other" actor to talk is very important. So is the actor's ability to stay within the

"safe zone." That is, their ability to stay on the correct side of the split without accidentally stepping across it or gesturing across it—either of which might potentially ruin the effect.

The Setting

The second factor is the setting. In order to pull the "twin thing" off convincingly, you should shoot the scene against a background that has a natural vertical line of some sort in the middle of the shot. This can be a wall, a flagpole, a telephone pole, a door, or anything of that nature that fills all or most of the frame.

The Timing

If the actor does a good job—allows enough time in the pausing, reacts correctly to what the other "twin" had said, and stays within his or her "world," in other words, their side of the screen—all that's left is to sync up the timing.

Pauses that are too long (such as when one twin asks a question and then the other twin just stares at him or her too long before answering) are easy to fix. Just trim the clip to remove the extra pause time. Pauses that are too short are harder to fix, but they can sometimes work for you. If the actor starts talking too soon, but you can still hear both "twins," it actually better imitates natural conversational speech. So, encourage shorter pauses rather than longer ones.

Lighting and Other Considerations

Another consideration when shooting "twins" or "triplets" is to be aware that natural light changes more quickly than you realize. So don't wait too long, or at all if possible, between shoots of the first twin and the second twin. Also, watch for shadows, which can change over time resulting in the two twins casting shadows in different directions, creating an unnatural look to the scene. When shooting outdoors, be aware of action—people, dogs, cars, kites—in the background. Remember, this is a composite and you risk having a dog running across the scene in the background and suddenly "disappearing" right at the midpoint of the screen, where your crop is.

If you are working with "triplets," finding a suitable location to film may be more difficult, but you can get creative. Find a wall where two hallways meet, or a street location where there are two signs together, or the side of a building that's also near a telephone pole, allowing the actor to first stand on the left side of the building, then on the right, and then to the right of the telephone pole, thus giving you your two vertical lines "in nature" to run your crop up against.

Here's an ideal starting point for setting your split screen scene, the perfect place for a couple of twins to hold a conversation! Notice the sharp vertical line created by the edge of the wall right down the middle of the shot. What also makes this location ideal is that the left and right sides are slightly different in terms of lighting. The left side, because it's a hall, is slightly darker than the right side, because the wall is reflecting light.

Shoot the actor and have her act out all of the dialog and reactions for the twin on the left side of the screen. The only direction you'll need to give her is to remember that the wall represents the border of where she can move. She should not walk or even gesture beyond that point (or even get too close).

Now that actor plays the part of the second twin, on the other side of the shot. As before, she should act out all of the dialog and reactions for her part in the "dialog." Again, she should be alert to the wall demarking the edge of her "world."

In the thumbnail at the top of the **Properties panel**, you can see how the clip has been cropped: the entire right half is black .

In Premiere Elements, the two clips are stacked one on top of the other. In this case, the LEFT CLIP is in the **Video 2** track above the RIGHT CLIP, which is in the **Video 1** track. The **Crop** effect has been applied. Notice in the illustration how the crop has been adjusted so that it falls exactly on the edge of the wall, creating the perfect illusion of there being no crop at all.

18

Applying the Crop Effect to All Clips ▶

Apply the Crop Effect

1 Click the **Effects and Transitions** tab on the **Media** panel to switch to the **Effects and Transitions** panel.

2 Type **crop** in the text box to bring up the **Crop** effect.

3 Drag the **Crop** effect from the **Transform Video Effects** and drop it onto the **TRIPLET1** clip on the **Video 1** track.

4 Back to the **Effects and Transitions** panel. Once again, grab the **Crop** effect, and again drag and drop it, this time on the **TRIPLET2** clip on the **Video 2** track.

5 The third time's the charm: Drag and drop the **Crop** effect one more time, this time onto the **TRIPLET3** clip on the **Video 3** track.

Did You Know?

You can search by name or by navigation.
The quickest way to find a given transition or effect in the **Effects and Transitions** panel is to search for it by typing all or part of its name in the text box at the top of the panel. However, if you don't know the name, you can navigate to the effect or transition by using the triangles next to each transition or effect category to reveal the subcategories, then use the triangles next to each category to reveal the choices there. For example, the Crop effect can be found by navigating to **Video Effects**, then to the **Transform** category. This is a category that contains, along with the **Crop** effect, the additional effects of **Camera View**, **Clip**, **Edge Feather**, **Horizontal Flip**, **Horizontal Hold**, **Roll**, **Vertical Flip**, and **Vertical Hold**.

We have our clips split, separated, renamed, and stacked on their own tracks. Now, to really make this effect kick in (other than some fine-tuning, which we'll do a bit later), we need to apply the **Crop** effect to each of the clips. We'll next adjust each of the crops so that what we have are three "thin" bars, side-by-each, which appear to anyone viewing this clip to be one "normal" clip, thanks to the magic of video editing with Premiere Elements 3.

Adjusting the Crop Effect for Each Clip

Now that we have applied the **Crop** effect to each of the clips, we need to make adjustments to each clip individually. We'll start with the **TRIPLET3** clip. Why? Because we have the clips stacked now, and **TRIPLET3** is the topmost clip in the stack. **TRIPLET3** is currently the only clip visible in the Monitor (and would be the only thing we'd see if we were to view the movie full screen or export the movie at this point). We'll adjust **TRIPLET3**'s crop first, since it's the topmost clip, and work our way down the stack of our clips.

Make the Adjustments for TRIPLET3

1 Click on the clip, **TRIPLET3**, to make it the active clip.

2 In the **Properties** panel for **TRIPLET3**, click on the **Crop Effect** name bar to select it.

> **TIP** *You don't need to click on the triangle next to the **Crop** effect as we won't be using the controls there. However, if you want to check that your settings are correct, or optionally use the effect controls, twirl the triangle next to Crop to reveal them.*

> **NOTE** *Notice that when you click on the **Crop Effect** name bar in the **Properties** panel, control handles appear in the **Monitor** panel at the four corners of the clip. Take a closer look, if necessary, because the appearance of the handles is a bit subtle.*

3 Grab one of the **handles** on the **right** (top or bottom, it doesn't matter) and drag it across the Monitor until it gets close, but doesn't touch, the actor sitting on the floor.

4 Now, grab one of the **handles** on the **left**. Again, it doesn't matter which one. Drag it a bit to the left until it comes near, but doesn't quite touch, the actor (as shown in the illustration).

> **NOTE** *If you are using the effect controls, the here are the **Crop Effect** settings for **TRIPLET3**:*

- ◆ **Left:** 40.0%
- ◆ **Top:** 0.0%
- ◆ **Right:** 25.0%
- ◆ **Bottom:** 0.0%

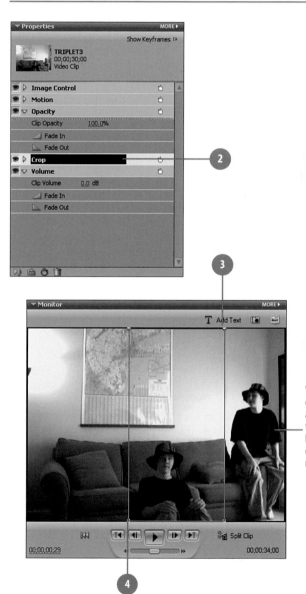

What's this? Triplet #2, or rather the same actor, this time playing the *role* of Triplet #2, has appeared! The effect has begun to reveal itself...

18

5 Click on the clip, **TRIPLET2**, to make it the active clip.

6 Just as we did for **TRIPLET3**, in the **Properties** panel for **TRIPLET2**, click the **Crop Effect** name bar to select it.

7 Grab one of the **handles** on the **left** (top or bottom, it doesn't matter) and drag it across the monitor screen until it gets close, but doesn't touch, the actor sitting on the floor.

NOTE *If you are using the effect controls, the settings for the **Crop** for TRIPLET2 are:*

- ◆ **Left:** **40.0%**

- ◆ **Top:** **0.0%**

- ◆ **Right:** **0.0%**

- ◆ **Bottom:** **0.0%**

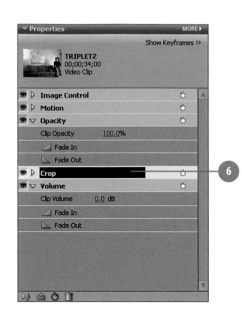

And so we find yet again the same actor, this time playing the role of Triplet #1! The effect is complete, but for some fine-tuning (which comes next...).

Fine-Tuning the Timing of the Conversation

Because all three "triplets" aren't actually sitting in the room talking together at the same time, you may encounter synchronization ("sync") problems after all the clips are stacked. For example, the actor in one part of the clip might delay unnaturally in answering a question from the actor in the other clip. Obviously, this is because the "triplets" weren't actually in the room at the same time. To correct this, you simply need to trim one, two, or all of the clips so that the dialog and action syncs up naturally. Remember, the more carefully you plot out your dialog and when the actor should pause and for how long for each of the positions in the scene that he or she are in, the less tweaking you'll have to do (and the less dramatic the tweaking will be).

Adjust the Clips in Each Track as Needed

1 Return the **CTI** to the beginning of the tracks (if you haven't done so already) by pressing the **Home** key on your keyboard.

> **NOTE** *If your cursor is in another panel in Premiere Elements, such as the **Properties** panel or the **Media** panel, pressing the **Home** key has no effect. If that's the case, click anywhere in the **Timeline** panel first and then click the **Home** key.*

2 If necessary, for more accuracy click on the **Zoom in** button (the magnifying glass with the plus + sign on it) or use the slider to zoom in on the clips. You can also use the + key on your keyboard. This is the key on the number row that has both the equals sign (=) and the plus sign on it, not the + key on the numeric keypad.

> **NOTE** *The scale of the timeruler changes as you change the zoom level. You'll notice that once you have zoomed in all the way, each "tic" on the timeruler now represents a single frame.*

3 There's an unnatural-feeling pause here after triplet # 1 has finished talking and triplet # 2 begins talking. So, we want to trim the first few seconds of this clip. Therefore, select the clip, **TRIPLET2**, in the track, **Video 2**, and drag the front (head) of this clip forward **six seconds** (+**00;00;06;00**); that is, drag the head of the clip to the right.

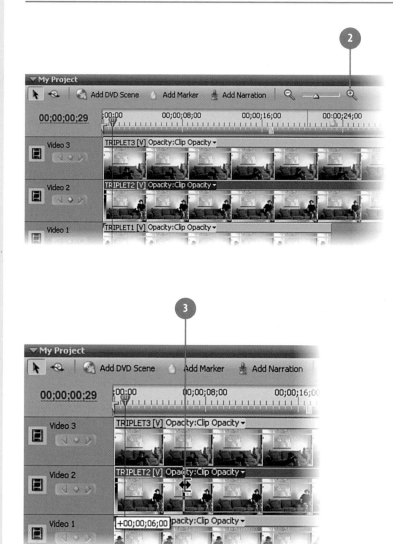

18

You should notice as you drag it that Premiere Elements counts off the frames in a yellow popup.

NOTE *We're working with the sample clips here, of course. In the footage that you take, the degree of adjustment you'll need to make may be far greater or far less.*

4 Select the clip, **TRIPLET3** in the track, **Video 3**. This triplet also has a bit of a delay before he beings "interacting" that makes it seem as if he just wasn't listening to the conversation. We need to fix that so that he joins in in a natural way. As you did with the **TRIPLET2** clip, drag the head of the **TRIPLET3** clip forward **six seconds** (+**00;00;06;00**).

5 The final problem we have is that the clips all end at different times, causing some of the "triplets" to suddenly pop right out of the scene and disappear. Fortunately, this is easy to fix. All we need to do is make sure that all three of the clips end at the same time. So, select the tail **end** of the **TRIPLET3** clip.

TIP *You may want to zoom in first so that you can see the entire project. One quick way to do that is to press the backspace key, \, on your keyboard.*

6 Next, drag the end of the **TRIPLET3** clip back so that it lines up with the **TRIPLET1** clip.

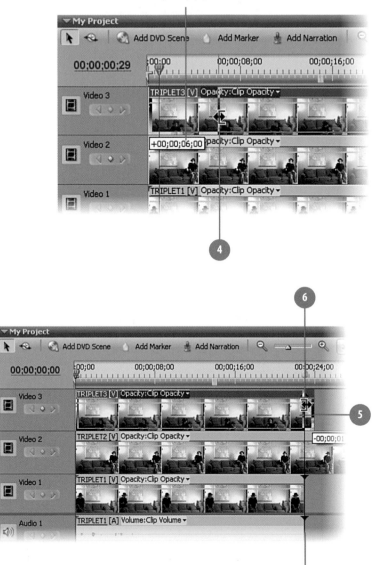

Line up the end of the **TRIPLET3** clip with the end of the **TRIPLET1** clip.

7 Next, select the tail end of the **TRIPLET2** clip.

8 Drag the end of the **TRIPLET2** clip back so that it lines up with the **TRIPLET1** clip.

> **NOTE** *The clips are now lined up visually on the Timeline, indicating that they are all the same duration; that is they start at the same time and end at the same time.*

All of the clips on the Timeline, synchronized so that they start at the right time, and all end together.

18

Making Adjustments, Rendering, and Exporting

Your final step in any project is to render and save. (Of course, you can render and save as often as you want throughout the development of the project. As for saving, you can't do it too many times!) You may want to optionally add a "fade out" to all of the clips as a nice way to end the movie. To do so, just select each clip in turn, and in the **Opacity** property for each, click the **Fade Out** button. (Be careful here. This can be a bit tricky as your clips are stacked and you may have "twins" disappearing in strange ways, but it can be done.) After that, make any final tweaks as needed, and your ready to save, render, and export your movie.

Finishing the Project

1 After you have played back your clip and made the necessary adjustments, press the **ENTER** key on your keyboard to render your project.

2 Press **CTRL-S** to save your project (or you can select **File, Save** from the menu).

3 Finally, export your work as an AVI file. To export the clip, select **File, Export, Movie**.

> **TIP** You can optionally bring this clip into a larger project, show it on your computer, upload it to an Internet video sharing site, or burn it to a DVD.

As your "triplets" project renders, Premiere Elements provides you with status information, including estimated time to complete and a status bar.

The finished project running in Windows Media Player.

The Super Hero Effect

MEDIA:

ACB101.mov
superboy.avi
supermusic.wav
superwind.wav

19

COMPLEXITY:	Simple	Moderate	Complex
SKILL LEVEL:	Novice	Intermediate	Advanced
MATERIALS:	None	Some Props	Greenscreen

Introduction

Superman returns! One of the most popular special effects of all time is creating of the illusion of a superhero flying through the clouds or over the sea or across a city skyline. With Premiere Elements and any acceptable greenscreen or bluescreen, this dream can be yours to achieve: human, or superhuman, flight!

There is virtually no child who wouldn't love to see themselves flying across the sky on the television screen, and there's virtually no child alive who doesn't know how to act this one out: how to stretch out across a dining room chair, how to place their arms in "flight" mode, how to look around at the "earth" below. It's almost as if we are born with the ability to "fly," at least in the special effects Superhero definition of the word.

When you're ready to shoot your own super hero scene, be sure to set up a greenscreen or bluescreen background as flat (wrinkle-free) and as evenly-lit as possible. Make any additional equipment (such as a table or a chair) greenscreen-friendly; that is, paint it "greenscreen green". Plastic patio furniture or kids' furniture can often work well "as is," if the color is right. The Chroma Key can key out any color, so you could match the background color (a sheet or paint) to the furniture, if that's an option.

When you create your own clip, consider dressing your hero in a super costume (or at least a cape) instead of leaving your hero in street clothes, as we've done in this project. You could optionally add a fan to cause the the cape to ripple in the wind—just be careful not to cause ripples in the greenscreen.

What You'll Do

Add the Superhero Clip to the Timeline

Remove the Green Background from Behind Superboy

Add the Chroma Key a Second Time

Remove the Last Remnants of Green

Learn About Royalty Free Video Clips

Add the Cloud Background

Brighten the Super Hero in the Sky

Adjust the Direction and Speed of the Clouds

Set Our Hero's Flight in Motion

Add Super Sound Effects

Add a Super Soundtrack

Adjust the Starting Point for Superboy's Appearance

Adjust the Fade In and Fade Out for the Soundtrack and Clouds

Make Adjustments, Render, and Export

Adding the Superboy Clip to the Timeline

The first thing we'll do with this project is bring in the hero of our clip, who resides in the **superboy.avi** clip, and add him to the Timeline. Once he's safely there, we'll strip away the greenscreen background as the next step in making you believe a man—well, a boy—can fly.

Add the Superboy Clip

1. Start Premiere Elements and create a new project called **superhero**.

2. Click the **Get Media from** button on the **Media** panel to access the **Get Media from** view, if it's not already active.

3. Select **DVD, Digital Camera, Mobile Phone, Hard Drive Camcorder, Card Reader**.

4. When the **Media Downloader** displays, click the **Advanced Dialog** button to switch to Advanced mode.

5. Select the **superboy.avi** clip.

6. Click the **Get Media** button. Premiere Elements copies the **superboy.avi** clip from the DVD onto your hard drive and adds it to the **Available Media** list for this project.

7. For this project, we'll need to be in **Timeline** view because we are working with multiple clips on multiple video tracks. So, If the **My Project** panel is not already in **Timeline** view, click the **Timeline** button to switch.

8. Drag and drop the **superboy.avi** clip on the **Media** panel onto the Timeline of the **My Project** panel onto the **Video 2** track. Line up the head of the **superboy.avi** clip with the start of the **Video 2** track.

   TIP We're placing the **superboy.avi** clip on the second video track because later we'll be adding the background clip to the timeline, and the **superboy.avi** clip needs to be above the background clip.

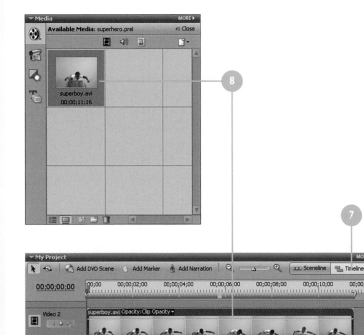

Removing the Green Background from Behind Superboy

Here we'll "clean the green" background from the **superboy.avi** clip. Because of the way that this particular greenscreen clip was filmed, it's a bit problematic. There are what are known as "hot spots"(places in the background on which light shown brightly) and shadows. The more uniform the green color is in your greenscreen clips, the more successful the **Chroma Key** effect will be when applied. Shadows and "hot spots" effectively create such variations on the green-screen color that they are practically completely different shades of green and are very difficult to remove. But we have a solution...

Apply the Chroma Key

1. On the **Media** panel, click the **Effects and Transitions** button to switch to the **Effects and Transitions** view.

2. Type **chroma** in the text box to bring up the **Chroma Key**.

3. Select the **Chroma Key** from the Keying category of **Video Effects**.

4. Drag and drop it onto the **superboy.avi** clip on the **Video 2** track.

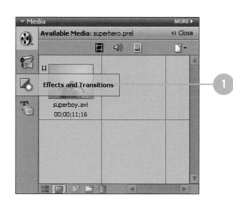

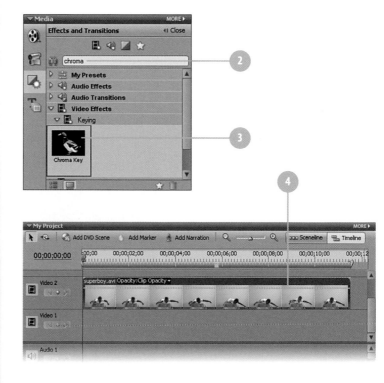

Did You Know?

Premiere Elements has 9 "Key" effects.
You have at your disposal with Premiere Elements nine effects in the Keying category, each of which can help solve any unique problem that a clip might present to you in your projects. There are three "garbage matte" keys. These are simply keys that let you crop out what is literally referred to as the garbage; that is, any part of the clip that you don't care about and are willing to throw away—just like garbage. The garbage matte keys include the Four-Point, the Eight-Point, and the Sixteen-Point Garbage Matte. The points refers to how many control handles, or points, each has. There is an additional matte key here, the **Track Matte Key**, whose purpose is to create transparency in a superimposed clip. There are also four keys related to chroma—or color—keying. These are the **Green Screen Key**, the **Blue Screen Key**, the **Non Red Key**, and the **Chroma Key**. The final keying effect in this category is the Alpha Adjust.

Fine-tune the Chroma Key

1 In the **Properties** panel for the **superboy.avi** clip, click the **triangle** next to the **Chroma Key** to twirl it down and reveal the effect's controls.

2 Select the **eyedropper tool** and click in the upper right corner of the greenscreen background of the **superboy.avi** clip in the **Monitor** panel.

3 Back in the **Properties** panel, set the **Similarity** to **30.0%**.

4 Set the **Smoothing** to **High**.

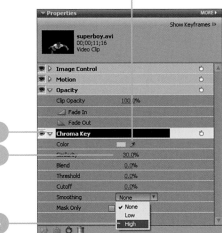

Did You Know?

The Chroma Key can key any color.
Chroma actually means color. Therefore, unlike the **Blue Screen Key** or the **Green Screen Key**, you can actually use the **Chroma Key** to key out *any* color in the color spectrum that you want to remove from the background. You can use the eyedropper tool to select the color directly from the background. Alternatively, you can click on the color swatch to bring up the **Color Picker** dialog box. From here, you can pick the color from the color spectrum, or enter the numeric value for the color if you know it. You can enter the numeric color as RGB (red, green, blue), HSB (hue, saturation, brightness), HSL (hue, saturation, luminance), YUV (luminance, blue, red), or even as a hexadecimal number.

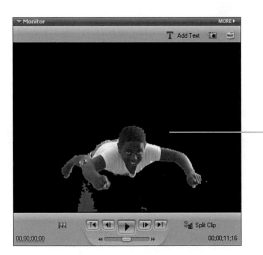

Note that now in the **Monitor** panel, most of the green in the background has been removed. However, there is still some green remaining.

Adding the Chroma Key a Second Time

This particular background is a difficult one to remove. If we use just the one **Chroma Key** effect and keep increasing the Similarity setting, we will eventually chip away at the foreground image, superboy, in our attempt to get rid of all the green. (Eventually, if you go high enough, every color in the spectrum is "similar" to green.) Fortunately, there's an easy solution because Premiere Elements lets you apply as many instances of the **Chroma Key** as you need, each one targeted at a specific color.

Once More with the Chroma Key

1. Once again, select the **Chroma Key** from the Keying category of **Video Effects**.

2. Drag and drop it for a second time onto the **superboy.avi** clip on the **Video 2** track.

3. In the **Properties** panel for the **superboy.avi** clip, click the **triangle** next to the *second* **Chroma Key** effect to twirl it down and reveal the effect's controls.

   TIMESAVER *To avoid confusion, first close the effect controls for the first **Chroma Key** by clicking the **triangle** next to it to twirl it up.*

4. Select the **eyedropper tool** again, and click to select the **dark green area** on the greenscreen background from the frame from the **superboy.avi** clip in the **Monitor** panel.

5. Back in the **Properties** panel, set the following:

   ◆ **Similarity: 10.0%**

   ◆ **Blend: 3.0%**

   ◆ **Smoothing: High**

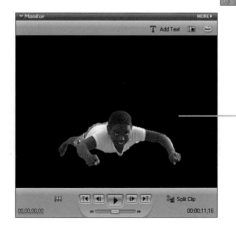

By applying the **Chroma Key** twice, and targeting the two very different types of green in the background, all of the green background has been successfully removed, without degrading the quality of the actor's image.

Removing the Last Remnants of Green

We're almost done perfecting our hero. We've successfully removed the greenscreen background (the black that you see is the "window" where blue sky and white clouds will soon be showing through), but a bit of green "tinge" remains. To remove it, we'll use the **Non Red Key**.

Apply the Non Red Key

1 On the **Media** panel, click the **Effects and Transitions** button to switch to the **Effects and Transitions** view, if it's not already the current view.

2 Type **red** in the text box to bring up the **Non Red Key**.

3 Select the **Non Red Key** from the Keying category of **Video Effects** and drag and drop it onto the **superboy.avi** clip on the **Video 2** track.

4 In the **Properties** panel for the **superboy.avi** clip, click the **triangle** next to the **Non Red Key** effect to twirl it down and reveal the effect's controls.

5 From the **Defringing** drop down menu, select **Green**.

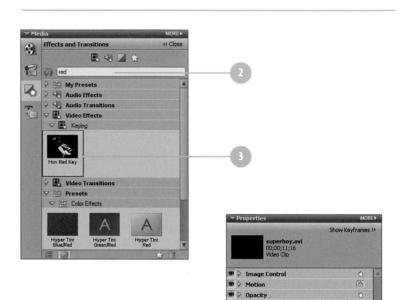

Superboy before the Non Red Key is applied. Note the green tinge around his arms and especially on his leg and foot.

Superboy after the Non Red Key has been applied, with Green as the Defringing option. The green is gone.

Learn About Royalty Free Video Clips

What Does "Royalty Free" Mean?

Royalty free footage refers to any video (or music or sound effects) footage that you purchase for use in your own projects. By the way, the "free" in royalty free doesn't mean that you don't have to pay for it. It means that you don't have to pay *again* each time you use it. You only pay for the initial purchase of the footage. After that, you can pretty much use the footage over and over again, for whatever you want; it's called "unlimited use."

However, there are typically some restrictions to use. For example, if used in a for-profit project, you may need to credit the clip's producers or there may be a limit to how much royalty free content you can include. It's standard, too, that you don't have the right to resell or to repackage the clip.

About Artbeats

Artbeats is one of the most respected sources in the industry for royalty-free content. Their source material is actually 35mm film, which Artbeats digitizes into high quality footage and distributes in two formats: NTSC (the format used in the United States and Canada) and PAL (the format used in most of Europe, as well as in Japan).

To help us create some of the projects in this book, as well as give you a taste of the kind of clips they have available, Artbeats supplied six of the clips included on the DVD supplied with this book. Screenshots from those clips are shown below and are on the DVD in Apple™ QuickTime™ format (.mov). You'll find hundreds more clips for purchase in many more categories at **www.artbeats.com**.

19

Artbeats Clips on this Book's DVD

D811-03.mov

TC107.mov

ACB101.mov

RF307.mov

TL302.mov

ANT113.mov

Adding the Cloud Background

For the superhero to fly free and powerful through the sky, as only a true hero with superpowers can, we have supplied you with a clip from Artbeats. The clip, **ACB101.mov**, is a swooping flight through a blue sky filled with puffy white clouds. Perfect for a relaxing flying break for a busy superhero.

Add the Clouds

1. Click the **Get Media from** button on the **Media** panel to access the **Get Media From** view, if it's not already active.

2. Select **DVD, Digital Camera, Mobile Phone, Hard Drive Camcorder, Card Reader**.

3. When the **Media Downloader** displays, click the **Advanced Dialog** button to switch to Advanced mode.

4. Select the **ACB101.mov** clip.

5. Click the **Get Media** button. Premiere Elements copies the **ACB101.mov** clip from the DVD onto your hard drive and adds them to the **Available Media** list for this project.

6. Drag and drop the **ACB101.mov** clip onto the Timeline of the **My Project** panel onto the **Video 1** track.

    IMPORTANT *Be sure to line up the head of the **ACB101.mov** clip with the start of the **Video 1** track.*

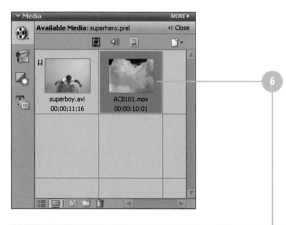

With the addition of the sky clip to the **My Project Timeline**, suddenly he's floating on air.

Brightening the Super Hero in the Sky

Now that are hero is up, up, and away, he doesn't look quite bright enough for someone so much closer to the sun. We'll need to make a couple of adjustments to our hero's Contrast and Saturation to give him a more convincing look, as if the sun were shining on him up there. We want to make fairly small adjustments to avoid washing him out or creating an artificial look.

Adjust the Contrast

1. In the **Properties** panel for the **superboy.avi** clip, click the **triangle** next to **Image Control** to reveal the effect's controls.

2. Set the **Contrast** to **110.0**.

Here's how our hero looks in the sky before adjustments.

Did You Know?

The Lens Flare effect is a bright idea.
If you're not familiar with the **Lens Flare** effect in Premiere Elements, you should be. Try it on those occasions when you want to emphasize a bright, sunlit scene. The **Lens Flare** effect creates a glare which just isn't appropriate for this project, but which can be quite appropriate in outdoor scenes where reflective material—such as a car bumper or a street sign—is in the scene. You'll find the **Lens Flare** effect under **Video Effects**, Render in the **Effects and Transitions** view of the **Media** panel. Test it out and see how the three types of flares are different: 50-300mm Zoom, 35mm Prime, and 105mm Prime. You can interactively set both the brightness and the location (Flare Center) of the lens flare, as well, for true control of just how the flare looks in your clip.

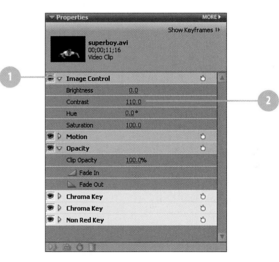

After a few small adjustments, he looks much brighter, more as if he's lit by the sun in the sky.

Adjusting the Direction and Speed of the Clouds

We'll be adjusting our superhero so that he flies towards us from the distance. Unfortunately, our clouds in the **ACB101.mov** clip were filmed moving in the wrong direction (away from us). This would work fine if our superhero were flying away from us, too. No problem, though. With Premiere Elements it's a simple thing to reverse a clip. In addition to reversing this clip, we want to slow the clip down just a bit so that it lasts as long (actually, just a bit longer than) the superboy.avi clip. Otherwise, he'll be flying against the sky background for awhile, and then suddenly against a mysterious black background.

Use Time Stretch to Make the Changes

1. **Right-click** on the **ACB101.mov** clip in the Video 1 track on the Timeline.

2. From the contextual menu, select **Time Stretch**.

3. In the **Time Stretch** dialog box, set the **Speed** to **50%**.

4. Mark the **Reverse Speed** check box.

5. Click **OK**.

> **TIP** Since the *ACB101.mov* clip does not contain any audio, we don't need to worry about the *Maintain Audio Pitch* setting.

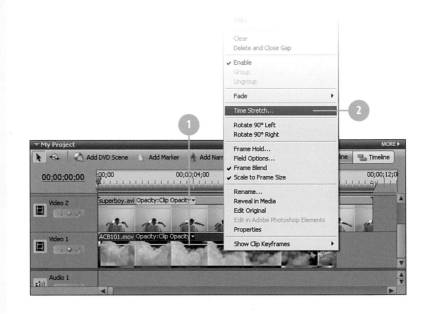

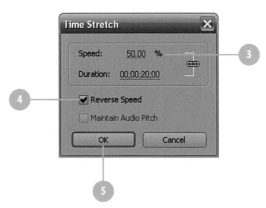

Setting Our Hero's Flight in Motion

In this task, we will really be making Superboy fly. We'll resize, move, and set a flight path for our hero, all using the **Motion** effect in Premiere Elements and keyframes.

Change Superboy's Size

1 Select the **superboy.avi** clip on the **Video 2** track in the Timeline.

> **TIMESAVER** *Be sure the CTI is in the home position at the start of the Timeline. If it isn't, you can drag it there with your mouse, or simply press the Home key on your keyboard.*

2 Click the triangle next to **Motion** on the **Properties** panel for the **superboy.avi** clip to reveal the effect's controls.

3 Click on the word **Motion** in the **Properties** panel for the **superboy.avi** clip.

> **TIP** *You should see a box appear around the clip in the Monitor panel.*

4 Grab one of the **corner handles** of the **superboy.avi** clip and **drag** it to resize the clip, as shown in the illustration.

> **TIP** *Resize the clip to about 25%. You can also do this by typing 25 for the Scale setting in the Properties panel.*

Selecting **Motion** in the **Properties** panel causes a box around the clip, complete with resizing handles, to appear in the **Monitor** panel.

Resize our hero to about 25%.

Change Superboy's Starting Location

1 **Drag** the **superboy.avi** clip over to the upper left of the **Monitor** panel screen, as shown in the illustration. It should be roughly in **Position 54.0, 112.0** or thereabouts.

2 Click the **Show Keyframes** button on the **Properties** panel to reveal the workspace for adding keyframes. Expand this area as needed.

TIP *The* **Show Keyframes** *button, once clicked, becomes the* **Hide Keyframes** *button and its function changes to match.*

TIMESAVER *Adjust the horizontal size of the* **Properties** *panel as needed so that you can work most effectively with keyframes. To do so, drag the left side of the panel to the left. You want to see as much of the* **Properties** *panel timeline as possible.*

3 Set the position and scale to be:

- ◆ **Position:** -80 40

- ◆ **Scale:** 0.0

4 Click the **Toggle animation** button to turn on the animation functionality of Premiere Elements.

TIP *Premiere Elements automatically places the necessary keyframes at this point for all of the Motion-related settings.*

To start, drag the **superhero.avi** clip over here, to the upper left of the monitor screen.

The superhero clip should be roughly in this position on the monitor screen.

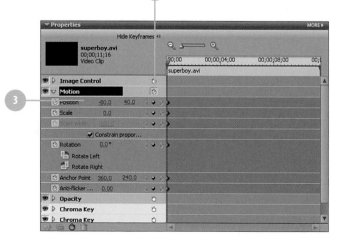

Set a Midpoint Marker for Adjusting Superboy's Size and Location

1. Drag the **CTI** over to the 4 second mark, **00;00;04;00**.

2. Drag the **superboy.avi** clip over to the center of the monitor screen.

Notice that our superhero is off-screen here for his starting point. He's also vanished, now that his Scale is set to 0.0

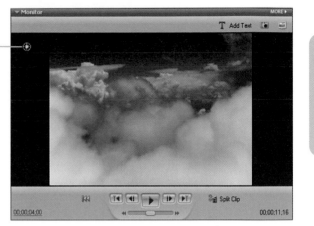

Did You Know?

Place a keyframe whenever and wherever you want to make a change. As you work on your projects, whenever you need an animation (time)-related change—such as a change to the size of an object, its orientation (rotation), or its location—move the **CTI** to the point in the Timeline where you want that change to occur and, with the animation function active as we have it here in this chapter, make your change. Remember, the more keyframes you use, the more control you have over the object (clip) that you are morphing. Remember, too, that Premiere Elements fills in the blanks, so to speak (known as "tweening") between each of the keyframes and their settings, in sequence.

3 Set the **Position** property for the clip as follows:

◆ **Position:**   320   180

4 Set the **Scale** property for the clip as follows:

◆ **Scale:**   50

TIMESAVER *After you adjust the position of the **superboy.avi** clip, Premiere Elements automatically drops a keyframe for the **Position** property. After you adjust the scale, Premiere Elements will then drop keyframes for both Scale and Scale Width.*

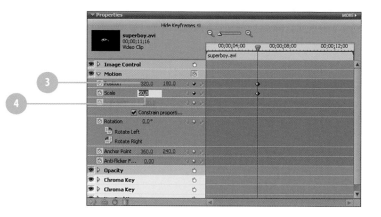

Change the Monitor Panel View

1 **Right-click** on the **Monitor** panel screen.

2 From the contextual menu that displays, select **Magnification**.

3 From the **Magnification Fly-out** menu, select **50%**.

IMPORTANT *In order to see the black areas outside of the visible clip, you may need to first resize the **Monitor** panel.*

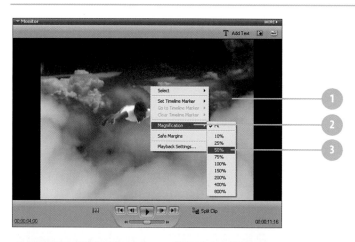

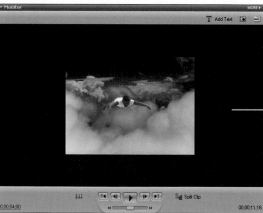

Note that we can now see more of the outside area surrounding the screen, which will allow us to drag the clip "off camera."

Set the Final Locations and Sizes for the Super Hero

1. Drag the **CTI** over to the 8 second mark, **00;00;08;00**.

2. Drag the **superboy.avi** clip over to the left of the monitor screen, as shown in the illustration. The clip should now be roughly at this position:

   ◆ **Position:** 250 315

3. Adjust the scale as follows:

   ◆ **Scale:** 100.0

   TIMESAVER *Premiere Elements automatically places keyframes for you for the **Position**, **Scale**, and **Scale Width** properties.*

4. Drag the **CTI** to the end of the **superboy.avi** clip (**00;00;11;16**).

5. Drag the **superboy.avi** clip over to "off camera" down to the bottom right of the monitor screen, as shown in the illustration. The clip should now be roughly at this position:

   ◆ **Position:** 760 480

6. Adjust the scale as follows:

   ◆ **Scale:** 150.0

   TIMESAVER *Again, after you adjust the position of the **superboy.avi clip**, Premiere Elements automatically places a keyframe for the **Position** property. This is also true when you adjust the scale. Premiere Elements places keyframes for both the **Scale** and **Scale Width** properties.*

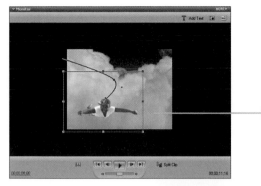

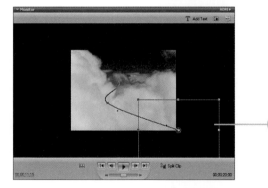

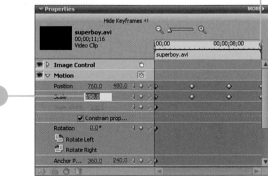

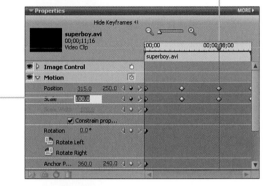

Adding Super Sound Effects

You can't have a super hero streaking through the sky without him or her generating the sound of a strong wind blowing. We've included a wind sound effect to add to the project that simply needs to be dropped onto the **My Project Timeline** and it's ready to go. To save time, with this task, we'll be grabbing both audio files, the wind sound effect file, **superwind.wav**, and the music file for this project, **supermusic.wav**.

Add the Wind Sound

1 Click the **Get Media from** button on the **Media** panel to access the **Get Media From** view, if it's not already active.

2 Select **DVD, Digital Camera, Mobile Phone, Hard Drive Camcorder, Card Reader**.

3 When the **Media Downloader** displays, click the **Advanced Dialog** button to switch to Advanced mode.

4 Select the following two sound clips:

- ◆ **superwind.wav**

- ◆ **supermusic.wav**

5 Click the **Get Media** button. Premiere Elements copies the clips from the DVD onto your hard drive and adds them to the **Available Media** list for this project.

6 Drag and drop the clip onto the Timeline of the **My Project** panel onto the **Audio 1** track.

IMPORTANT *Again, be sure you line up the head of the **superwind.wav** clip with the start of the **Audio 1** track.*

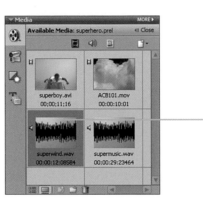

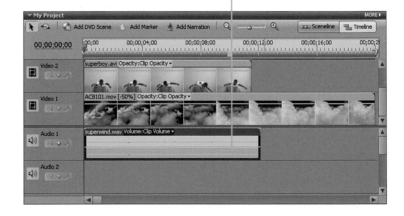

Adding a Super Soundtrack

Thanks once again to the folks at SmartSound® and their Quicktracks™ software, we have some great music for our super hero to fly by. It's more in the style of the theme music for Neo in the Matrix movies than Superman, but it works. We've renamed it **supermusic.wav**, but it's original name in the Quicktracks software is "SmartSound - Subterfuge - Shamus [00;29;16].wav."

Add the Super Music

1 With your mouse, select the **supermusic.wav** clip from the **Available Media** view of the **Media** panel and drag and drop the clip onto **Audio 2** track on the Timeline.

> **IMPORTANT** *As before, line up the head of the supermusic.wav clip with the start of the Audio 2 track.*

2 Grab the tail end of the **supermusic.wav** clip, and drag it back to shorten its duration. You want to have it be just a bit longer than the **ACB101.mov** track (the Artbeats footage of the sky and clouds). The **supermusic.wav** track should end at about 22 seconds or so.

3 The super music is a bit too loud. So, in the **Properties** panel for the **supermusic.wav** clip, set the **Volume** to **-8.0 dB**. Doing so will let viewers hear both the wind and the music at the same time, without one overpowering the other.

> **TIMESAVER** *If you're using Quicktracks and prefer to grab the music yourself right from the software, start Quicktracks from within Premiere Elements and choose the Futuristic style and select the Subterfuge track from the Maestro screen. Then, on the Quicktracks screen, choose the Shamus variation.*

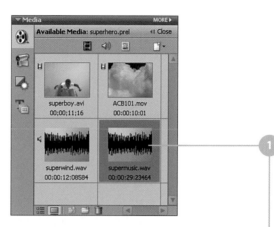

Adjusting the Starting Point for Superboy's Appearance

We want the clip to open to the sound of music and the sight of the clouds moving through the sky. Then, after a short pause, we want our super hero to appear off in the distance and fly towards us, with the sound of wind accompanying his flight. To achieve this, we simply need to move both the **superboy.avi** and **superwind.wav** files a bit later in the Timeline. Later, in Timeline terms, means to the right.

Move Superboy and the Wind Sound to the Right

1. Click the **superboy.avi** clip on the **Video 2** track.

2. Holding down the **Shift** key on your keyboard, click the **superwind.wav** file on the **Audio 1** track.

3. Now, release the **Shift** key and with your mouse, drag the two clips to the right until the head (front) of the clips is at the two second mark (**00;00;02;00**).

   TIP *To make it easier to drag the clips to the two second mark, move the **CTI** there first as a placeholder (as shown in the illustration). Then, move the clips and they will snap into place. (If necessary, activate the **Snap** function by selecting **Snap** from the **My Project MORE** menu.)*

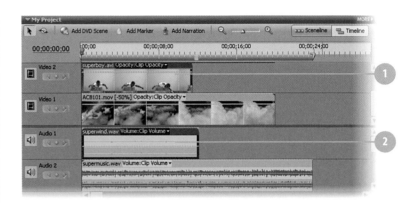

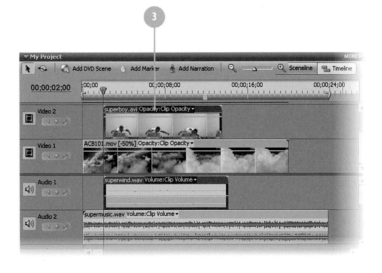

Adjusting the Fade In and Fade Out for the Soundtrack and Clouds

It will be a cool final effect to have the clouds fade to black after our super hero has flown out of the scene. We'll let the music continue to play over the black background (a great place to run end credits, if we were using them, by the way). Finally, we'll fade out the music at the end of the clip, and our project is over.

Select the Fade In and Fade Out Buttons

1 Click the **ACB101.mov** clip on the **Video 1** track to select it.

2 On the Properties panel for the **ACB101.mov** clip, click the **Fade In** button so that the clouds and sky fade out.

> **HUH?** *Yes, you read that right. You want to click the* **Fade In** *button so that the clip fades out. If you remember, we reversed this clip in an earlier task. By doing so, we effectively made the back of the clip the front, and the front of the clip the back. So to fade out the "back" of the clip (which is really the front, reversed), we need to apply a Fade In.*

3 Click the **supermusic.wav** clip on the **Audio 2** track to select it.

4 On the **Properties** panel for the **supermusic.wav** clip, click the **Fade Out** button under **Volume** so that the music fades out.

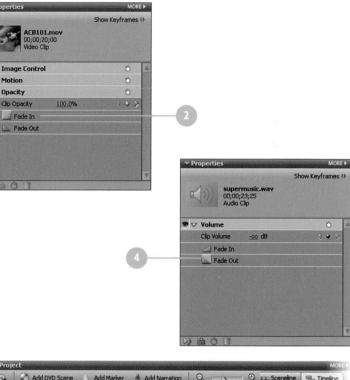

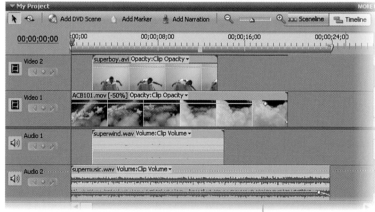

Notice the "fade outs" for both the sky and the music tracks, represented by the descending rubberbands.

Making Adjustments, Rendering, and Exporting

You've done a super job! All the pieces are in place. You've learned how to create the illusion of a superhero in flight using chroma key, motion effects, keyframes—not to mention sound effects and music. Save your work one more time, and then render and export your project so that you can show people what you've created.

Finishing the Project

1 After you have played back your clip and made the necessary adjustments, press the **ENTER** key on your keyboard to render your project.

2 Press **CTRL-S** to save your project (or you can select **File, Save** from the menu).

3 Finally, export your work as an AVI file. To export the clip, select **File, Export, Movie**.

TIP *You can optionally bring this clip into a larger project, show it on your computer, upload it to an Internet video sharing site, or burn it to a DVD.*

The finished project "flying" along in Windows Media Player.

The Around the World Effect

MEDIA:

fallfoliage.avi
hawaii.avi
Hawaii_reporter.avi
islandparty.wav
NE_reporter.avi
sanfranpaintedhouses.avi
SF_reporter.avi

20

COMPLEXITY:	Simple	Moderate	Complex
SKILL LEVEL:	Novice	Intermediate	Advanced
MATERIALS:	None	Some Props	Greenscreen

Introduction

Without leaving the relative comfort of your home studio—be it your den, basement, garage, office, attic, kitchen, or bedroom—you or your loved ones can travel the world to frolic in the fields in France, rock out the outback in Australia, make it big in New York, New York (if you can make it there virtually, you can make it virtually anywhere), or even march with the penguins in Antarctica.

With the international clips available from such vendors as Artbeats and the Footage Firm, you can purchase (for a surprisingly reasonable price) beautiful and interesting, high quality (even HDV versions) clips of virtually any location in the world, both of cities and the countryside, for you to go to. For example, you could "visit" Chicago, Illinois; Las Vegas, Nevada; Sydney, Australia; Toronto, Canada; Athens, Greece; London, England; Paris, France; Rome, Italy; or even Papua New Guinea. Like Johnny Cash, you'll be singing, "I've been everywhere, man..."

By using the Green Screen Key in Premiere Elements, you'll be able to drop out, or "key out," the green background behind the actor to reveal any location that you choose. While the location in the background can be a still photograph, especially in cases where the actor is standing in front of a building or monument, using video clips adds to the realism. One factor to consider when using the Around the World Effect is the lighting. If the light on your actor appears to be coming from the east, and the light in the background clip is coming from the west, it looks strange, especially if shadows are noticeable. In this chapter, you'll learn how to use Premiere Elements to brighten your traveller and help match the actor to the background clip.

For this project, we'll be "travelling" to New England in the fall, then to the city of San Francisco, and finally to a beach in the beautiful state of Hawaii. We'll be dealing with some unique challenges matching the clips up in terms of lighting, movement, and other considerations. You'll learn a lot along this journey that you'll apply to your own projects ahead.

What You'll Do

Load the Travel Clips for the Project

Load the New England Clips to the Timeline

Apply and Adjust the Green Screen Key for the New England Reporter Clip

Make Adjustments to the New England Scene

Load the San Francisco Clips to the Timeline

Apply and Adjust the Green Screen Key for the San Francisco Reporter Clip

Make Adjustments to the San Francisco Scene

Load the Hawaii Clips to the Timeline

Apply and Adjust the Green Screen Key for the Hawaii Reporter Clip

Make Adjustments to the Hawaii Scene

Add a Little Travelling Music

Make Adjustments, Render, and Export

Loading the Travel Clips for the Project

For this exercise, we have clips of three travel reporters. One reporting from San Francisco, one from New England, and one from Hawaii, each with their own corresponding "location" clip. Once the clips are brought in to the project, we'll then load each of these on the Timeline in the **My Project** panel in turn, along with its corresponding background location. Each clip has its own unique challenge, which we will discuss and remedy later in this chapter.

Add the Video Clips to the Project

1. Start Premiere Elements and create a new project called **aroundtheworld**.

2. Click the **Get Media from** button on the **Media** panel to access the **Get Media From** view, if it's not already active.

3. Select **DVD, Digital Camera, Mobile Phone, Hard Drive Camcorder, Card Reader**.

4. When the **Media Downloader** displays, click the **Advanced Dialog** button to switch to Advanced mode.

5. Select the following clips:
   - ◆ **fallfoliage.avi**
   - ◆ **hawaii.avi**
   - ◆ **Hawaii_reporter.avi**
   - ◆ **NE_reporter.avi**
   - ◆ **sanfranpaintedhouses.avi**
   - ◆ **SF_reporter.avi**

6. Click the **Get Media** button. Premiere Elements copies the clips you selected from the DVD onto your computer's hard drive and adds them to the **Available Media** list for this project.

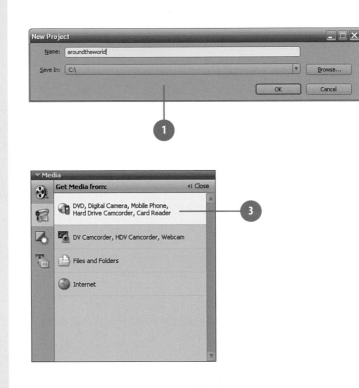

All of the files for this project, loaded in the **Media** panel ready for use.

Loading the New England Clips to the Timeline

Our journey starts on the East Coast, moves to California, and ends in Hawaii. So the first clips that we are going to add to the **My Project** panel Timeline are the two East Coast clips, **NE_reporter.avi** and **fallfoliage.avi** We have a unique problem with the **fallfoliage.avi** clip. The camera zooms in on the pumpkin stand. This would surely give it away that our "reporter" really isn't at the scene. However, we can solve this by syncing the zoom in the **fallfoliage.avi** clip with a zoom on the reporter that we create in Premiere Elements.

The Trip Starts in New England

1 Drag the **fallfoliage.avi** clip onto the **Video 1** track on the **My Project** panel. Line up the head of the **fallfoliage.avi** clip with the start of the **Video 1** track.

> **TIP** *If you are in Sceneline view, just drop the clip onto the first scene placeholder.*

2 Drag the **NE_reporter.avi** clip onto the **Video 2** track. Again, line up the head of the clip with the start of the track.

> **TIP** *These two clips happen to be the same length. This is typically not the case.*

3 If the **My Project** panel is not already in **Timeline** view, click the **Timeline** button (shown below) to switch.

> **TIP** *We need to be in Timeline view because we'll be working with multiple video tracks.*

Did You Know?

There are two ways to preview available.
Premiere Elements has two ways for you to take a quick look at any clip in your project. One way is to activate the **Preview Area** in the **Media** panel (select the **MORE** button at the top right, and then select **View, Preview Area**). Select a clip and click the tiny **Play** button up by the **Preview Area** to watch a thumbnail version. View a larger preview by double-clicking any clip in the **Media** panel or on the Timeline to open the **Preview** panel, a resizeable panel similar to the **Monitor** panel.

20

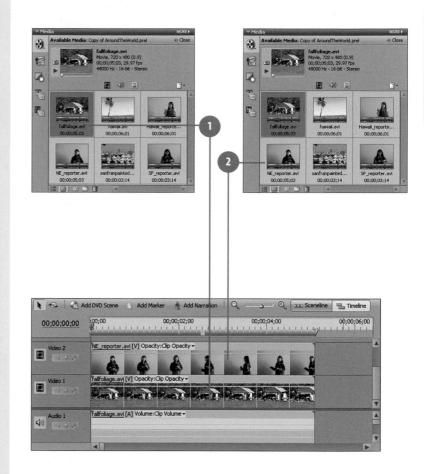

Applying the Green Screen Key to the New New England Reporter Clip

In order to "transport" our reporter from one part of the world to another, we need to apply the **Green Screen Key** so that we can remove the green background and reveal the world behind her. We then adjust the **Green Screen Key** a bit so that all of the green background is gone. If you worked your way through this book chapter by chapter, you should be already familiar with this technique. And if not, just follow the steps that follow to learn how it's done.

Find and Apply the Green Screen Key

1 Click on the **Effects and Transitions** button in the **Media** panel, to switch to the **Effects and Transitions** view.

2 Type **green** in the text field.

3 Select the **Green Screen Key** effect from the Keying effects in the **Video Effects** list and drag and drop it onto the **NE_reporter.avi** clip on the **Video 2** track.

4 In the **Properties** panel, click the **triangle** next to **Green Screen Key** to view the effect's controls.

5 Adjust the effect as follows:

◆ **Threshold: 31.0%**

◆ **Cutoff: 31.0%**

◆ **Smoothing: High**

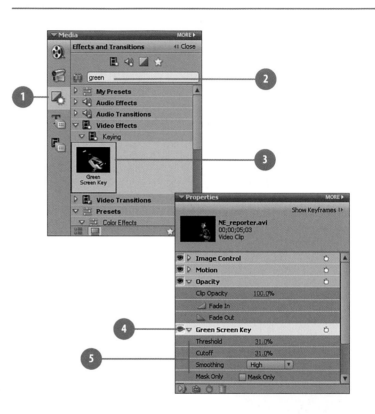

The reporter clip before the **Green Screen Key** has been applied.

The same reporter clip after the Green Screen Key has been applied.

Making Adjustments to the New England Scene

When the clip of the pumpkin stand was recorded, the videographer zoomed in on the scene. This is fine and makes for an interesting clip. However, if we simply leave our "reporter" standing as she is, then the illusion that she's on the scene is broken. In order to create a convincing scene, we must also zoom in on the reporter at the same time, and to the same degree. In that way, it appears as if the cameraman zoomed in on a scene in which the reporter was actually present. We are also going to make a slight adjustment to where the reporter stands. We want her to stand a bit closer to the camera, and a bit off to the right (her left). We'll do that first.

Adjust the Location of the Reporter

1. To move our reporter, first click on the **NE_reporter.avi** clip on the **Video 2** track to select it.

2. In the **Properties** panel, click on the **Motion** effect to select it (it reverse highlights to show that it is selected).

    TIP When you select the **Motion** effect, you should see a box appear around the **NE_reporter.avi** clip in the **Monitor** panel.

3. Click anywhere inside the box around the **NE_reporter.avi** clip in the **Monitor** panel and drag the clip slightly down and to the right, as shown in the illustration.

    TIP You can use the **Motion** effect controls to type in exact coordinates for **Position**, which are **450, 270**.

Zoom in on the Reporter

1. The zoom action starts in the background clip, **fallfoliage.avi**, at **00;00;01;10**, so we'll place a keyframe at that spot. Do do so, first click the **Show Keyframes** button to view the keyframes workspace.

2. Then, move the **CTI** (either the one in the **My Project** panel timeline or the one right in the keyframes workspace) to **00;00;01;10**.

3. Click the **Toggle Animation** button (shown below) for the **Motion** effect to activate **Motion** controls.

1. Clicking the **Show Keyframes** button changes it to the *Hide* **Keyframes** button.

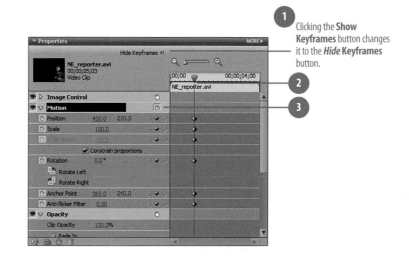

TIP *You may need to click the **triangle** to twirl open the **Motion** effect controls, if they aren't already visible.*

TIP *Keyframes should drop automatically. In case they don't, you can add a keyframe manually by clicking the **Add/Remove Keyframe** button (shown below).*

4 Press the **Page Down** key on your keyboard to move to the end of the clip (your **CTI** should be at **00;00;05;03**).

5 Click the **Add/Remove Keyframe** button for **Scale** (under **Motion**).

6 Change the **Scale** from 100.0% to **130.0%**.

TIP *Now, when you click the **Play** button on the **Monitor** panel, or press the **Spacebar** on your keyboard, you'll see that as we zoom in on the pumpkin stand, we appear to be zooming in on our intrepid reporter as well.*

The reporter, standing in her new location, a bit to the side.

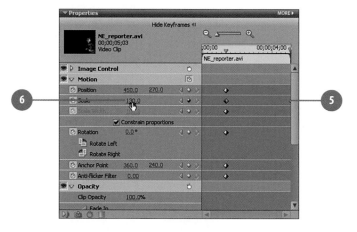

With the scale changing over time to match the zoom action of the background clip, the camera appears to be zooming on both the pumpkin stand and the reporter!

Loading the San Francisco Clips to the Timeline

Off We Go to California

① Drag the **sanfranpaintedhouses.avi** clip from the **Media** panel onto the **Video 1** track on the **My Project** panel, directly to the right of (and touching) the **fallfoliage.avi** clip.

TIP *It's easier to work with clips that you want to "stick together" if you have the **Snap** function turned on. To turn on **Snap**, select it from either the **My Project** panel's **More** button or from the **Timeline** menu at the top of the screen.*

② Drag the **SF_reporter.avi** clip from the **Media** panel onto the **Video 2** track on the **My Project** panel. Again, you want it directly to the right of (and touching) the clip that's already there, **NE_reporter.avi**.

The next clip, of San Francisco, has a sunny setting, with a shade tree towards the front of the clip, casting a shadow. As it turns out, the clip of the reporter is a bit dark, which is good since it will appear that the reporter is standing in the shade. If that wasn't the case, we'd have to adjust the **Contrast** or **Brightness** settings to darken the reporter clip a bit.

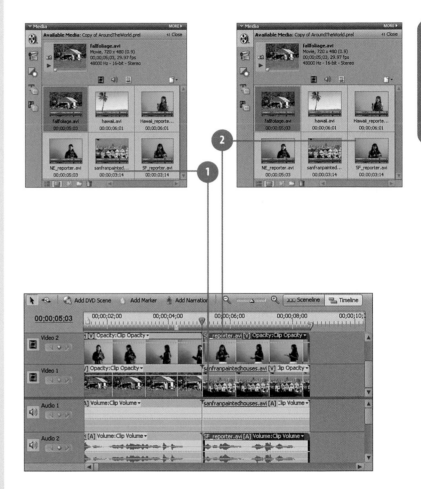

20

Applying the Green Screen Key to the San Francisco Reporter Clip

Our intrepid reporter, after a grueling day at virtual airports and in the air, is to arrive in San Francisco for her next report, "live on location." Just as for the New England clip, we need to strip away the green background from the **SF_reporter.avi** clip. To do so, we again employ the Premiere Elements effect, the **Green Screen Key**.

Find and Apply the Green Screen Key

1 Click on the **Effects and Transitions** button in the **Media** panel, to switch to the **Effects and Transitions** view.

2 Type **green** in the text field.

3 Select the **Green Screen Key** effect from the Keying effects in the **Video Effects** list and drag and drop it onto the **SF_reporter.avi** clip on the **Video 2** track.

4 In the **Properties** panel, click the **triangle** next to **Green Screen Key** to view the effect's controls.

5 Adjust the effect as follows:

- ◆ **Threshold:** 35.0%

- ◆ **Cutoff:** 35.0%

- ◆ **Smoothing: High**

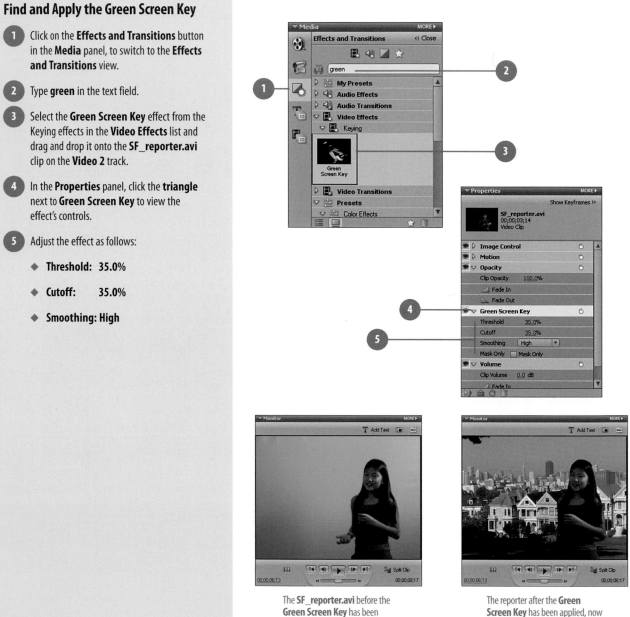

The **SF_reporter.avi** before the **Green Screen Key** has been applied.

The reporter after the **Green Screen Key** has been applied, now reporting live from San Francisco.

Making Adjustments to the San Francisco Scene

Unfortunately, once we apply the **Green Screen Key** and adjust it to remove the green background, the clip appears to have a slightly purple tint to it, especially in the actor's hair. We'll need to remove this, which we'll do using the **Non Red Key**.

Find and Apply the Non Red Key

If it's not already the current view, click the **Effects and Transitions** button in the **Media** panel, to switch to the **Effects and Transitions** view.

2 Type **red** in the text field.

3 Select the **Non Red Key** effect from the Keying effects in the **Video Effects** list and drag and drop it onto the **SF_reporter.avi** clip on the **Video 2** track.

4 In the **Properties** panel, click the triangle next to **Non Red Key** to view the effect's controls.

5 From the **Defringing** drop down, select **Blue**.

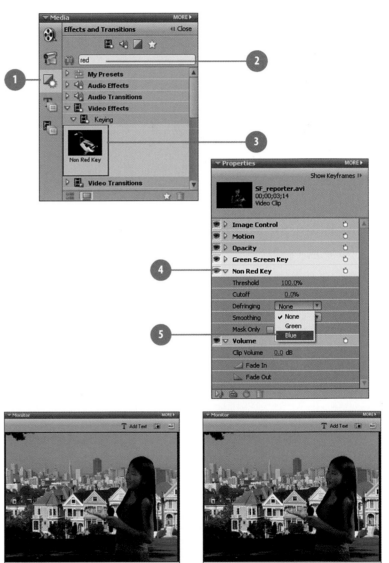

The **SF_reporter.avi** before the **Non Red Key** is applied. Notice the purple tone on her skin and hair.

The reporter after the **Non Red Key** has been applied. Her skin and hair now look just fine.

Loading the Hawaii Clips to the Timeline ▶

Well, we're almost at the end of our journey. We're just about at our final destination, the Hawaiian islands. To set up our reporter there, we'll need to drop both the reporter clip for Hawaii as well as the Hawaiian beach background. Then, as before, we'll strip away the green background to reveal the location and make some other adjustments to the clips as needed.

Our Journey Together Concludes in Hawaii

1 Drag the **hawaii.avi** clip from the **Media** panel onto the **Video 1** track on the **My Project** panel, directly to the right of (and touching) the **sanfranpaintedhouses.avi** clip.

2 Drag the **Hawaii_reporter.avi** clip from the **Media** panel onto the **Video 2** track on the **My Project** panel. Again, you want it directly to the right of (and touching) the clip that's already there, **SF_reporter.avi**.

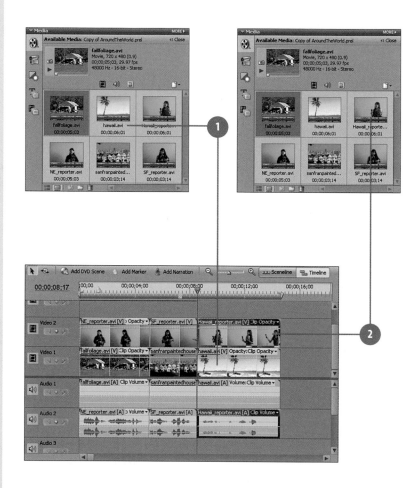

Applying the Green Screen Key to the Hawaii Reporter Clip

We have our actor, complete with pineapple drink, saying the right things about Hawaiian beaches. But until we remove the green background and replace it with the beach she's describing, not only will the scene not be believable, it just won't make a whole lot of sense.

Find and Apply the Key

 Click on the **Effects and Transitions** button in the **Media** panel, to switch to the **Effects and Transitions** view.

2 Type **green** in the text field.

3 Select the **Green Screen Key** effect from the Keying effects in the **Video Effects** list and drag and drop it onto the **Hawaii_reporter.avi** clip on the **Video 2** track.

4 In the **Properties** panel, click the **triangle** next to **Green Screen Key** to view the effect's controls.

5 Adjust the effect as follows:

◆ **Threshold:** 35.0%

◆ **Cutoff:** 35.0%

◆ **Smoothing:** High

The reporter, with props, in front of a green-screen, pre-**Green Screen Key**.

The clip after the **Green Screen Key** has been applied. Aloha! Welcome to Hawaii!

Making Other Adjustments to the Hawaii Scene

Because our actor is supposed to be standing in the sand on a sun-drenched beach in Hawaii, the fact that she appears to be lit like she's indoors (which she was, actually) is causing this scene to be a bit unbelievable. What we'll do here to brighten up our actress (other than actually sending her to Hawaii) is to increase the brightness of the clip just a touch.

Adjust the Brightness to Give the Actor an Outdoor Look

1 Select the **Hawaii_reporter** clip on the **Video 2** track to make it the active clip.

2 In the **Properties** panel, click the triangle next to **Image Control**.

3 Set the **Brightness** to **8.0**. Leave all of the other **Image Control** settings exactly as they are:

- ◆ **Contrast:** **100.0**
- ◆ **Hue:** **0.0°**
- ◆ **Saturation: 100.0**

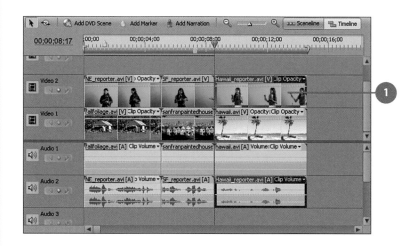

Create a Freeze Frame to End the Video

① Move the **CTI** to the very last frame of the **Hawaii_reporter.avi** clip.

> **TIP** *The last frame of the clip is at* ***00;00;14;17***.

② In the **Monitor** panel, click the **Freeze Frame** button.

③ On the **Freeze Frame** dialog box, set the duration to **10 seconds**.

④ Click the **Insert in Movie** button.

Adding a Little Travelling Music

Music is always a good thing when creating movies. Find any excuse you can to add music to your projects and you will instantly improve your video by leaps and bounds. For this project, what would be better than a bit of travelling music with an "island" feel? We'll be using another clip generated from Quicktracks™, **islandparty.wav** (or, as it is known officially in the Quicktracks library, SmartSound - Island Party - Pool side [00;30;00].wav). We need to modify the volume for this track so that it starts off very quietly, playing softly through New England, building up just slightly in San Francisco, and then—*bam!*—when we're in Hawaii, we'll bring it up loud for the end of the clip. If we were running credits, we would continue the music right on through the end credits playing.

Add Some Music to the Soundtrack

1 Click the **Get Media from** button on the **Media** panel to access the **Get Media from** view, if it's not already active.

2 Select **DVD, Digital Camera, Mobile Phone, Hard Drive Camcorder, Card Reader**.

3 When the **Media Downloader** displays, click the **Advanced Dialog** button to switch to Advanced mode.

4 Find and select the **islandparty.wav** clip.

5 Click the **Get Media** button. Premiere Elements copies the **islandparty.wav** clip you selected from the DVD onto your computer's hard drive and adds it to the **Available Media** list.

6 Select the **islandparty.wav** clip on the **Media** panel and drag on drop it onto the **Audio 3** track.

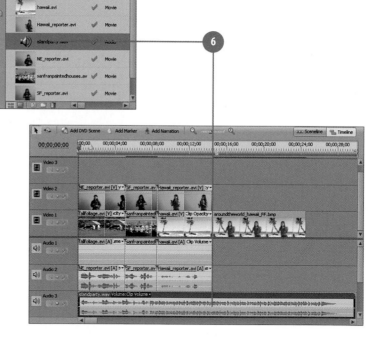

Adjust the Music's Volume to Match the Clips

1 With the **islandparty.wav** clip still selected, go to the **Properties** panel and set the **Volume** to **-10 dB**.

> **TIP** *Click the triangle to twirl open the volume controls, if they aren't already visible.*

2 Click the **Show Keyframes** button.

3 Move the **CTI** (either the one in the **Properties Panel** timeline or the one in the **My Projects** timeline) to the start of the San Francisco clip, at the **00;00;05;00** mark.

4 Click the **Toggle Animation** button.

> **TIP** *A keyframe should automatically be placed for Volume. In case it doesn't, you can place a keyframe manually by clicking the **Add/Remove Keyframe** button.*

5 Change the **Volume** to **-3.0 dB**.

6 Move the **CTI** to the start of the Hawaii clip, at the **00;00;08;17** mark.

7 Click the **Add/Remove Keyframe** button.

8 Change the **Volume** to **0.0 dB**.

9 Move the **CTI** to the middle of the Hawaii clip, at the **00;00;12;00** mark.

10 Click the **Add/Remove Keyframe** button.

11 Change the **Volume** to **3.0 dB**.

> **TIP** *Now, when you click the **Play** button on the **Monitor** panel (or press the **Spacebar**), you'll hear the music gradually increase in volume, swelling to a full-blown island party by the time the reporter has finished speaking.*

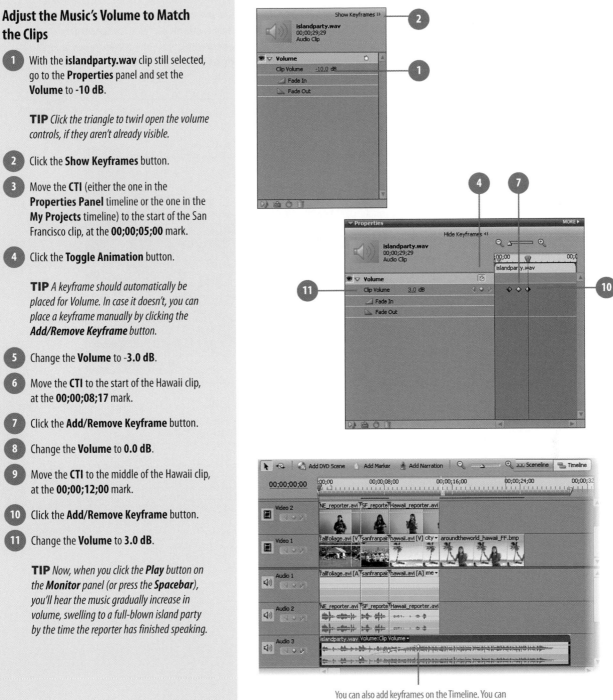

You can also add keyframes on the Timeline. You can adjust the markers by moving them up and down or back and forth along the yellow volume rubberband.

Making Adjustments, Rendering, and Exporting

We're now ready to render all of our effects, save our project one more time, and create our output file. Before we do so, you might want to play the clip (press the **Spacebar** on your keyboard or click the **Play** button on the **Monitor** panel) to see how it looks. If you need to, make any final tweaks as necessary. After which, you'll be ready to save, render, and make your movie.

Finishing the Project

 1 After you've played back your clip and made the necessary adjustments, press the **ENTER** key on your keyboard to render your project.

2 Press **CTRL-S** to save your project (or you can select **File, Save** from the menu).

3 Finally, export your work as an AVI file. To export the clip, select **File, Export, Movie**.

> **TIP** *You can now optionally bring this clip into a larger project, show it on your computer, upload it to an Internet video sharing site, or burn it to a DVD disc.*

The finished project running in Windows Media Player. What an exciting trip it was!

Index

Peachpit
Essential books for the creative community

Visit Peachpit on the Web at www.peachpit.com

- Read the latest articles and download timesaving tipsheets from best-selling authors such as Scott Kelby, Robin Williams, Lynda Weinman, Ted Landau, and more!

- Join the Peachpit Club and save 25% off all your online purchases at peachpit.com every time you shop—plus enjoy free UPS ground shipping within the United States.

- Search through our entire collection of new and upcoming titles by author, ISBN, title, or topic. There's no easier way to find just the book you need.

- Sign up for newsletters offering special Peachpit savings and new book announcements so you're always the first to know about our newest books and killer deals.

- Did you know that Peachpit also publishes books by Apple, New Riders, Adobe Press, and palmOne Press? Swing by the Peachpit family section of the site and learn about all our partners and series.

- Got a great idea for a book? Check out our About section to find out how to submit a proposal. You could write our next best-seller!

You'll find all this and more at www.peachpit.com. Stop by and take a look today!